# A Requiem for Hitler

KLAUS SCHOLDER

# A Requiem for Hitler

and Other New Perspectives on the
German Church Struggle

SCM PRESS
London

TRINITY PRESS INTERNATIONAL
Philadelphia

Translated by John Bowden from a selection of articles
contained in *Die Kirchen zwischen Republik und Gewaltherrschaft*,
published 1988 by Siedler Verlag, Berlin 1988

Copyright © Siedler Verlag 1988

Translation copyright © John Bowden 1989


First published 1989

SCM Press                                Trinity Press International
26–30 Tottenham Road                     3725 Chestnut Street
London N1 4BZ                            Philadelphia, Pa. 19104

British Library Cataloguing in Publication Data

Scholder, Klaus, *d. 1985*
    A requiem for Hitler and other new perspectives on the
    German church struggle.
    1. Germany. Christian church, history
    I. Title.   II. Die Kirchen zwischen Republik und
    Gewaltherrschaft. English
    274.3

    ISBN 0–334–02295–9


Library of Congress Cataloging-in-Publication Data

Scholder, Klaus.
    [Kirchen zwischen Republik und Gewaltherrschaft.  English.
    Selections]
    A requiem for Hitler : and other new perspectives on the
    German church struggle / Klaus Scholder.
        p.        cm.
    Bibliography: p.
    Includes index.
    ISBN 0–334–02295–9
    1. Germany—Church history—1933–1945.    2. Church and state—
    Germany—1933–1945.    I. Title.
    BR856.S34372513    1989        89–4505
    200'.943—dc20

Photoset by Input Typesetting Ltd, London
and printed in Great Britain by
Richard Clay Ltd, Bungay, Suffolk

# Contents

# Introduction

It was summer 1977. Both the University of Tübingen and the University of Uppsala were celebrating their quincentenaries, and to mark the occasion, among other things, they had arranged an international congress of church historians. Klaus Scholder was given the difficult task of writing and presenting a final summary of fifteen very different papers and the discussions which had followed them, with only a lunch hour in which to prepare it. He achieved in one and a half sides what many people had thought impossible, and did so in such a deceptively simple way that in retrospect it seemed the most natural thing in the world. Scholder did not open up any metahistorical horizon on a philosophical foundation, but operated simply with the concepts of the universal and the particular. So at various levels and in differing degrees of depth he was able to show in a comparative historical survey what he felt to be the aim of the whole enterprise: 'to see more clearly and to understand better the course of the many churches and the one church of Jesus Christ in this world'.[1]

This little episode is in many respects characteristic of the work and activity of Klaus Scholder, in his professional world and in his contacts with the general public. He never forgot the universal in dealing with the particular, and his eye for the universal always made him aware of the particular. To lay stress on what critics, above all after his death, increasingly felt obliged to do,[2] was in fact his strength. The real secret of his success was not just his enormous vigour and self-discipline, his interdisciplinary approach, his own personal investigation of archive material from Warsaw to Washington, or his brilliant literary style, but also specifically that eye for the particular and the universal and their interconnection. His bold theses, his overall view, almost naturally shaped events which often enough were well known into a new whole as he wrote. All at once, the dynamic of what had previously been a wilderness of facts and information apparently not adding up to anything became clear and obvious.

If we ask what made him more able than many of his contemporaries to produce a living, synthetic picture from the fragments of past reality which have been come down to us, two things come to mind.

All his life Scholder maintained a lively interest in almost everything that was going on in the world around him; he followed political discussions and controversies, literary and cultural developments. But he did not do so like any well-informed middle class person; for the most part he also connected his newly-acquired information and insight with his teaching and research. Thus for example after the appearance of Solzhenitsyn's *The Gulag Archipelago* he immediately rewrote the chapter on 'The Orthodox Church and the Revolution' in his lectures on 'Basic Problems of Church History in the Twentieth Century', because he thought that reading this book had given him a completely new perspective on events. And he could correct himself or allow others to correct him just as quickly and readily. So as a result of conversations or other stimuli he would often write two or three versions of a chapter, each completely independent of the other, until he was finally convinced that he had got the most important features right.

Scholder's other striking characteristic was the wealth of his ideas. One occasionally got the impression that he was almost being pursued by his own ideas; he had more of them than he could make use of (or than other people thought he ought to make use of), and his range of interests was so wide that more than once he broke through the classic division of scientific disciplines. But even within his 'own' discipline, church history, his ideas and projects ran far ahead of what he could accomplish. So even while he was writing the second volume of *The Churches and the Third Reich* he was toying with the idea of writing a history of the orders.

Of course those around Scholder profited from this wealth of ideas and his constant productivity. He was never at a loss for a theme, and in his best periods he could inspire a good dozen doctoral students simultaneously with suggestions and proposals. At the beginning of the 1970s, when he himself was writing the first volume of his church history of the Third Reich, he was already encouraging dissertations on post-war church history – not just because it was an interesting field still quite untouched by historians, but also because at a very early stage he foresaw the shift in interest which is now unmistakable.

Scholder was aware of the public, but again the nature of his awareness characteristically distinguished him from many of his contemporaries. It was not personal vanity which drew him to the public, but the conviction that he had something to say. Of course he was delighted when his arguments were successful, but he certainly did not 'enjoy' public appearances – though perhaps he did not give that impression. Moreover, stage fright tormented him and also stimulated him far too much – there was a deep excitement which always gave his voice a rather hoarse tone at the beginning of lectures.

Although Scholder's sphere of research in church history extended from the Enlightenment to the present, his own pioneer work lay in the establishment of contemporary church history as an independent scholarly discipline. Here on the Protestant side he overcame the monopoly of those who had been involved in the church struggle and were writing their own history – his liberal convictions made him question any monopoly!

In the course of a discussion with Catholic colleagues in 1978 he wrote: 'Such monopolies naturally tend to a certain one-sidedness. As a rule only those works are encouraged and published which fit into existing frameworks: outsiders with contrary views hardly stand a chance. That, moreover is the strength and weakness of all scholarly schools...'[3] So he was always deeply sceptical about the formation of schools and watched with antipathy and indeed contempt the attempts of others to form parties. It is probably no exaggeration to say that Scholder himself was an outsider – however, he was an outsider whose originality, achievement and public success indisputably put him in the forefront. The convinced individualist ultimately kept only loosely in touch with his immediate fellow-historians: social contacts and the exchange of academic ideas seldom led to any real co-operation of any substance. He always went his own way, even in the choice of his publisher.

Scholder was also one of the first German church historians, without denying his confession, to begin an integral account of the history of both churches in the Third Reich; this not least brought substantial gains in understanding Hitler's church politics.

The Tübingen theologian, historian and politician of culture wanted to understand our past better, not to excuse it or condemn it. His concern was supported by the requirement of historicism 'to show what really happened'; and he did this with an incorruptibility which his closeness to his church did not exclude, but in fact entailed. 'Truth may be painful for the church,' he wrote in the Preface to the first volume of his *The Churches and the Third Reich*, 'but untruth is even more so.'[4] For the convinced liberal, doing history also meant providing descriptions without any moralizing connotations which thus furthered a capacity for judgment in the present. In a lecture 'On Dealing with our Most Recent History', given in 1979, he said: 'We do not get anywhere with slogans like Fascist, neo-Fascist, crypto-Fascist. The important thing is, rather, to recognize not so much the goals of a political movement as how it describes its opponents and how far in principle it is prepared to tolerate them. No immediate political and social goals can be derived from the experiences of our history, but rather criteria on which all parties, groups and movements can orientate themselves.'[5] In his last major article, 'The Theological Foundation of the Church Struggle. On the Origin and Significance of the Barmen Declaration', Scholder also made clear his own theological standpoint on the political action of the church in the world: 'Even where the church receives a political call, it is called as church and recognizes only the means of the church...', i.e. it addresses those in positions of responsibility through prayer and intercession. 'After Barmen, both false political activism in the church and false repudiation of politics derive from the same root, a lack of trust in God's promise.'[6]

Politically a liberal, theologically Scholder constantly remained indebted to the thought of the dialectical theology of Karl Barth and his circle. So Barth's *Theological Existence Today* of June 1933 and the Barmen Theological Declaration of May 1934 stood at the centre of his theological judgment. He was fully in accord with his Tübingen colleague Eberhard Jüngel in his interpretation of Barmen: the two of them held a joint seminar on Barmen in the winter semester of 1983/1984 and presented the results of their historical and theological reflections to the Rhineland Landessynode in January 1984.[7] Beyond question Scholder's historical judgment shaped his theological position, but he never sought to hide that in any way.

In his last years Scholder constantly and with increasing urgency spoke on the question of fate and guilt in history. He used the concept of fate to denote 'the fact that we have only limited possibilities of controlling history. Even if we are most vigorously and keenly aware of our responsibility, it is never possible to foresee the consequences of our decisions.'[8] But 'faith does not see faith as mere blind workings but as God's will'.[9] This was the theological basis for his rejection of moralism and pessimism, and for his confident, indeed sometimes optimistic, view of the future.

Two years before his death Scholder attempted to describe the features of a 'Protestant profile'. At that time he wrote: 'Dealing independently with Holy Scripture, being led unconditionally by the conscience and having an openness which is often very difficult to acquire – over the centuries these three characteristics produce the typically "Protestant profile".'[10] Scholder had it.

Klaus Scholder's death on 10 April 1985 struck all who knew him like a thunderbolt from a clear sky. He had concealed his illness, which he bore bravely and calmly, even from his closest friends. The great procession of mourners which went through Tübingen on a rainy 16 April from the Stiftskirche to the cemetery was utterly bewildered. His books were in the windows of the Tübingen bookshops, and no one could believe that this cheerful man, who had radiated such joy in life, was no more. That is still impossible to believe.

The attempt to make some of his scattered articles available to a wider public by collecting them together in this volume is therefore also prompted by a concern not only to preserve the memory of Klaus Scholder the man but also to draw attention once again to him and to his work.

The articles published here are all about contemporary church history. No theme since 1945 has called forth such a flood of publications as the history of the struggle of the Protestant and Catholic churches against the Third Reich – though struggle is perhaps a misleading term, since there was never any question of overthrowing the régime. The struggle was a conflict with an anti-Christian, racist system which saw both churches as relics of former times that had to be superseded as quickly as possible. To spare them, or even to come to some arrangement with them, was therefore possible only for a time; initially this régime was concerned to have a positive relationship to the churches only in order to consolidate its own rule. The régime also had a democratic basis, albeit perverted, and almost anxiously sought to avoid anything that could jeopardize a consensus with the majority of the population. Here was one possibility for the churches to oppose the new authorities, though it was recognized only by a few.

Neither church emerged unscathed from the twelve years under Hitler's dictatorship. That explains the many publications on this theme. Whereas the Protestant church confessed its failure in its Stuttgart Declaration on 19 October 1945, the Catholic church found it far more difficult to cope with the past. A mistaken aura of papal infallibility stood in the way of such a declaration. So for a long time those on the Catholic side acted as though no serious mistakes had been made in the church struggle.

It was the discussion of Hochhuth's play *The Representative* in 1962/1963 which marked a turning point here. On the Catholic side research was begun to clarify all the questions, prompted by the publication of Vatican records and by the admirably presented series of publications from the Commission for Contemporary History. This was matched on the Protestant side by an overwhelming number of publications, but these could not always keep up with Catholic research. Most publications on the church struggle were not concerned to point out failures, but to justify actions and describe the persecution that had been suffered and the accusations of a régime whose anti-Christian attitude had made it capable of the most monstrous crimes.

That was as it were the starting point for Scholder's researches. It very soon became clear to him that a move had to be made beyond the pattern of research which hithertho had been divided by confessions, in order to bring out the common features of developments. In his view, this was the only way to demonstrate the National Socialist policy against Christianity *per se* and to highlight links which otherwise could not be shown. This position did not go undisputed, because Scholder showed up some 'assured knowledge' as legend.

This approach taking in both churches led, for example, to his account of the prehistory of the Reich concordat, which in Germany provoked a passionate challenge from Konrad Repgen. In this discussion, in which Scholder engaged with a mixture of amusement and amazement, because for him and others it had the all too evident features of Wilhelm Busch's well-known dictum that what may not be cannot be, both sides produced new insights; though neither

Scholder's view that Hitler exchanged a promise to conclude a Reich concordat for Rome's promise to abandon the Centre Party, nor Repgen's view that the abandoning of the Centre Party had nothing to do with the Reich concordat, can be supported from the records.

In dealing with his theme Scholder also had another clear conviction. The great theme of the churches in the Third Reich could not be described without a readiness to survey considerable periods of time. Thus the relationship between the churches and the state during the Weimar Republic was as important for the years 1933 to 1945 as a survey of the whole development. So while he had to present his work chronologically, because the particular events could only be explained from the situation, the problem of what the Nazi dictatorship ultimately planned for the churches and Christianity could only be resolved if one took the whole period into account. That meant that Scholder did not limit his collection of material to the time which he was working to describe. This gave rise to an extensive collection of documents on contemporary church history which is now with Gerhard Besier in Berlin; he and Jörg Thierfelder, who want to continue the work begun by Scholder, will be glad to be able to make use of it.

This approach also explains the slow progress of the work. The manuscript of the second volume was two-thirds finished when in 1983 Scholder became aware that he was seriously ill. He wanted to get over this insidious illness before he went on working. Only when it became clear that this would not be possible did he resume work in December 1984; however, he was unable to complete the volume. The second volume appeared in German in autumn 1986, but without the concluding chapter on developments in the Catholic sphere during 1934 which he had planned.

It was not just the extensive collection of material, though, that meant that progress on the work was slow. From the beginning Scholder's interests had been broad. Born on 12 January 1930 in Erlangen, the son of the Professor of Inorganic Chemistry, Dr Rudolf Scholder, he grew up in a climate to which all specialization was alien. After his Abitur in 1948 he was resolved to become a theologian. He began his theological studies, which throughout his university days were combined with German studies, in Tübingen in 1949 and moved from there to Göttingen in 1951, returning to Tübingen for his doctoral work in 1954, the year in which he was ordained. During this period he also developed an interest in politics

and had connections with the Federal Democrats. He initially
planned to produce his Habilitationsschrift on a topic of modern
German history, but eventually wrote it on 'Origins and Problems
of Biblical Criticism in the Seventeenth Century. A Contribution
to the Rise of Historical-Critical Theology'; it was published by
Christian Kaiser Verlag in Munich in 1967. The title does not give
a full idea of the content of the book, which is really about
the problem of the historical conditioning of the non-theological
statements in the Bible, a problem which oppressed both churches as
a result of the scientific knowledge of the sixteenth and seventeenth
centuries. The Catholic church sought to ward off the new insights
with the trial of Galileo; Scholder now demonstrated that Protestant
theology also spent a long time struggling with the problem. Protestant orthodoxy avoided such spectacular measures as the condemnation of Galileo or the burning of Giordano Bruno, but basically
it was no more tolerant than Catholicism. This slow process of the
reconciliation of theology with the insights of the natural sciences
was resolved, as Scholder impressively demonstrated, in the Nether-
lands, with its great tradition of tolerance. This was to be one of the
presuppostions for the activity of the Protestant church in the
modern world.

No one had really expected this work from a man who was so
interested in contemporary history and politics, and the theological
faculty did not make things easy for Scholder, who had meanwhile
also made a name as a journalist and television commentator. The
faculty gave him recognition, but required him to observe the
restrictions imposed on a junior lecturer. Others were quicker to
acknowledge his qualities and he was invited to join the editorial
boards of several distinguished scholarly periodicals; and in 1968 he
received a call to the chair of church history in the University of
Bonn.

Only then did Tübingen begin to take seriously its junior lecturer
whose public reputation had by that time surpassed that of many
professors. So it called him to the chair for church order which had
meanwhile become free. However, his real subject was contemporary church history, and from now on his research interests were
concentrated on the history of the struggle of the two churches
against National Socialism. The appearance of the first volume of
his *magnum opus The Churches and the Third Reich* in 1977 brought
him a call to the University of Hamburg, but he turned it down.

Scholder remained true to his Württemberg descent and a group of students gathered around him in Tübingen.

Despite Scholder's great success in teaching and research, the work of a university professor was only part of his interests. His political activity and his appearances as a television commentator had brought him too much of an audience beyond Tübingen for him to be able to resist the temptations of public life. Indeed in due course the University of Tübingen began to fear that it would lose him completely to politics, and that might have happened had the political climate been more favourable. Moreover from 1969 he had become involved in environmental questions and was given important posts on several expert committees. All this involved so much work that it is a miracle that he had any time left for research.

Despite all this activity and the wide range of positions that he held, Klaus Scholder never became a politician or a journalist. Research generally, and the continuation of his great work in particular, had priority. As a scholar he would not compromise. There was a connection betwen his Habilitationsschrift and his work on the churches in the Third Reich. At that time it had become clear to him that an overall view of developments in both churches, which hitherto had hardly been regarded as a research task by church historians with confessional ties, was an extremely fruitful approach.

Despite this clear focal point, it may be permissible to ask at what point all Scholder's widely diverging interests came together. In scholarship he had distinguished himself as a theologian, a Germanist and a historian, but he maintained links with politics, commented in the media on current affairs as a journalist, and worked in the extremely complicated issues of environmental protection at a time when the importance of this issue had yet to be recognized. Where did Scholder's career ultimately take him?

It is impossible to understand Klaus Scholder apart from his deep roots in Christian belief. He was a theologian who was marked by his faith and did not chase after passing fashions. He was a Protestant theologian who was convinced that the church had to face all the problems of its time, but avoid the temptation of adapting to current trends. If his preoccupation with National Socialism had taught him anything, it was the insight that the churches had to fight against the seductions of the present where they were contrary to the gospel of Jesus Christ. He became increasingly more cautious in his judgments, not least on the attitude of the churches to the Third

Reich. His reconstruction of the past had made him very aware of the temptations which National Socialism had presented to those filled with nationalistic desires. That does not, however, mean that he accepted the shameful compromises of former ties; on the contrary, he saw the insights that he gained from his researches as a warning of how because of excessive adaptation to given circumstances and recourse to popular trends the churches could find themselves in situations which it should have been their task to resist.

It was this Christian self-understanding that gave Scholder's activity its inner coherence. Even as a commentator on political problems he never ceased to speak as a Protestant Christian, and he regarded the protection of the environment as a service to God's endangered creation. Klaus Scholder was a Protestant champion for Christ, and it would be remarkable if the Lord of this world did not delight in him.

Gerhard Besier
Karl Otmar von Aretin

# Translator's Postscript

I first came across the writing of Klaus Scholder in early 1967, while I was waiting to see a German publisher in Munich. The newest publications of Christian Kaiser Verlag were displayed on a table in their lobby and I picked up the book about the origins of biblical criticism in the sixteenth and seventeenth century mentioned in the introduction above and found it impossible to put down. The publisher, Fritz Bissinger, kindly gave me a copy; since then I have read the book several times and have it, heavily marked, on my shelves.

I have always regretted that we never published a translation of it; for all its interest much of it had seemed too technical at the time. I looked out over the years for further works by this exciting author but never found anything, until to my great surprise a publishing colleague told me that Klaus Scholder was working on a history of the churches in the Third Reich. Since I had read widely in that area, I awaited the publication of the English edition eagerly, but it seemed very long in coming.

It was in Tübingen in the summer of 1986 that I discovered from Frau Scholder the problems which had been associated with producing the English edition, and later that year, to my great delight, had the chance of making the translation. I have translated many books from a variety of languages over the years, and comparisons may seem invidious, but I do have to say that I have never enjoyed working on any books so much as on the two volumes of *The Churches and the Third Reich* and this book, and this delight has clearly been shared by my colleagues and by reviewers. There are not many major books of church history that one can read all the way through and then just want to go back to the beginning and start all over again. But that is the effect that Klaus Scholder can have; parting company with him, even as he is present in print, induces severe withdrawal systems.

I wanted to take this opportunity of adding my own personal tribute to Klaus Scholder, and with it my deepest thanks to Frau Carola Scholder for all her help and friendship, to Professor Gerhard Besier and his colleagues, and to everyone at Siedler Verlag, Berlin, for their warm co-operation.

Because the size and invevitable expense of the two volumes of Klaus's Scholder's *The Churches in the Third Reich* is likely to limit their circulation, we have tried to keep this book, which is in some ways an introduction and sequel to them, as compact as possible. Specialist readers should know that four essays contained in the German original have been omitted, not least because they are more technical or of more specifically German interest. So too has the bibliography to the present chapter 6 and the bibliography of Klaus Scholder's own works. (The present introduction is made up of parts of the original Preface and Postscript.) But those who want the complete book will prefer Scholder's splendid German to my English, anyway.

*Christmas 1988*                                         SCM Press Ltd

# 1

## History and Hope
### Nuremberg and the Twentieth Century*

If I interpret the conversations which have preceded this lecture rightly, those who are gathered here have very different expectations. There are older ones among us for whom my subject, the history of Nuremberg in the twentieth century, is still a vivid memory; it is a part, often a painful part, of their own life. They are expecting, if not consolation, at least gentle treatment; if not an excuse, at least understanding in dealing with what has happened to this city and to them over past decades. Then there is a second large group, the middle generation, which is probably looking above all for information; they would like to know what happened and how those events came about which have been and still are such a fearful burden on Nuremberg and on German history. And finally, there are many younger people among us who are passionately concerned with the question what their generation can learn from all this; what they have to do to prevent the same thing or anything like it happening again in Germany.

As we know, historiography can do all these things. It can clarify memories; it can provide information, reveal who was involved, and not least be mobilized to a special degree for actions and decisions. But to do this it has to pay a high price, namely making the happiness and suffering of whole generations a means to an end, and using them for particular desires, aims and purposes. Certainly no historiography is free from that. But the fate of Nuremberg warns almost more than any other against making history in this way

*This study originally appeared in H.Uhl (ed.), *Deutscher Evangelischer Kirchentag Nürnberg 1979. Dokumente*, Stuttgart and Berlin 1979, 286-301.

merely the means to a particular end. And so today I do not want
to present Nuremberg as an example of what the inhabitants of this
city and the inhabitants of Germany in the twentieth century should
have done or tolerated; I want to investigate what they did in fact
do and tolerate. And I want to do this more by asking questions
than by passing judgment; judgments will certainly not be absent,
but they will be made in the awareness that in the end God's
judgment and God's grace apply to us all.

The theme that governs this history, which I shall mention again
explicitly at the end, is the ease with which people can be led astray.
Nuremberg's history in the twentieth century is a history of how
people have been led astray and how they can be led astray. And
precisely in that respect it is also our history.

## 1. Views of Nuremberg in the 1920s

If we attempt to get a picture of Nuremberg in the years which
followed the First World War and preceded the Third Reich we
come upon three different views.

The first view is the one which we are also likely to have met first:
the view of old Nuremberg which is loved and marvelled at by both
the people of Nuremberg and the numerous visitors to the city; the
view that is preserved in picture books and popularized on leaflets.
Granted, almost all the old city was destroyed in the war; but what
was left or has been rebuilt is still enough to show the splendour and
beauty of this incomparable city. This view of old Nuremberg is not
a chance one. Rather, it reflects the special role that the city on the
Pegnitz once played in the history of the old German Reich, which
bore the remarkable title of the Holy Roman Empire of the German
Nation.

From the fourteenth century, Nuremberg was a centre of this
empire. We can see that from the particularly striking privileges that
it enjoyed. So it was here at a Reichstag in January 1356 that the
famous 'Golden Bull' was laid down and accepted, that constitutional law of the old empire the principles of which lasted 450
years until the end of the empire in 1806. And the city fathers of
Nuremberg did not fail to keep recalling this constitutional law; in
the future, each German king had to hold his first Reichstag in
Nuremberg.

Certainly no one was thinking of the Golden Bull when the

National Socialist German Workers Party held its first open party meeting in Nuremberg in September 1923. But as the Party became increasingly aware of itself, it also became increasingly aware of the significance of symbolism. Reichstag and Reich Party Conference, old and new Reich, seemed bound together by Nuremberg.

About a century after the Bull, in 1424, the city was given a further historical privilege. It was chosen in perpetuity as the place where the Reich insignia were to be kept. So from then on these imperial insignia lay in its treasury: the German imperial throne, the imperial orb, sceptre, sword and mantle. In 1806, after the end of the empire, these insignia were moved to the Hofburg in Vienna. But in 1938, when with the Anschluss of Austria Hitler believed that the old empire had risen again in the new, he had the Reich insignia brought back to Nuremberg; this was a further sign of the historical context in which he wanted to be seen.

Around 1500 the great and prosperous imperial city had reached the height of its power and reputation: politically, economically and artistically. The artists and craftsmen of this time played a special part in shaping the later view of old Nuremberg. It was also in this period that the city made a decision of world-historical significance: its early support of Luther's cause substantially strengthened the Reformation movement and made Nuremberg one of the centres of German Protestantism, as it continued to be until the end of the Second World War.

For almost 150 years Nuremberg faded into the background of German history, but then a new life began at the beginning of the nineteenth century. It was a thoroughly romantic one. For out of all these elements, out of persons and events, out of the image of the city and its history, the nineteenth century created that first view of Nuremberg that we all know: the view of a city of German imperial glory, German artistic sense and German piety: the view of Nuremberg as 'the most German city', as Hitler called it in 1931.[1] We can leave right out of account here what this view had to do with the real Nuremberg of the fifteenth and sixteenth centuries. For the twentieth century was influenced not only by the historical reality of this city but also by the view that the nineteenth century gave it and which the twentieth century took over, namely that it was the embodiment of what is German, 'the most German of all German cities'.[2]

Historical traditions are real political power for those who can use them. Hitler could. Without the seductive power of the old imperial tradition embodied in Nuremberg, the Third Reich would hardly have become what it did become.

Alongside this view, however, at this time there was a second quite different view of the city. In the course of the so-called industrial revolution in the second half of the nineteenth century and the beginning of the twentieth Nuremberg had risen to become one of the most significant industrial cities in Germany. This new role of the old imperial city can best be read off the truly breathtaking increase in the size of the population. In 1806, when it was incorporated into the kingdom of Bavaria, Nuremberg had precisely 25,000 inhabitants; by 1880 this figure had quadrupled, and in the following fifty years it quadrupled again. In 1932, the year of crisis, the city had around 416,000 inhabitants.[3] In addition to traditional crafts like toy-making and pencil manufacture, large modern industrial factories had arisen for making machines and automobiles, electrical goods and metalware; these were established in the new suburbs to the south and west. Almost half of Nuremberg wage-earners in the 1920s were industrial workers, and the political attitude of the city was in line with this. As in all Protestant industrial cities, so in Nuremberg the Social Democrats held the field unchallenged until 1930. True, in 1932 they soon lost their majority to the National Socialists, but even before the March weeks of 1933, at around thirty-three per cent their share of the vote was almost twice as high as the national average; whereas in the city in which the Reich Party Conferences were subsequently to be held, the National Socialists even remained some points under the national average.[4]

This second view of Nuremberg is of great significance. It corrects the widespread notion that Hitler went to Nuremberg above all because the city particularly favoured National Socialism. Before 1933, as the election results clearly show, that was by no means the case. Nuremberg was an industrial city, and as in all industrial cities, the NSDAP found it difficult to make headway against the organized work force. However, once the breakthrough had been achieved, the situation in Nuremberg was like that in other areas of the Reich. The newly created Workers' Festival on 1 May showed that Hitler was now also beginning to gain ground among the workers.

Alongside the views of the old imperial city and the modern industrial city of Nuremberg, since the 1920s there has, however, been a third view, the darkest. Nuremberg became a centre of

German antisemitism. This was essentially the work of one man, the self-appointed Führer of Franconia and later Gauleiter, Julius Streicher. Of all the leading members of the Party, Streicher was the one whose antisemitism most resembled that of Hitler. Not a few Party leaders never in fact completely understood Hitler's hatred of the Jews and tended more to fall in with the general tendency than to act on their own account in this respect. But with Streicher, things were different. In his memoirs, which he composed in summer 1945 in an internment camp as his 'confession', he described the same experiences as those which shaped Hitler. To begin with there were abstruse things, rumours, gossip, the first intimations of the Catholic, on being told the passion story in his religious instruction, that the nature of the Jews was 'quite different'.[5] To begin with, in pre-war Germany there was no more than muffled discontent here and there, malicious and stupid talk – and this would probably not have amounted to anything more without the First World War.

Antisemitism only became a blazing torch in Germany when *völkisch* circles made the Jews responsible for the downfall of the German Reich. That struck home like a thunderbolt, and anything that could not be explained by a German unpreparedness, national limitations and political stupidity all at once seemed clear and obvious. Who was responsible for the War, for the defeat, for the miseries of the post-war period, for the Treaty of Versailles, for the continuation of German wretchedness? It was not the former German leadership, the Kaiser, the military and the Germans as a whole who had at least shared responsibility for the war; it was the Jews. And so if Germany was to be saved, it was necessary first and foremost to fight against the Jews, inexorably, mercilessly, to the last man, woman or child. We shall not understand the further course of German history unless we are clear that this was Hitler's deepest conviction, as it was Streicher's; and that both held firm to this conviction from the first days of their political activity to their last. National Socialism had a great many faces and aspects, but in Germany this was its nucleus: the fight against the Jews in all circumstances and with all means.[6]

Ideologies take little account of reality, and totalitarian ideologies take no account of it at all. In fact the Jewish question had nothing at all to do with the German problems of the post-War period. But that did not disturb either Hitler or Streicher. And there are moments in history when anything seems credible, even what is most absurd. For example, in 1944 anyone who said that the Führer had deliberately alllowed the invasion in the West to succeed so that he could be all the more certain of destroying the Americans in France could still find a credulous audience for his assertions. And the period after the First World War was another such moment.

To begin with, Nuremberg had no more to do with this than other cities in Germany. There was no particular antisemitism here before the First World War. An 'Antisemitic Association for Nuremberg and its Environs' was dissolved in 1901;[7] in June 1913 the antisemitic Theodor Fritsch's Nuremberg 'Hammer Community' numbered a miserable twenty-three members with an annual income of 94.64 Mark.[8]

The reason why Julius Streicher began in Nuremberg was there-fore not because this city was particularly prone to antisemitism, but quite simply because Streicher was a schoolteacher there. Already a convinced antisemite, when in autumn 1922 he and his Nuremberg group offered allegiance to Hitler, there was no doubt about his concern: 'The aim of National Socialism is the transform-ation of Germany from the roots, a revolution, not a brave and meek rebuilding. We are concerned to fight to the last. And the central issue in this fight is and remains the Jewish question.'[9]

A year later, in August 1923, Streicher founded the weekly which was very soon to become the embodiment of National Socialist antisemitism. It was called *Der Stürmer*, and at first bore the sub-heading 'Nuremberg Weekly for the Fight for the Truth'. It was *Der Stürmer* that made Nuremberg the centre of antisemitism.

It is hard to think of a journal which was more shameless, mean and despicable than Streicher's weekly. Supported by a notorious cartoonist, who portrayed the Jews with every conceivable repulsive-ness, *Der Stürmer* disseminated an unparalleled pornographic anti-semitism. Though it was initially published in editions of a few thousand, in its heyday in 1938 its circulation had reached almost half a million, and special numbers even had editions of several million.[10] After 1933, even those who did not want to have anything to do with the paper would find it in countless showcases in city and country, which zealous officials supplied with the latest edition.

The witchhunt did not fail to have consequences in Nuremberg. At the end of the 1920s there was an increasing number of antisemitic incidents and excesses – above all in connection with the Party

Conferences. By deliberate denunciations *Der Stürmer* generated a climate of hatred and fear which businessmen and house-owners, associations and the bourgeois press found increasingly difficult to avoid as time went on – nor did they want to. Even the Protestant church did not protest. Granted, in general people were agreed that racial witchhunting was to be condemned, but they thought that the Jews were to some extent guilty, and would not stick up for them.[11]

*Der Stürmer* was the decisive feature of that third view of Nuremberg. In the 1930s the paper became known far outside Germany, and found many imitators in world-wide antisemitism. With it, the name of Nuremberg became widely known as the home of antisemitism in its worst form.

As early as 1921, Joseph Wassermann, a very well-known writer of the time, wrote in his book *My Career as a German and as a Jew*: 'It is useless to take the venom out of the poison. They brew a fresh dose. There is no point in living and dying for them. They say: he is a Jew.'[12]

As far as Streicher and his *Stürmer* were concerned, this was literally the truth.

## 2. The city of the Reich Party Conferences

These three views of Nuremberg – the city of old imperial glory and the most German of all German cities; the modern industrial city; and the city of *Der Stürmer* – moulded the history of the city in the 1930s and 1940s. If ever history became destiny, it did so here.

In retrospect we will feel that these three views are irreconcilable, that they must inevitably resist any form of integration: the old Franconian city romanticism set against the modern industrial world, and this in turn set against a quite retrograde, irrational hatred of the Jews. But this retrospect is deceptive – at least to begin with. For these three views were not just views of Nuremberg; in one respect they were the three views of the Third Reich generally. Indeed, the desire to use the term 'Third Reich' already betrayed a concern to exploit the old imperial tradition; at the same time, with his acute realization of the future possibilities of technology, Hitler accelerated the development of this Reich into a highly industrialized society, and both tradition and technology furthered the battle against Judah, the omnipresent, imaginary enemy of the world.

If we want to know how Hitler succeeded in fusing these elements

into a unity which was called the National Socialist world-view, at
least for a few years, we again can see this in Nuremberg, at the six
Reich Party Conferences which took place here between 1933 and
1938.

These Party Conferences were far more than just meetings of the
Party; they were and increasingly became grandiose demonstrations
by the régime, which repeated year by year both for those who took
part in them and for the whole people what Hitler felt to be the basis
of his rule: the spontaneous and ecstatic assent of the masses to him
as their only, unconditional and undisputed leader. The unity of the
Third Reich and its world-view lay in this assent; and unless all the
pictures, the reports and the recollections lie, it was also confirmed
in Nuremberg year by year.

Leni Reifenstahl, who with a brilliant eye shot the film of the 1934
Reich Party Conference, convincingly depicted the function of the
Party Conferences. At Hitler's wish the film bore the title 'Triumph
of the Will', and there is no doubt that what he meant was his own
will.

'The Führer over all!', was the way in which she later described
her impression. 'Over the tremendous symphony of massed people,
marching columns, conferences, honours, marches and congresses
– his word over the present – for the future.'[13] And this was the
feeling not only of this woman but obviously also of the many
millions who were ready to follow this man.

I want to insert a brief theological reflection at this point. In June
1931 a young pastor whose theology was strongly influenced by Karl
Barth gave a lecture entitled 'Political Messiahship'. In it he stated
that Hitler had now become for many of his followers the real 'Myth
of the Twentieth Century', and that the Nationalist Socialists were
now the ones who were reaching the ears and hearts of men and
women with their political prophecy. 'But the prophecy of the
church,' he continued, 'is so completely quenched that even Protestant pastors confuse the secularized eschatology of the völkisch
movement with the legitimate eschatology of the church's proclamation and enthusiastically fall in with the National Socialist camp'.
However, this argument concluded, the political prophecy of the
right and the left could be coped with neither by 'an individualistic
Christianity of bliss' nor by any form of 'religious and moral activism',
but only by 'the legitimate prophecy of church proclamation.'[14]

'The Führer over all...' – 'his word over the present – for the future'. Why had the church's word become so weak and helpless that millions of people, all baptized Christians, followed the political Messiah?

Back to the Reich Party Conferences. Anyone who traces them down the years will gain the impression of a grandiose, deliberately planned crescendo. That can already be seen from the number of those taking part. The first Party Conference after the seizure of power, the 'Victory Conference', brought around 400,000 participants to Nuremberg. That in itself was an enormous organizational achievement – and not just for that time. Five years later, in 1938, at the 'Greater Germany' conference, already more than 1.6 million people came to Nuremberg in a thousand special trains and hundreds of thousands of cars and buses.[15] And with the number of participants, the number, size and extent of the Party Conference buildings grew, those buildings which Hitler commanded and his architect Albert Speer planned and executed.[16] Everything was now on a gigantic scale: platforms and parade grounds, congress halls and stadia were all to surpass anything there had ever been in the history of the world. Speer did not fail to utilize any of the most impressive and most modern technological solutions and possibilities here – including the famous cathedral of light which he constructed above the evening Party Leaders' demonstration from 150 anti-aircraft searchlights and which even to foreigners seemed to have an incomparable, almost unearthly, effect.[17] And it was Hitler himself who incessantly spurred on the architect and the buildings. Year by year he wanted to lay new foundation stones, though the foundation stones were then brought back to the city building yards to await their future use.[18]

And all this was connected with Nuremberg and its history. The city, Hitler declared in 1933, was to be the 'place of our Reich Party Conferences' in perpetuity;[19] and four years later, in 1937, he assured his followers in the Nuremberg Rathaus: 'So this city, perhaps anticipating the rest of Germany, is the first to be given its future and thus its eternal shape.'[20]

'Future and thus eternal shape': anyone who follows the development of the Party Conferences will recognize in retrospect that this was in fact the aim, not just of the buildings but also of the ritual, which year by year became more powerful, stricter and more impersonal. There was still a good deal of spontaneity and improvisation, much personal sacrifice and enthusiasm, in the first Party

Conferences, but later this retreated more and more into the background. When after the end of the 1938 Party Conference Hitler once again discussed with Speer the whole course of events, he made it clear that in his view it had now reached a final form and was to become an 'unchangeable rite'. 'I had long believed,' Speer later recalled, 'that all these marches, processions, and hours of dedication were part of a virtuoso propaganda revue: now it became clear to me that for Hitler it almost amounted to the founding of a church.'[21]

As the development of the Party Conferences made clear, that finally raised Hitler above all criticism. He led people astray, but he was also led astray by them. Year by year the ecstatic devotion of the masses, bewitched into the strict forms of a grandiose ritual, increasingly confirmed him in his belief in a mission and election which finally lost all proportion, all sense of reality, all humanity and all reason. And there was no longer anyone who could contradict him, whether Gauleiter, minister, general or business leader.

It is difficult to overestimate what Nuremberg meant for this process of inner co-ordination.

The insignia of the old Reich and the military power of the new Reich were meant to demonstrate the past, present and future of Germany in Nuremberg. And through all this, from the first Party Conference to the last, Hitler never let the Jewish question out of sight. So it made sense that during the 1935 Party Conference he surprisingly ordered the Reich Ministry of the Interior to draft within two days a law on the Jews which was to be passed in the Reichstag convened in Nuremberg for the last day of the Party Conference. This was the origin of the notorious Nuremberg laws: the 'Law concerning Reich Citizens', which excluded so-called 'full Jews' from important civic rights, and the 'Law for the Protection of German Blood and German Honour', the most important clause of which forbade marriage between Germans and Jews. It is not at all easy to determine the significance of these Nuremberg laws. For the officials in the Ministry of the Interior succeeded in drafting the laws in such a way that they affected as few people as possible, so that to some degree half-Jews had some security under the law. Many Jews in the Reich also saw them in this light in the wake of the wild campaigns of hatred orchestrated by the Party which had preceded them. On the other hand these laws and the framework within which they were passed and proclaimed undoubtedly marked a further development in the growing antisemitic campaign carried on in the Third Reich.[22]

It was sheer coincidence that the Nuremberg laws were passed in Nuremberg. As far as we know, Streicher had no direct part in them. Nor is there any direct causal link between these laws and the holocaust, the great murder of the Jews. But in retrospect we can see connections which go deeper than direct causality. Where people had not prevented things beginning, later they had to be content if they were able to mitigate the greatest injustices even a little.

### 3. The other Nuremberg

The place in which year by year the Party held such overpowering demonstrations must raise the question of another Nuremberg. Was there only the city of the Reich Party Conferences and *Der Stürmer*, the city of wild Aryan demonstrations and an evil National Socialist clique over which, to Hitler's sorrow, in the end even Streicher himself was to fall, or was there also another Nuremberg? What about the people of Nuremberg themselves, of whom as late as March 1933 more than forty per cent had voted for left-wing parties? The question is hard to answer, but I want to refer to at least two aspects of this problem.

First of all, in Nuremberg, too, there were attempts by both the Communists and the Social Democrats to carry on an underground campaign against National Socialist rule. However, as early as 1934 both groups were virtually finished – for two reasons. The first was purely external. The political police succeeded very quickly in breaking into the underground organization and arresting all the important people. From the beginning of 1935 more than 150 Social Democrats were brought to trial and condemned to shorter or longer periods of imprisonment; later some of them were put in Dachau concentration camp. Neither the Communist Party nor the Social Democrats could recover from this blow. And this brings us to the second, more important, reason for their failure. The left-wing groups in general expected an imminent uprising of the workers or at least broad support for their political activity under Fascist rule. The opposite happened. The undoubted economic success of the régime, especially its reversal of the unemployment trend which could be seen from the middle of 1933, largely deprived the left-wing opposition of its basis. The ideology of the right-wing Workers

Party and Hitler's persistent and deliberate wooing of the German working class also helped to destroy all hopes of an effective left-wing revolt. There were still individual small groups and circles, which went on meeting in Nuremberg, but there was no further organized political resistance before the end of the war.[23]

Things looked quite different in the Protestant church. Even the starting point was quite different here. For at no stage was this an underground rebellion; everything that happened in the church happened in public. Nor was this an active political process with the aim of ending Hitler's rule; what the church could do and sought to do in the best instance was to preach the gospel without falsification and without omission, even in the Third Reich. One may question whether this should be counted as political resistance, though to an increasing degree that is how the Third Reich came to understand it.

Be this as it may, it was possible in Nuremberg to organize a kind of mass movement against the Party under the impact of which Streicher, the Bavarian government and in the end even Hitler in fact gave in. The occasion was the attempt in October 1934 to depose the Bavarian Landesbischof Hans Meiser and to co-ordinate the Landeskirche with the Reich Church, which was dominated by the German Christians. So on 16 October 1934 thousands went from the Confessing services in the Lorenz and Sebaldus churches to the chief market place in the city; moreover on subsequent days the people of Nuremberg made it quite clear that they wanted to support their bishop.[24]

However, these clashes did not have many more wide-reaching consequences. There were only isolated expressions of protest and opposition in the next few years, even in Nuremberg. 13 November 1937, the day on which Wilhelm Geyer preached from the pulpit of St Lorenz, where he was a pastor, against the Jewish pogrom, and all the pastors of the church joined in reminding their congregation of the Ten Commandments, remained an isolated instance.[25]

So there was another Nuremberg, but as far as we can now tell, its voice was gentle and weak. And the louder the crescendo of the Party Conferences, the gentler and weaker became the voice of the other Nuremberg. So what was written to a friend by Wilhelm von Pechmann, one of the most eminent members of the Protestant laity and President of the Protestant Kirchentag held in Nuremberg in 1930, was all the more to the point: 'I know that I am free from any trace of arrogance when I say how happy a later church historian will be about each one of those who have not bent the knee before the Baal of this era.'[26]

## 4. The downfall of the old Nuremberg

Is the world's history the world's judgment? I would hesitate to follow Schiller's idealistic maxim. We have seen too much unatoned injustice, too much triumphal power. But it is certain that in Germany after 1941, after the rumours of the German atrocities in the East became known, quite a number were convinced that we could not win this war – not for military reasons but for reasons of a higher justice, which would not let evil triumph. This was also preached here and there during the war in the ruins of our cities; not as a historical law but as an insight and recognition of faith: 'Do not deceive yourself. God is not mocked. For what a man sows, that will he reap' (Gal.6.7).

The last Reich Party Conference to be planned in Nuremberg was to have taken place on 2-11 September 1939. It was to have been called the 'Reich Party Peace Conference' and thus once again to have done more to conceal and veil what Hitler had sought and wanted from the beginning: war. On 26 August 1939, when thousands were already on their way to Nuremberg, the Party Peace Conference was cancelled.[27] And just five days later, on 1 September, at 4.45 a.m, they were already 'shooting back'. The Second World War had begun.

Nuremberg's experience of the first years of this war was like that of the rest of Germany: it was the time of a triumph of German arms which removed the last doubts about Hitler's mission. Probably at no time did Hitler have the Germans closer to him than in summer 1940, after the brief and brilliant campaign against France which seemed at last to have done away with the defeat of the First World War.

However, this was only a prelude. With the beginning of the German attack on Russia on 22 June 1941 it became clear that Hitler had planned this war not just as a war of conquest but also as a war of annihilation, a war of the annihilation of all that was not German and Aryan: the Jews above all, but also the Poles, the Russians and all those who were termed 'subhuman' in the language of the régime.

The war of annihilation did not remain a one-sided one. It was in the logic of things that the enemy should respond to annihilation with annihilation. And so in 1941 there began the attack on the German cities: the only attack on the Germans themselves that the Allies could then launch.

On 20 February 1941 the British War Cabinet resolved to begin an 'intensive air offensive' against Germany. Soon afterwards, Sir Arthur Harris was named head of Bomber Command. He took over responsibility for an unprecedented kind of war in the air. His goal was the destruction of the German will to resist by the large-scale annihilation of German cities and their population.[28] It was a concept which proved to be mistaken in its aim, and its basically terrorist approach was disputed even among the Allies themselves. But its effect on the German cities was frightful.

As a significant industrial city, Nuremberg was on the list of allied bomber targets from the beginning. In addition, in the view of Bomber Command at the same time it was 'also a political target of the first order and one of the holy cities of the Nazi creed'.[29] But the first great air attacks of the new offensives in 1942 and 1943 had still left the city centre of Nuremberg and its industry – and indeed the Party buildings – largely intact. So at the end of March 1944 Harris decided to send his whole fleet of bombers, almost a thousand four-engined planes with high explosive and incendiary bombs, on a major attack which would totally destroy the city.

This attack turned into a catastrophic defeat for Bomber Command. In the biggest night air battle of the Second World War the German defence shot down almost one hundred four-engined planes; the heart of the city remained almost undamaged.[30]

It met its fate only at the beginning of 1945. A low-level attack with more than a million incendiary bombs, thousands of high-explosive bombs and air mines destroyed historical old Nuremberg in a fire storm. It was the worst catastrophe that the city had suffered in more than a thousand years of history.

The Allied bombing of Germany is still one of the most disputed chapters in our history. When the guilt or innocence of the Germans is discussed, it is still the favourite argument with which to point the finger at others. But it is quite unsuitable for doing that. For what this merciless counter-attack by the Allied bombers teaches us is only the fearful truth that evil provokes evil and that all our consciences succumb to this evil. The German soldiers were probably no more aware of the ethical problems of the war that Hitler had wanted than the English pilots and bomb-aimers were clear about the questionable character of the strategic bomber offensive.[31] This too is part of the theme of leading astray and being led astray. And I hope that no one here is so certain of his or her conscience as to feel that the same thing might not happen to them.

## 5. The Nuremberg trial

The unparalleled war and the unparalleled crime were followed by an unparalleled trial, the trial of the so-called major war criminals. It took place in Nuremberg because of the symbolic power that this name had meanwhile taken on all over the world. To begin with, the Russians had insisted on Berlin as the setting for the trials, but the Americans succeeded in the choice of a city in their occupation zone. Where National Socialism had celebrated its greatest triumphs and where the ruins of the city demonstrated its terrible end was to be the place where others would sit in judgment on it.[32] The seat of judgment was fixed in July 1945, and the main hearing began on 20 November 1945 at 10 a.m.

Almost every aspect of the Nuremberg trial has been challenged: its politics, its legality, the individuals involved, its content. And yet more than a generation later we can clearly work out what this unparalleled trial achieved and what it did not.

What it did achieve can perhaps be summed up in the following three points.

First of all it should be stressed that this trial was not a show trial, but in fact an open legal hearing. Though there may be many problems about the legal norms of the proceedings, there can be no doubt that the accused had an opportunity to defend themselves and that the judges were resolved that justice should be done within the limits laid down.

We need to know the plans which had previously been considered in the victors' camp in order to assess the extraordinary significance of this trial. In Tehran in 1943 Stalin had proposed shooting 50,000 or even 100,000 German officers, and had only backed off this idea after Churchill's bitter protest.[33] But in America, too, there was a group around Minister of Finance Morgenthau which called for the immediate execution of the main known German war criminals.[34] By contrast, the fact that a court was meeting here made it unmistakably clear that it was the will of the victors not to let revenge rule, but law. This law was very incomplete, and it did not extend to countless Germans in the West and above all in the East. But an attempt was made to implement it at least in Nuremberg, and that people did not give way to the countless voices which called for vengeance here too was in itself already a significant event which had a wider effect.

Because a court was meeting here which was in search of the truth, and not a show tribunal which already knew the truth, in Nuremberg in fact parts of the truth about the Third Reich came to light which would not otherwise have been believed. Those who work their way through the important protocols and the incriminating evidence of the forty-two volume documentation of the trial will not understand how there could ever be, and indeed still are, people in Germany who doubt the truth of the crimes of the Third Reich. One can argue over many individual issues and their evaluation. But after Nuremberg one can no longer argue about the criminal character of National Socialism.

One can also learn something else from the records of this trial: an important insight for the younger generation. Even among the chief defendants in Nuremberg there were some who only realized the extent of the crime gradually as the trial went on, and were deeply affected when they did so. In the face of the evidence and statements presented at the trial, at least here and there blindness, fanaticism and folly gave place to insight into personal guilt and complicity, regardless of whether the individuals concerned recognized the Allied court or not. Only a few of the accused were still convinced supporters of Hitler at the end of the trial. One of them came from Nuremberg. He was Julius Streicher, the Führer of Franconia.

Since this was the victors' court – and this is the third important point – it has often been accused of depriving the Germans of the opportunity of sitting in judgment on the sins of their fellow-countrymen themselves. But anyone who knows what the situation was in 1945/46 will hardly be able to imagine how such a German court could have been made up and in accordance with what law it would have acted. That the Allies took upon themselves this utterly necessary and unavoidable task of making a first discovery of the truth and passing judgment proves in retrospect to have been a contribution towards the new beginning which Germany sought after 1945.

However, there is one thing that the trial did not achieve, and for the International Court of Justice that was the most important thing. Nuremberg has not become the name for the new foundation of an international law making aggressive wars, war crimes and crimes against humanity, including genocide, universally recognized criminal actions. A generation after Nuremberg the world is as helpless and powerless here as before.

Of course we cannot turn this into an argument against the Nuremberg trials. In truth it is only an argument against ourselves and our inability to preserve justice and peace in the world.


## 6. Called to hope

We have come to the end of our journey through Nuremberg's history in the twentieth century, which was in fact a journey through our own, German history. The theme under which we have gathered here is 'Called to hope'. But the history of our century – particularly as reflected in this city – seems to give little reason for such hope.

On the contrary, if we want to sum up the results of this history, what emerges is an insight into the evidently almost unlimited capacity of people for being led astray. For in retrospect what we have to say is that among the hundreds of thousands who came to Nuremberg year by year, full of enthusiasm, hardly anyone actually wanted all that subsequently happened – perhaps even nobody among those who arranged the Party Conferences. Perhaps they too only went further along the way of evil year by year because they were borne up by the enthusiasm of the masses, just as the masses thought that they were being borne up and led by them. The capacity of human beings to be led astray is what perhaps becomes most stubbornly evident here: their capacity for madness, for hatred, for blindness, for superstition. In these circumstances, what can it mean that we are called to hope?

I think that two things can be said here.

The hope mentioned here is hope for God's future. Where that is proclaimed and believed in, it is constantly present, and is always new help against our capacity to be led astray. The 1934 Theological Declaration of Barmen said that the church 'reminds men of God's kingdom, God's commandment and righteousness, and thereby the responsibilty of rulers and ruled'. If the church does this; if we, Christians, do this, actively and passively, reminding and being reminded, then we are doing the most important thing that can be done against being led astray and our capacity to be led astray.

And secondly: the green stem of hope grows out of the trunk of the cross. It grows where we do not expect it and it grows from powers which are not our own. That is also true of history. Hope also grows in history where we do not expect it, from powers which are not ours.

This is one of the reasons why we as Christians can and must act politically: threatened by being led astray, like all other people, and yet called to hope for God's kingdom, God's command and God's righteousness.

# 2

# Fate and Guilt in History*

It is well known that nothing is more difficult to answer in science than very simple questions. Two such simple questions will be concerning us at the beginning of this lecture. Is history shaped by human interests and plans, decisions or actions? Or is it shaped by chance, i.e. by events which simply cannot be foreseen, the necessity for which we are unable to recognize?[1]

That as a rule we now answer the first question unreservedly in the affirmative, perhaps asking at the same time what else could shape history, is more a result of our rational and moral attitudes than of our experience. Reason and morality require history in principle to form a rational whole in which the same moral categories hold that we use elsewhere. However, experience teaches that in our own lives, and even more in the world in which we live, a great, indeed possibly even a dominant, role is already played by developments that we have not planned and could not plan – though as a rule we are reluctant to assign this role to events which are usually described as fortune or misfortune, precisely because of their irrational character. But it is evident – to take just this one point – that we cannot choose either our parents or the time or country in which we are born. And as we all know, this is what determines our lives. So whatever the individual circumstances may be, such an experience also requires us to take into account the possibility that history is shaped, against all reason and morality, by chances which are in principle unpredictable, however disturbing this possibility may seem to us.

It is clear that both these questions are very closely connected

*A lecture given at the solemn annual session of the Wittheit in Bremen on 20 October 1981. First published in *Jahrbuch der Wittheit zu Bremen* XXVI, 1982, 105-21.

with my theme. For it is only if we understand history as a realm shaped by human interests and plans, decisions and actions, that we can speak in the strict sense of historical guilt, whether this is the guilt of individuals, the guilt of élite leaderships, or the guilt of whole states and peoples. If, however, we begin by supposing that history is shaped by chance events, we will not speak of guilt but rather of fate. Anything that befalls us by chance, unwanted, unforeseen and unavoidable, clearly cannot be associated with any concept of guilt. We then describe what happens as fate, if along with other chance happenings it creates constraining situations and quite unpredictable consequences. So not all chance historical events have the character of fate. But when we speak of fate, we always mean a series of chance events: events which take place or do not take place by chance, fortuitous constellations and fortuitous developments.

However, the question what shapes history, will or chance, is not so much a real question as a hermeneutical question. In other words, we do not ask it in the expectation that at the end our reflection on it we shall be able to say a clear yes to one alternative and therefore a no to the other – nor should we have such an expectation. Rather, the question is meant to open up a way to an understanding of history which does justice not only to its rationality but also to its enigmatic character. For in all our experience of life there is no guilt which does not involve fate at least at some remove, and no fate in which it is impossible to find any guilt. So the theme of this lecture is not fate *or* guilt, but fate *and* guilt.

Now if this is the case, one of the most important tasks of the historian must be to define more closely the relationship between fate and guilt in periods in which the two of them seem as it were to have allied to produce catastrophe, and the degree to which they are involved in the origin, progress and outcome of events.

Beyond question the time between 1914 and 1945, the time between the beginning of the First and the end of the Second World War, is one such period, a period which we are increasingly learning to understand as an era of its own, a kind of second Thirty Years' War.

So in what follows I shall attempt to approach the question of fate and guilt in history through some historical chapters from this period.

## 1. War-guilt and the question of war-guilt in connection with the First World War

The question of where guilt lies for the outbreak of the First World War is still one of the most discussed historical problems of our century. Despite all specific efforts and despite an almost overwhelming number of attempts at explanation, a completely clear answer has yet to be given.[2]

It is certain that everything was ready for this war in Europe – and that was far from being fortuitous: the plans had been made, and the weapons and above all the hearts and heads of the nations were ready. It is a legend to claim that at that time the national leaders incited their people into a war against their knowledge and their will. The opposite is the case. The people, too, were ready for war and the frenzy of enthusiasm in August 1914 seized not only Germany but also Russia and France.

If we consider the particular role of Germany in the events leading up to this war, again there can be no question of chance. Rather, we find here a long list of items of guilt. In first place certainly comes the German effort for a so-called 'place in the sun'. It was probably not, as Fritz Fischer though, a 'grab at world power' which deliberately caused the war, but rather a readiness to fight if need be, and if there was no alternative, for this 'place in the sun'.[3] In addition there were political errors which may be counted as guilt: a misguided foreign policy which increasingly isolated the Reich and by its fleet building programme challenged England in particular; the militarization of public life and, worse, of thought, doubtless a legacy of Prussia; and finally the tendency to arrogance typical of the Kaiser himself and of the whole of his Reich, which was combined with a catastrophic ignorance and underestimation of their opponents. All this and much more combined to make the war seem a possibility, indeed sometimes even a necessity, in Germany. And the weight of the items of guilt is not lessened by the fact that more or less long lists could be compiled for most of the other European powers involved.

Nevertheless – and this is the decisive factor in our context – all that we know indicates that the First World War did not break out because Germany or some other power deliberately planned and wanted this particular war at this particular time.[4] Rather, this war broke out because of events and combinations of factors which could not be foreseen and therefore could not be avoided. That is true, of course, of the assassination of the Austrian Crown Prince, which only acted as a catalyst but nevertheless cannot be detached from the chain of causality.

By way of an exception we must now do what the historian is usually forbidden to do, namely ask 'What would have happened if...?'So what would have happened if that assassination had not taken place? Of course any answer must be hypothetical. It is possible and even probable that sooner or later there would have been a war in Europe anyway. But we certainly cannot rule out the possibility that the Great War, at any rate, could have been avoided.

For unfortunately the July crisis broke over a group of statesmen not one of whom evidently had the above-average capabilities needed for coping with it. No one has described the situation more clearly than Lloyd George, later to become Prime Minister of England during the First World War. After the War he had this to say on the question of guilt. 'Had a Bismarck been in power in Germany, a Palmerston in Great Britain, a Roosevelt in America or a Clemenceau in Paris, the catastrophe could have been – and in my view would have been – avoided. But in none of the great states was a man of this quality there at the helm... None of the leaders at this time in fact wanted the war. To some degree they slid into it, or rather they staggered or stumbled into it, perhaps out of folly.'[5] So in addition to the guilt for this war there is something else which we simply cannot explain but can only recognize in retrospect as fact: the impact of the assassination on a group of responsible people, none of whom was fully able to see the consequences of his decisions. It was only because of this combination that the crisis became a catastrophe. How little people knew what they were letting themselves in for with this War is evident from the simple reflection that at least the governments of Russia, Austria-Hungary and Germany would have prevented a war at any price had they only guessed that it would end up in revolutions which marked the end of the old régime.

But, it might be asked, were there no warnings? Certainly, there were warnings enough. But they all recall the terrifying story of Cassandra, Priam's daughter. As is well known, Apollo had granted her the gift of foretelling, and when she rejected it he punished her by making no one ever believe her true prophecies. So she helplessly foresaw the downfall of Troy, the downfall of the house of Atreus and her own end.[6] The appeals of the Bureau of the Socialist International and of the representatives of the World Alliance for Promoting Friendship between the Churches met with the same fate in July 1914.

In closing his account of this period, Theodor Schieder therefore concluded: 'The idea of the nation had priority over internationalism. The Europeans were agreed on this at the very moment when they were in process of putting an end to all the material and spiritual possessions they had in common. Here all criteria of scientific explanation or moral arrogance fail at a time which could hardly have been better equipped culturally and morally to cope with the problems of war and peace which faced it; here history appears to us as an overwhelming fate.'[7]

The so-called war-guilt question cannot be separated from this question of the proportion of guilt and fate in the outbreak of the First World War, but it can be distinguished from it. There was nothing more necessary for Europe to do after the end of that cruel war than to consider the question of guilt seriously, in order if possible to make a new beginning on the basis of its insight into guilt and fate.

Instead of this, the so-called question of war-guilt itself obstructed this necessary course from the beginning.

Even before the War broke out, the question who was to blame for it played an important role for all those involved. Both the Central Powers and the powers of the Entente attempted to present themselves as the victims and their opponents as the aggressors. Only a defensive war offered a guarantee in Germany, as in Austria, Russia, England or France, that in fact the whole people would rise against the enemy with a feeling that justice had been violated and honour insulted. Both sides succeeded here so convincingly that the troops of both the Central Powers and the Entente, along with their respective peoples, fought in the unshakeable conviction that they were fighting for indubitable justice against injustice.

Nothing made an understanding more difficult even during the War, and nothing more hindered a reasonable peace than those reciprocal assertions of guilt which made every act of compromise seem immoral.

So it was impossible to insult and humiliate the conquered Germans more deeply than by forcing them in the Peace Treaty to acknowledge that they alone were to blame for the war.

This is precisely what the victors demanded; and as is well known, this is what they got. In Article 231 of the Peace Treaty of Versailles the Germans had to sign the statement 'that as the originators of the war, Germany and her allies are responsible for all losses and damage which the allied... governments and members of their states have suffered as a result of the war forced upon them by Germany's attack.' The German Peace delegation thereupon declared with complete conviction on 13 May 1919: 'The German nation did not want the war and would never have embarked upon an offensive war. In the consciousness of the German people this war has always been a defensive war.' However, the Allied answer in the notorious covering note of 16 June 1919 ruled out any further discussion. It stated that in the judgment of 'the whole of the civilized world' the war had been 'the greatest crime against humanity and against the freedom of all peoples which a nation claiming to be civilized has ever consciously committed'. And Germany alone was to be made responsible not only for the unleashing of the war but also for 'the rough and inhuman way' in which it was waged, so that the covering note ended by saying that the behaviour of Germany was 'almost without parallel in the history of humanity'.[8]

Eighteen years later, in June 1937, the author of this covering note, the Englishman Philip Kerr, remarked that in working out this position the Allies had been the victims of their own propaganda. He said that he was firmly convinced that Germany bore more responsibility for the outbreak of the war than anyone else, but that there could be no question of its sole guilt.[9] However, at this time the question of war-guilt had already done its work. Possibly insight into the German guilt for the war would have saved the life of the Weimar Republic. In the first six months after the end of the war there were the beginnings of such an insight not only among the Social Democrats but also for example in the Protestant church. But all that came to an end with the signing of the Peace Treaty on 28 June 1919. Now the question of war-guilt itself, instead of contributing towards a clarification and a settlement, had become a weapon in the hand of the right wing and therefore a link in the fateful chain of events which finally led to the fall of the Weimar Republic.

Here, too, there was no lack of warnings. Max Weber, who among other things had been one of the sharpest critics of German politics in the pre-War period and during the war, prophesied as early as

1919 what in fact happened in the 1930s. A peace like the one planned, he wrote, 'would naturally make the most politically radical worker in Germany – not now, but after a year and a day, when the present tumult and subsequent exhaustion have passed – chauvinist, so that along with the intellectuals of the nation he will inevitably reflect on those revolutionary means of self-determination which any Irredentist had used and which a people of seventy million can naturally use more widely and more impressively than Serbia or Italy ever did'.[10]

Nine months later, in September 1919, Corporal Adolf Hitler for the first time formulated the connection between the fight against Judaism and the 'Rebirth of the moral and spiritual powers of the nation'.

## 2. The downfall of the Weimar democracy and the rise of Hitler

In the late Schleiermacher we occasionally find the melancholy observation: 'One age bears the guilt of the others, but rarely knows how to absolve it other than through new guilt.' Anyone who follows the course of events between 1914 and 1945 cannot but be struck by the truth of this observation. Germany's guilt in the war was followed by the guilt of that treaty which did not create peace in Europe, but sowed bitterness, hatred and revenge. However, it was not the peaceful revisionary policies of Stresemann or Brüning which absolved this guilt, but Hitler with a new and monstrous guilt which far transcended anything that had gone before. At the same time, though, here too fate is intermingled with what in retrospect are clearly incriminating items of guilt, in the form of chance events the unpredictable occurrence of which left a decisive mark on the course of history.

I shall attempt to clarify the combination of guilt and fate in this period by means of a few examples.

One of the manifest faults of the victorious powers, France and England, was that despite an increasingly better insight into the character of the Versailles treaty they held firm to its basic conception. This placed an almost intolerable burden on the Weimar Republic and at the same time gave Hitler the starting point for his revisionist policy which was approved of far beyond the circle of his immediate supporters. This guilt is intensified by the fact that on the other hand – and we should be particularly attentive to this

argument today – it failed to counter the possible explosive consequences of such a policy in Germany by producing a military
deterrent. In 1947, André François-Ponçet, the French Ambassador
in Berlin, who was in a better position than anyone else to follow at
close quarters the development of German politics berween 1931
and 1938, described this in his memoirs as the complicity of the
Allies in the outbreak of the Second World War. In connection with
his repeated warnings in Paris about German rearmament he
observed: 'When Hitler was guilty of the first breach of the treaty,
it would without doubt have been better immediately to have taken
counter-measures. For quite understandable reasons – the desire to
avoid a new war, the nation's profound pacifism, the firm ties with
the League of Nations and a belief in its mission..., the inadequate
military apparatus which was constructed only for defence – for
all these reasons our governments did not have the necessary
courage.'[11] And no less a figure than Karl Barth was still agreeing
with him in 1950 when, speaking of his call to the Czechs in autumn
1938 to defend themselves by force of arms against the German
invasion, he repeated his conviction that 'Much that was inhuman
and un-Christian which took place subsequently could have been
prevented at that time relatively painlessly, simply by the demonstration of armed steadfastness, had the state order in the West been
responsibly defended at the right time.'[12]

The growing inability of the democratic parties to come to any
agreement or compromise is no less clearly one of the elements in
German guilt for the downfall of democracy and the rise of Hitler.
The last parliamentary government of the Weimar Republic, the
Müller cabinet, supported by a major coalition, fell on 27 March
1930 over the question of cover for unemployment insurance. Rarely
can the cause for the resignation of a government have been more
blatantly disproportionate to the consequences. For from this point
on until March 1933 it was no longer possible to find a parliamentary
majority for a government. It was not just that Hitler claimed that
the democratic parties were incompetent; they *were* incompetent.
And the consequences were what might have been expected. At
that time, in March 1930, of the 491 Reichstag delegates 12 were
National Socialists and 54 were Communists. Only six months later,
on 14 September 1930, 107 were National Socialists and 77 were
Communists.[13]

Only examples of these items of guilt have been cited here. While completely understandable in terms of the time, they do not seem to have been the result of ill will and in some respects seem to have been almost unavoidable, though in retrospect they can be recognized as evidence of guilt. To them was now added a series of fateful events; these sealed the fate of the Republic.

We find a particularly dramatic example of an event of this kind in Churchill's memoirs. If the Republic was still to be saved from the National Socialist advance, then in addition to economic consolidation, this was most likely to come about through success in foreign politics. And it was precisely this success which was within Brüning's grasp in Geneva in April 1932, with an agreement on a partial revision of the Treaty of Versailles.

In conversations with the English Prime Minister and the American Foreign Minister, a German Chancellor had succeeded for the first time in gaining the agreement of the Allies to a new level of armaments. Only France's assent was still lacking. Churchill tells us that 'Norman Davis, the American Ambassador-at-Large, telephoned to the French Premier, Tardieu, to come immediately from Paris to Geneva. But unfortunately for Brüning, Tardieu had other news. Schleicher had been busy in Berlin, and had just warned the French Ambassador not to negotiate with Brüning because his fall was imminent. It may well be also that Tardieu was concerned with the military position of France on the formula "equality of armaments". At any rate, Tardieu did not come to Geneva and on 1 May Brüning returned to Berlin.' Shortly afterwards, Tardieu was succeeded by Herriot, who immediately declared his readiness to discuss the new proposals for negotiation with Brüning. At noon on 30 May 1932 Brüning received an invitation to Geneva with an indication of the French readiness to negotiate. A few hours later he officially resigned. 'So,' Churchill concludes, 'ended the last Government in post-war Germany which might have led the German people into the enjoyment of a stable and civilized constitution and opened peaceful channels of intercourse with their neighbours. The offers which the Allies had made to Brüning would, but for Schleicher's intrigue and Tardieu's delay, certainly have saved him. These offers had presently to be discussed with a different System and a different man.'[14]

Even if Churchill's 'certainly' should be replaced with a 'possibly', the element of fate in this story is clear. Certainly, here too one can also find specific mistakes and omissions, by Macdonald and

Tardieu, by François-Ponçet and Schleicher, by Hindenburg and by Brüning himself. But there is no historical theory which could explain why in the Weimar period all the possibly decisive shifts like this one came too late, too slowly and too half-heartedly; and why all the mistakes and omissions added up to a chain of fate under the burden of which the Republic finally collapsed.

The list of items of German guilt which brought Hitler to power is a long one. No less long is the list of weaknesses, errors and mistakes which kept him in power. And whatever the individual knew or did not know, one certainly cannot exclude any adult German from complicity in the fact that the Reich which he served was an unjust state.

The fateful character of this period comes out all the more clearly when we see the contrast between the unfortunate Republic and the no less fateful good fortune which Hitler enjoyed between 1933 and 1940. Not only Germany but the whole of Europe at this time was under the impression that Hitler was being fortunate in all the things in which the Weimar government had been unfortunate; and in addition to that he realized within a few years political goals which people did not even dare to mention in the 1920s. That was ultimately what attracted the Germans, what made them renounce more and more rights and freedoms and close their eyes to injustices: the successes of a man who apparently succeeded in everything to which he set his hand.

Even Dietrich Bonhoeffer, who from the beginning did not waver for a moment in his verdict on the régime, was not unimpressed by the success. It must remain an open question whether he really called for a change of attitude to Hitler in the Council of Brethren of the Prussian Confessing Church after the German victory over France, because events had proved 'that God is with him'.[15] But it is certain that at this time he inserted a section into his *Ethics* called 'The Successful Man', which stated: 'The world will allow itself to be subdued only by success. It is not ideas or opinions which decide, but facts. Success alone justifies wrongs done. Success heals the wounds of guilt.'[16]

Moreover, Hitler himself knew that very well. When he was preparing the senior officers of the three sections of the Wehrmacht for war in a secret speech at the Kroll Opera in Berlin on 10 February 1939, he called for the unconditional obedience of the army with the argument: 'For six years now, gentlemen, we have had one good fortune after another. In these six years we have really pulled off miracles. Gentlemen, things might easily have gone very differently.'[17]

Again there is a wealth of explanations for this series of successes. But anyone who follows through in detail the unpredictable coincidences, the combinations of events which no one could plan, that were necessary for Hitler's success will also see this series of successes which did not fail once until 1940 as a fate against which it seemed impossible to act.

It was the opponents of Hitler who felt their impotence here particularly clearly, and almost painfully. And in fact there is a further indication of the fateful character of this time, namely the ill star which shone over all the attempts on Hitler's life.

In August 1936 Friedrich Reck-Malleczewen, an ardent opponent of Hitler, who was murdered in Dachau in February 1945, recorded this sense of impotence against fate in his *Diary of a Desperate Man*. He recalled a scene from autumn 1932, when he happened to be dining one evening with Hitler in the Munich restaurant Osteria Bavaria. At that time, Reck noted four years later, 'I had come by car into the city and as the streets... were then already very unsafe, I had a loaded pistol with me. On that occasion I could have shot him without further ado in the almost empty inn. I would have done so on the spot had I been certain of the role of this vituperous man and of our future years of suffering.' Reck did not shoot because he still did not take Hitler seriously at that time, and he added: 'Even here, where in the counsels of the highest our martyrdom is already decided on, it would have been no use; and even if at that time he had been bound to a railway line, the approaching express would have been derailed before it got to him. Nowadays we hear a good deal about attempts on his life, all of which have failed. That will go on, and he will have good fortune until his time has come. But when it has come, disaster will creep upon him from every corner...'[18]

We can only understand the prophetic significance of this comment from 1936 when we recall the long series of attempts on Hitler's life by desperate Germans in subsequent years, which did indeed all fail without exception and against all probability. On 8 November 1938, for example, Hitler unexpectedly left the Bürgerbrau Keller just thirteen minutes before Georg Elser's bomb exploded. On 13 March 1943 the fuse failed in a bomb in Hitler's plane; soon afterwards an attempt failed in the Berlin armoury because Hitler left the room quickly, contrary to his previous habits. And on 20 July 1944 only a few yards made the decisive difference between the life and death of the dictator.[19] These were certainly all chance happenings, the unpredictably fateful consequences of which for subsequent history can easily be seen.

### 3. Resistance and confession of guilt

In view of the overpoweringly fateful character of these years, which increasingly impressed itself on contemporaries as the war went on, the question arises whether and in what sense one can talk of guilt here. For if we are delivered over to events which we cannot influence in any way, there no longer seems to be any guilt in terms of decisions which have been freely chosen.

But that is a pseudo-argument. Rather, what matters above all in the right understanding of the relationship between fate and guilt is to grasp that there is a category of guilt which asserts itself against all fate. It is that guilt which is experienced and confessed either by the individual alone or a community as his (her, its) own guilt. If so far we have seen fate and guilt working as it were alongside each other in history, we now come to a point where we can define the relationship between the two more closely. The overwhelming majority of Germans, including the German leaders, doubtless followed Hitler without any sense of guilt and thus entered the war. That was not just a consequence of the way in which discussion of guilt for the First World War was hampered by the war-guilt question, but that question was also a factor here.

However, in the course of the war that changed. It was not a change which took place overnight; far less one which could in any form become common property. For both the law of war and the terror of the régime stood in the way.

Nevertheless, there can be no question that here and there in Germany awareness was aroused of a personal guilt and complicity in the course of events which was not prompted by any propaganda and which no propaganda could assuage: an awareness of one's own guilt and complicity which, once it had risen to consciousness, began to understand fate itself as a consequence of guilt. No matter how hidden it had to be, by nature and because of external circumstances, this change was nevertheless one of the most important developments which took place at this time.

We find it in a simple form in the memoirs of an old pastor, written above all for his children and grandchildren, which he sent me some time ago. In them he described, among other things, his experience of the advance into Russia in 1941 as a lieutenant in the Second Panzer Division and how by chance he was witness to a mass shooting in Berdichev. Hundreds of Jews, men, women and children, were murdered before his eyes and the eyes of other soldiers. Almost all the soldiers, he wrote, were distraught, and looked away with horror and revulsion. The lieutenant himself, helpless and bewildered, decided against all military rules to take the case to his most senior officer. In fact he succeeded in getting through to the general. The general listened to the lieutenant's report, equally deeply moved and shaken. But when the lieutenant asked him to do something, he replied; 'What can I do? You have too much respect for the power of a general. Do not suppose, chaplain, that what you have told me does not move me. But what can I do?' And soon afterwards he repeated yet again: 'What can I do? I cannot simply make the police batallion stop its criminal activity; it is not under my command. I cannot carry on a private war against orders all of which come from above.'[20]

Despite this experience, both the lieutenant and the general continued on active service. To this degree the dialogue did not have any consequences. But it is impossible for it not to have affected their awareness. Rather, here and in countless similar conversations people became ready to speak of their own guilt and complicity, even if they were not themselves murderers or directly guilty.

This was evidently the starting point for Hans Asmussen, one of the leaders of the Confessing Church, when he wrote to Visser't Hooft during the catastrophe which befell the Sixth Army in Stalingrad. He said that after the war the church would have to speak to the world about its guilt: 'It is one of the most impressive experiences of recent years that great disaster comes about when the question of guilt is simply left to propaganda. For propaganda is concerned to find just one scapegoat. But in so doing it heaps up injustice and sows fearful dragons' seed, which shoots up one day.' He went on to write that he found in Germany today, and not just among the theologians, 'a readiness to hear of guilt' which was very much greater than after the First World War.[21]

The higher form of this readiness 'to hear of guilt' developed in the resistance. For the resistance to Hitler was quite simply the purest declaration of an intention not to (or no longer to) be accomplices in the misdeeds of the régime. The readiness 'to hear of guilt' led to a sense of responsibility for putting and end to the régime and thus risking one's own life in atonement for the guilt.

When Major-General Henning von Tresckow, who made a decisive contribution to the military resistance, took leave of his friend Schlabrendorff after the failure of the attempt on Hitler's life in the early hours of 21 July 1944, he said: 'If God once promised Abraham that he would not destroy Sodom if only ten righteous men were found in it, I hope that God will not destroy Germany for our sake. None of us can lament our own deaths. Anyone who has joined our circle has donned the cloak of Nessus. A person's moral value begins only when he is ready to give his life for his convictions.'[22]

These remarks show that there is only one authority which can clarify the ambiguous relationship between fate and guilt, and that is our own conscience. Only where historical guilt is identified by the conscience of an individual or a community as his or its own guilt is clarity achieved. And only here can responsible action which seeks repentance and expiation arise from the insight.

It is in this insight that the special, indeed the incomparable, significance of the German resistance lies.

No denazification, no re-education, no Nuremberg trial could have moved the Germans after the war to an insight into their guilt had not individual consciences made their own judgments within Germany itself. Many of the victors' decisions were more prone to make the Germans deny their guilt and lament their fate, as after the First World War. The reason why that did not happen lies in the change which began during the war and which took on tangible form in the resistance in all its guises. But it was also precisely this change whch in 1945 led to the Stuttgart Declaration of Guilt and its two central statements: 'With great sorrow we say that through us, infinite sorrow has been brought upon many peoples and lands', and, 'We regret that we did not confess more boldly, pray more loyally, believe more cheerfully and love more ardently.'[23] As we know, this declaration was not generally accepted at the time. But it became such an effective new experience that it shaped the new beginning after the war more strongly than any thought of hatred and revenge.

## 4. Guilt and fate as categories of political action

To conclude with, I would like to attempt to indicate briefly a possible significance of the categories of guilt and fate for our present political action and decision.

There are two aspects of the insight into the character of guilt in history. First of all it shows that in history there is in fact a demonstrable constellation of guilt: from the outbreak of the First World War, caused by a readiness to wage war, by arrogance, national blindness, claims to power and much else, a complex of guilt – guilt for acting and for failing to act – leads to the collapse of the Weimar Republic, to the rise of Hitler, to the murder of the Jews and to the catastrophe of the Second World War. If I say that here we recognize a demonstrable complex of guilt, that means that in my view nothing here was determined, nothing was unavoidable, but in retrospect it is possible to identify and name the wrong decisions and those who made them, whether individuals or groups.

If that is correct, then there can be only one conclusion from our insight into the character of guilt in history; we must take responsibility for political decisions with all the watchfulness and sensitivity to their aims and possible consequences that we can command.

Politics, the stuff of which history is made, is practised by human beings. It is our hopes and desires, our prejudices and impatience, our fears and anxieties, which enter into the political decisions of the present. We are responsible for them, and will be held to account for them by subsequent generations. Insight into the character of guilt in history is therefore the foundation of our political responsibility for history – the responsibility for creating peace, freedom and justice and not unrest, lack of freedom and injustice. It is not to be expected that we should emerge guiltless from this responsibility. But that does not change it in any way.

All this is immediately understandable and clear nowadays in connection with the category of guilt.

The character of history as fate is, however, another matter. From our rational and moral standpoint we prefer to take as little notice as possible of this element of history. But we only deceive ourselves if we deny this element – a piece of self-deception which must belong in the category of guilt. Similarly, insight into the character of history as fate also has two aspects.

First of all the concept of fate simply denotes the fact that we have only limited possibilities of controlling history. Even if we are most vigorously and keenly aware of our responsibility, it is never possible completely to foresee the consequences of our decisions. At any point unpredictable incidents which we could not have planned for take place to thwart all good plans and intentions. The history of the world is full of such chances, which always have the character of fate. That history can look like fate indicates that while human beings make history, they are not its lords. For the great statesmen, this was never in doubt. Thus on 20 July 1864 Bismarck wrote to his wife, in the middle of the Danish war: 'The lesson of this business is that one can be as wise as the wise men of this world and yet at any point go into the next minute like a child into the dark... perhaps in eight days we shall have peace with the Danes, and perhaps the war will still be on this winter.'[24]

In my view, one consequence of this insight is that no absolute claims should be made in the political sphere. No decision can guarantee the right way into the future with absolute certainty.

The other question is how we deal with this insight into the character of history as fate. One can deny this character; one can also seek to make it philosophically innocuous, as happens in the major ideological programmes of modern times.

The answer given by Christian faith is rather different. Faith does not see fate as mere blind workings but as God's will. To end with, here is one illustration of this. On the rear wall of St Mary's Church in Osnabrück there is a picture of the great fire in the city in 1613. Houses, churches and towers are in flames.

Underneath, the parish of St Mary's put the following text:

On 11 March 1613
in this city
through God's fate
942 houses and
this church and tower were
burnt.

On 7 May
Lord, Lord,
but spare
who will help Jacob further,
for he is so small.

# Modern German History and Protestant Theology
## Aspects and Questions*

### 1. The Weimar Republic in crisis and the beginnings of dialectical theology

The beginnings of dialectical theology without doubt form one of the most moving chapters of the history of modern theology. The early speeches, articles and polemic which have now been collected into two volumes (a selection from which has been translated into English),[1] still show clearly the fascination which it exerted. But the historical distance which separates us from them also sharpens our eyes to the problems associated with that great departure from Fatherland and friends. The most visible expression of these problems is the parting of the spirits which took place in 1933. It is no coincidence that here a political date took on decisive significance. For from the beginning dialectical theology was very closely bound up with the cultural and political situation after the First World War. We shall be concerned here with some aspects of this association.

In his Foreword to the German edition, Jürgen Moltmann pointed out that it is 'certainly very interesting to read and interpret these "theologians of crisis" historically in the context of the whole crisis for culture, state and Christianity after the First World War'. But he does not regard this as 'very fruitful'. ('What is important is not the mood of crisis and the radicalism which "dialectical theology" communicated, but the theological insight that was gained in those critical years' (ixf.). That may be correct in principle, but I find dubious the impression that there is something like theological

*First published in *Evangelische Theologie* 23, 1963, 510-36.

insight in itself, which can be separated from the historical conditions of its origin. Whether or not an inquiry into the general historical context is 'fruitful', it does seem me in any case to be a necessary one to make. Moltmann's assertion that ' "Dialectical theology" does not derive from the mood of crisis in those turbulent years' (x),[2] put as baldly as that, hardly does justice to this complex problem. Or are the numerous references to the great crisis which appear more or less emphatically and explicitly in almost all the contributions really no more than interesting decoration?

I shall attempt to investigate this question, basing my comments above all on some recent publications relating to the cultural and political history of the Weimar period.

I

In recent years it is no coincidence that the unhappy First Republic has been the object of special interest: for the Federal Republic of Germany it is both democratic tradition and a warning. It is to this interest that we owe not only a vast flood of specialist investigations but also two excellent accounts on a larger scale, which discuss the stages of the collapse of the Weimar Republic and the seizure of power by Hitler.[3] Although their orientation is predominantly political, both works make it clear that the Republic did not just fail because of an extremely unfavourable combination of political circumstances at home and abroad; an important role was played by that movement which as the 'right-wing opposition' undermined all attempts at political consolidation. Kurt Sontheimer has now made his own detailed investigation of this movement, and I think that his book is one of the most significant contributions to the understanding of more recent German history.[4]

Sontheimer begins with an important distinction between the old nationalism which was still alive in the traditions of the Kaiser's Reich and the new nationalism which grew 'out of the World War as the beginning of a new era' (28), and which was often characterized by a 'vehement rejection of Wilhelmism' (30). In this connection Walter Bussmann had already referred to the great significance of the generation question.[5] This new nationalism, which has also been termed the 'conservative' revolution, was the real cultural nucleus of the anti-democratic movement.

If we attempt to work out the cultural foundations of this national-ist revolutionary movement, the first and most important characteristic that we come across is its passionate rejection of liberal democracy. This rejection was not so much of the Republic itself – though the Republic was often wide open to criticism – as of its foundation: the liberal and democratic 'system'. To this new opposition, liberalism stood for all forms of individualism, mechanism and atomism; it stood for the whole allegedly spiritless and corrupt social system of the West, which was regarded as dead formalism in contrast to the powerful liveliness of a new order. How deeply this anti-liberal thought had taken hold, above all of the young, is clear, for example, from a 1932 study of cultural attitudes; Sontheimer thinks that its author is not exaggerating when he declares that 'for the best part of German youth liberalism is dead' (186). A characteristic quotation from this study reads: 'These young men have only unspeakable contempt for the "liberal world", which describes an alienation from the world that is of little worth as an unconditional response to the spirit; they know that compromises in things of the spirit are the beginning of all kinds of vice and lies' (186f.). Here at the same time we can see clearly the solemnity of radical absolutism, which is so characteristic of this whole way of thinking.

They were all at one in their rejection of Western liberal ideas: Moeller van den Bruck, whose *Drittes Reich* is perhaps the most impressive document of this trend; the Jünger brothers, Oswald Spengler and Hans Freyer, Alois Dempf and Hans Zehrer's 'Tatkreis'.

It was a consequence of this way of thinking that the political manifestation of liberalism, parliamentary democracy, met with only hatred and contempt in these circles. Along with the parties it belonged on the side of utterly dead being.[6] What made liberal parliamentary democracy so hateful to the right was that feature which was its very essence: the pressure towards compromise, the relative truth of majority decisions, the legalization of group interests, and bound up with this the dull, unheroic nature of the decisions arrived at by democratic processes.

But what were the positive aims of the nationalist opposition?

Chief among them was a picture of the new state which was opposed to the party state of the 'system'. Sontheimer describes it as a 'strong, powerful state, a state which raises itself above party quarrels and economic interests and points out their limitations with a firm and if necessary indeed with an iron, hand' (244). The whole desire of the bourgeoisie for order and cleanliness, for authority and leadership, but also for national greatness and glory, was concentrated in the idea of the new state. Its characteristic types emerge in Othmar Spann as a class state, in Edgar Jung as an authoritarian state, led by a highly qualified élite; or in the writings of Carl Schmitt as a totalitarian state, as a unity of state and society. In it and through it everything will become different: an authentic Volk community will take the place of the pluralist society; the free decision of the charismatic leader, to whom his followers are bound in unconditional obedience, will take the place of anonymous majority decisions; and the new, great German Reich will take the place of a weak night-watchman state that has become a mockery. The new Reich will be the crown and fulfilment of the thousand-year history of Germany.

It was with these aims that the nationalist opposition went to war against the Republic. It did not achieve them. Instead, through the radicalism of its criticism and the demagogic and utopian character of its demands it systematically destroyed the cultural substance of the Republic, which was in any case weak, and in so doing made a substantial contribution towards preparing the ground for the 'Third Reich'. The conservative revolution may certainly not be simply be identified with National Socialism. But, as Sontheimer rightly asks at the end of his account, was not 'that weakening of the idea of humanity, that defaming of liberalism, that radical scepticism about reason, that readiness to give credence to the suggestive propaganda slogans of the new authorities, also the consequence of the anti-democratic cultural movement?' (398). It is in this respect that the nationalist opposition belongs in the immediate cultural prehistory of the Führer state.[7]

So far I have been essentially relying on Sontheimer's account; now I shall take from this complex a question which seems to be of particular significance in the present context.

The really astonishing thing about the conservative revolution is not so much the fact of its existence – a number of reasons can be given for that – as its extent and the extraordinary response that it provoked in the bourgeoisie and above all among the youth. It seems to me now that a decisive role was played in it by a feeling which was perhaps the basic feeling of the 1920s: the feeling of crisis. At that time there was incessant and indeed passionate talk and writing about the great crisis. That the times were out of joint, that in their womb a powerful yet still unknown force was in preparation which would do away with the everyday life of the Weimar Republic at a stroke, was a conviction which clearly dominated the thoughts and feelings of a whole generation. Without this sense of crisis the success of the nationalist opposition would have been unthinkable. With its mixture of radical criticism and irrational utopia it was the exact reflection of this basic mood. It was one, bourgeois-nationalist, answer to the crisis, just as Communism was the other.

However, this sense of crisis was not merely reflection on an objectively critical situation, as one might at first think. Rather, the solemnity with which it presented itself indicates that its roots are to be sought at a deeper level. And in fact here we very soon come up against a movement which had been gaining increasing influence even in the last decades of the Kaiser's Reich. Its rallying-cry was to the fight against the bourgeois liberal world of the nineteenth century, its main opponent the Enlightenment and the rationalistic thought of the West which that had dominated, and its arsenal above all Romantic ideas of all shades.[8]

Christian Graf Krockow has investigated these connections in a perceptive study.[9]

Krockow characterizes this movement as 'the struggle of the bourgeoisie against itself', as a kind of 'ideological class suicide' (28). It finds its expression in the philosophy of life which 'strove for liberation from a burden which had become intolerable' (31) – namely the burden of a civilized and mechanized bourgeois world – and also in its practical parallel, the youth movement, which in its search for allegiance and authority, in its longing for the experience of being 'us', found a supreme value in dedication to the community. The famous demonstration of support in August 1914 is a first climax of this development. The tumult and frenzy of those weeks, which were later also constantly evoked by the conservative revolution as the great hour of the nation, are the expression of an 'elemental feeling of liberation'.

'The beginning of the war brought the universal victory of the youth movement and showed that the alleged outsiders and rebels were in fact the representatives of the really dominant feelings' (39).

Ernst Troeltsch aptly described the irrational character of this demonstration of feeling when he wrote: 'The first and most powerful experience of the nation is now none other than this discovery of the spirit itself which lies in the experience of the return of the nation to faith in the idea and the spirit... Our opponents counted out the square kilometres, the population statistics and the financial resources of the peoples of the Entente and trusted in victory with the constantly repeated triumphal words, "c'est mathématique". We said, "It cannot be God's will that we should be obliterated from a world of nations that is to be strong for the future, nor is it our will", and that was our mathemathics.'[10] The war was also waged in this conviction by the best of the younger generation as a Kultur-krieg, as a war about the self-assertion of the German spirit over Roman/Anglo-Saxon thought.

Now it was precisely that which made the defeat a spiritual problem of the first order, quite apart from its immediate political effect. For to acknowledge the defeat also meant acknowledging the superiority of 'Western thought' to German ideology; it meant revising it in favour of an assimilation to the old humanitarian, natural-law tradition of the West. The older generation of the bourgeois liberals, men like Ernst Troeltsch, Friedrich Meinecke, Hugo Preuss, Max Weber, Friedrich Naumann and not least Thomas Mann, was ready to take this bitter way.[11] The younger, the spiritual élite of the generation which had been at the front, refused to draw these conclusions. They were not ready either to accept the defeat or to draw any conclusions from it. So their only way was into the 'philosophy of crisis'. It was the spiritual parallel to the 'And yet you have conquered', the attempt to salvage that irrationalist outburst by understanding the war merely as a stage in the era of revolution in world history. The loss of the war was a sign that the 'German idea' had not yet been worked out radically enough, with sufficient purity. 'For this War,' as Ernst Jünger wrote in 1922, 'is not, as many people think, the end, but the beginning of power. It is the hammer blow which smites the world into new divisions and new communities. It is the twilight glow of a time that is passing away, and at the same time the dawn in which preparations are being made for new, greater battles' (Krockow, 46).

Here we find talk of the great crisis being shown up as an enormous ideological expedient. It is the presupposition and at the same time the legitimation which enabled those who felt that they were in the right to hold fast to their ideas in the face of the historical fact of the defeat, and indeed to proclaim as the demand of the time that these ideas should be made stronger and more radical. The great crisis allowed, and indeed required, a radicality and absoluteness of spirit;

it prohibited any 'relative' or 'rational' solutions, which from the perspective of the powerful dimensions to which it constantly appealed it could easily mock. So a helpless bourgeoisie was told that its salvation and redemption lay in precisely that which had been a cause of the catastrophe: the destruction of the last traditions of humanity and natural law in favour of unconditional, heroic resolution towards the absolute. 'What is being experienced is the complete collapse of individualism; it is the absolute bankruptcy of humanitarian thought.'[12]

In the main part of his study Krockow points out the parallels in structure between Ernst Jünger's concept of struggle, Martin Heidegger's concept of decision and Carl Schmitt's concept of resolution. The same emptiness of content is characteristic of all these concepts: they are meant to 'be significant purely as such, to a certain degree "in themselves"' (2). And it is precisely in this respect, in this call to struggle, to decision, to resolution, without any why, against whom or where, that these three figures prove to be representatives of that philosophy of crisis in which the only value is revolution *per se*. No wonder that this 'decisionism' led both Carl Schmitt and Martin Heidegger to glorify the 'nationalist revolution' of 1933. Ernst Jünger's aristocratic opposition provides no proof to the contrary.

## II

I should have stressed something else in order to bring out some characteristic ideas from the years after the First World War. The aim of this account was to point to the parallels which exist between the outbreak of the nationalist revolution and the beginnings of dialectical theology.

The parallel is particularly striking in the case of Friedrich Gogarten.[13] The famous 1920 article which two years later gave the group's journal its title is doubtless one of the most impressive testimonies of the feelings of the young opposition. Gogarten spoke here in the name of the generation which felt it to be its destiny to stand 'between the times':[14] 'So we stand in the middle – in an empty space. We belong neither to the one nor to the other.' And in just that respect he precisely grasped the feelings of the 'lost generation'.

Moltmann understands the article as the 'passionate denial of traditional theology'.[15] It is certainly also that. But it is very much more. It is the denial of the world of the nineteenth century generally and of all its traditions: the proclamation of judgment on a dead, empty past which has become meaningless. 'Today we are witnessing the demise of your world. We can be as calm about all that concerns this decline as if we were seeing the extinction of something with which we had no connection at all... We do not wish to lift a hand to stop it [the destruction]. What is it that we should stop? And how should we do it? All these things have long since disintegrated.' Gogarten's criticism of the past is as radical as it is comprehensive: 'In all the world we see no form of life which is not being dissolved',[16] dissolved by historicism, rationalism, scholarship; dissolved ultimately by the human element which has established itself as far as 'to the most refined concept of God'.[17]

Gogarten is convinced that this 'refined, wise culture' stands like a wall between God and the people of his time. 'We raise the question, in all seriousness, whether today there are any men who can really conceive of God.'[18] Only the complete collapse of this culture can create the presupposition for a new, authentic question about God. Therefore at present there is no solution, there are no proposals, no spontaneous expedients; all there is is to remain between the times and be open to the word and the action of God.

Is this programme the theological equivalent of the criticism and demands that the young generation of the nationalist revolutionaries were making on state and society? There are many signs pointing in that direction. In both instances we are confronted with the same passion and radicalism attacking the same opponents: the rational, ordered, bourgeois humanitarian world of the nineteenth century. In both cases the death sentence is passed on this world and those who seek to rescue its traditions for the new time. And in both cases we encounter the vehement rejection of all concrete proposals and the demand for heroic endurance of the crisis as the presupposition of the new thing that is hoped for and desired.

The parallel even extends to details. For example the interpretation of the war as the sign of the dawn of a new era, with the help of which the nationalist opposition ideologically rose above the fact of the defeat and all its necessary consequences, finds its precise parallel in Gogarten: 'For after such an event as this war what person whose thought is directed towards human things would go on thinking as he had thought before? It was not a war like other wars; this war is the dawn of the end of a period of history, indeed of an era of humanity.' That was written in 1932.[19] And it is perhaps not superfluous to point out that here, fourteen years after the end of the war, Gogarten was still speaking of the war as a present event. The state of war had to remain permanent because the idea of its definitive ending and the reflection on the possibilities of a new beginning which was necessarily bound up with it simply could not be tolerated by the ideology of crisis.

If we look at Gogarten's intellectual career from this perspective, then the parallels with the ideas of the 'conservative revolutionaries' become even clearer. He, like them, is rooted in the irrational, anti-bourgeois movement of the decades before the First World War.[20] Under the impact of the war this beginning turned into the ideology of crisis with its demand for the radical endurance of the absolute as this is expressed in *Zwischen den Zeiten*. The attempt to overcome the crisis leads to the theological grounding of the community in the concept of readiness to listen, or obedience, which when related to the state constitutes the new form of freedom[21] and ends up not inconsistently in the decision of the year 1933.

The question arises whether or not *this* aspect of Gogarten's work, which is only one among many, can contribute anything towards the understanding of his theological approach and in addition also to an understanding of the beginnings of dialectical theology.

We may start from the fact that the group of young theologians who gathered round the new journal in 1922 recognized a picture of themselves in that self-portrait of a generation which was developed in the article 'Between the Times'. Otherwise the choice of this title is inexplicable. Gogarten later formulated the one original experience which bound this group together, as it were its theological distinctiveness, like this: 'It was not only another way in which people were asking here and there about God, but it was another God who was being asked about here and there... The God about whom people were asking in traditional theology was the highest thought or the highest good – that which brought human life to a rounded conclusion. The God about whom we were asking in the new theological approach was an uncanny reality, the question, the rift, the contradiction of which, running through all human life and through all that is in human life, was kept open to an intolerable degree.'[22]

Jürgen Moltmann surely grasps the essential point in supposing that here it becomes clear that 'with the theology of the Word of God is associated a programmatic opposition to that theology which begins with objects and elements present in human beings and their world, with religion or religious experience, history or saving facts'.[23] One could also say that this approach is connected with the programmatic opposition to any ideology, whether this is religious-social, conservative Western, liberal democratic or orthodox church theology. It is to this freedom to which the Word of God is a summons that Karl Barth was referring when he said at the end of his Tambach lecture: 'Without being disturbed by the inconsistent appearance of it we shall then enjoy the freedom of saying now Yes and now No, and of saying both not as a result of outward chance or of inward caprice but because we are so moved by the will of God, which has been abundantly proved "good, and acceptable, and perfect" (Rom.12.2).'[24] There is no need to say anything in support of the justification and the significance of this approach; they are evident. But the question now is whether in this struggle against binding the Word of God to any ideologies a new ideology did not to some extent creep in through the back door, namely the ideology of crisis. The question again applies to a special degree for Gogarten. The maxim of dialectical theology, that in the freedom of its power to judge and save the word of God is the crisis of all cultures and ideologies, cannot in any circumstances be reversed. That means that the Word of God cannot be discovered as the word of judgment and grace from any historical situation, however deeply critical that situation may be felt to be. Only God's word can produce crisis. And in the face of this crisis, all the crises of world history are equally important or unimportant, equally significant or insignificant. Where this relationship is reversed, talk of the Word of God as the crisis of culture becomes ideology. Here the positive-ideological bonds on the Word of God – Christian culture, Christian state, Christian morality, etc. – are simply exchanged for negative ideological bonds: the absolute No replaces the absolute Yes.

The article 'Between the Times' proclaims this absolute No. It understands its time to a special degree, indeed exclusively, as God's time. 'There was finally an opportunity to raise questions about God. The times fell asunder and now time stands still. For one moment? For an eternity? Must we not be able to hear God's Word now? Must we not be able to see his hand in his work now?'[25] Why? Because Germany lost the war? Because the humanitarian traditions of the West did not seem as strong as a century which believed in progress had once imagined? Because human wisdom to some extent seemed at an end? Or because God's Word was on the scene as the crisis of this time, as of all times?

There is much to indicate that for the Gogarten of the 1920s the crisis came first and God's Word as answer came second. That inevitably had ominous consequences: a particular historical moment with its particular spiritual, political and economic complex of events became 'God's time'. Marked off from a godforsaken yesterday and ready for a new tomorrow, this time seemed to have been taken out of the stream of history. The crisis in world politics directly became God's judgment on cultures and peoples. And any reason and good will aimed at overcoming the crisis appeared only as an attempt to escape this judgment. But in this way Luther's decisive *simul-simul* was surrendered in favour of an ideology of negative salvation history. The contemporaneity of the *kai*, 'and', in II Cor.6.9f., on which everything depends, now became a temporal succession which today allowed only repentance and perhaps might again allow a 'programme' tomorrow.[26]

It is interesting to examine Karl Barth's Tambach lecture from this perspective, since it too is something like a programmatic work. Barth too stressed the negative very strongly at that time:'We live more deeply in the No than in the Yes, more deeply in criticism and in protest than in naiveté, more deeply in longing for the future than in participation in the present.'[27] But at the same time the formulation shows that this No cannot in any circumstances be understood as an absolute, but remains related to the Yes, even if the Yes is often broken. Therefore where Gogarten radically rejected any proposal and any programme, in Barth there could be a confession of solidarity 'by frank criticism of particulars, by courageous decision and action, by forward-looking proclamation of truth and patient work of reform. Today there is a call for large-hearted, far-sighted, characterful conduct towards democracy – no, not towards it, as irresponsible onlookers and critics, but within it, as hope-sharing and guilt-sharing comrades; – and it is largely in this field that we must work out the problem of opposition to the old order, discover the likeness of the kingdom of God...'[28]

It would have been consistent with this line of thinking for Karl Barth, despite his extreme theological position at the opposite pole, to have joined up with that 'republican community of reason' which the leaders of the old liberalism attempted to create after 1919.[29] The concern was to form a broad democratic centre which would be as open as possible to both right and left, and which could bring together all the powers that supported the state. As we know, the Republic failed not least because this centre was never created.

That Karl Barth did not manifestly take this way – despite his deliberate alliance with social democracy – but rather (at least as many of the public saw it) was on the side of those who were shooting at the Republic during the years in which it was under fire is one of the remarkable features in which this period is so rich.[30] Closely connected with this question is another one: why did it evidently take Barth until 1933 to see what was really happening, though he had far more background knowledge here than Gogarten? Here one might object that it is in no way the task of theology to involve itself in the political struggle for or against a particular form of state. But the battle over the state in the Weimar period was only the superficial expression of a much deeper struggle, which now affected theology to the highest degree: a struggle over the image of man, his nature and his real destiny. At any rate, Karl Barth himself was probably the last to allow this objection in the present context. That is indicated by the lines which he wrote in 1945 in his letter 'To the German theologians who are prisoners of war': 'I want to confess to all of you that if I reproach myself for anything in connection with the years that I spent in Germany it is that at that time I concentrated purely on my task in theology and the church and, since I was a Swiss, had some hesitation about becoming involved in German affairs. This meant that I omitted to warn of the tendencies which had been clear and disturbing to me since 1921, when I set foot on German soil, tendencies both in the church and in the world around me. I should have warned not only implicitly, but explicitly; not only privately, but also publicly!'[31]

The formation of the 'Confessional Front' shows that the charge Gogarten felt that he must level against Barth in the preface to 'Judgment or Scepticism', namely that under his influence there was the dangerous threat 'of a timeless, self-sufficent theology',[32] is not tenable, at least in that form. On the other hand, Barth's indication that concentration on his 'church theological work' had made him keep silent where he should have spoken is not completely satisfactory either.[33] Does work in the church and theology, rightly understood in Barth's terms, have to be done in any other way than by always taking account of the No along with the Yes, the world along with the word of God which is addressed to it? Was that not the postulate of the Tambach lecture? It is a dangerous oversimp-lification of the problem here to summon the church to its own task and think, like Thurneysen: 'Its first concern should not be what then happens in state and society at the earthly human level of political and economic life. It is enough for it to know that the reflection of the eternal words which then shines out again will also show itself in the form of a new, other, better form of life at the level of this earthly event, in the "ordinances of sin" (Gogarten) under which the church as an institution finds itself.'[34]

One cannot avoid the suspicion that even with the shifting of the focal point into the realm of the church and theology in the narrower sense which characterizes the work of Barth during these years, the fascination of the crisis played the role of posing radical questions without being aware of its own questionable basis.

Perhaps we should attribute to this fascination the fact that terms like freedom and right, humanity and human worth, the relative significance of which for the world order should have been estab-lished and maintained from the beginning, seem almost without exception to have succumbed to the great spell – and to have done so at a time at which there was also extreme danger not only to these concepts but to what they represented (and theology could not be completely indifferent to this reality). Here the spirit of the time, which stood against these concepts and what they represented, was evidently stronger than political and indeed theological insight. In the decisive years the great No of the young theologians was certainly heard more than the Yes. For the time heard only what it wanted to hear: No to reason and humanity, to spirit and culture.[35] It understood and remembered this, for this seemed to be spirit of its spirit. And perhaps – we do not know – at that time people could already have suspected that where the No was so loud and clear and the Yes was so gentle and hard to grasp, there was a great danger that others would capture the position which was hardly defended by uttering an excessively loud and clear Yes.

One last question in this context, which I want only to hint at. In his last years Ernst Troeltsch continually sought to clarify the problem of the relationship between the 'German spirit' and 'West-ern European thought'.[36] In so doing he saw the 'German' spirit grounded in the romantic counter-revolution and characterized by concepts like individuality and development, organic division and creative productivity, Volksgeist and community. Over against this stood the Western European tradition: rational, influenced by natural law and humanitarian, it was based on the notion of the 'value of universal human reason in every individual'. 'On the one hand an eternal, rational and divinely appointed order which is the foundation for both morality and justice; on the other a constantly new and living individual embodiment of the historical and productive spirit: that is the ultimate difference.'[37]

At first glance, in its approach dialectical theology seems to stand beyond these two directions. And yet the different interpretation of this approach in Barth and Gogarten, which eventually led them to part company, raises the question whether different spiritual traditions were not also involved in these different interpretations. Despite Barth's powerful warning[38] that he wanted to ground and understand his 1933 decision elsewhere than in theology, it made a difference whether like Gogarten one had grown up in the tradition of the 'German spirit' and was indebted to it, or whether, like Barth himself, one had breathed the air of a traditional Western liberal country. It really goes without saying that this difference did not have to match one's birth certificate, and that is also confirmed by a series of examples, like Bergson or Houston Stewart Chamberlain. To this degree Barth's objection, 'that there are also Swiss, indeed Swiss living in Switzerland, who do not swear more highly than by Gogarten, and on the other hand good Germans who would not think of doing this', is no argument to the contrary.[39]

I am far from regarding this aspect as the substance of the matter. But it seems to me worth considering whether it may not have helped to clarify some decisions which otherwise would have to remain quite incomprehensible. For it is obvious that within the tradition of the 'German spirit' terms like individuality, freedom, Volk, community and nation had very different connotations and meanings from those they had in the sphere of Western European thought. If I see things rightly, the profound effect of this German tradition on theology and church is not only clear among those who responded positively in 1933 but also an influence on the formation of the Confessional Front. Here – as was the case for many people – 'obedience to God's word and commandment' at this moment at the same time represented a painful break with one's own origins and past.

## 2. The picture of history as a spiritual force in German Protestantism

If we look at the German Protestantism of the Weimar period as a cultural and political phenomenon, the trends which we have just been considering fade right into the background. Neither the Religious Socialists nor the Liberals nor dialectical theology managed to exert any profound influence on the church between 1918 and 1933. Rather, generally speaking, even after the War this church remained what it had been before war broke out: conservative and German nationalist. In its political stance it corresponded quite closely to what I have called 'old nationalism', and regarded it as an honour in this way to have opted for by far the most conservative of all possibilities. Gottfried Mehnert has recently investigated the questions in context for the first time.[40]

If we attempt to sum up his work, which is based on a wealth of source material, we find unqualified confirmation of the remark made by Erik Peterson in 1928 in a letter to Harnack. 'In cultural and sociological terms the Evangelical Church roughly corresponds to the cultural and sociological status of the German National Volkspartei.'[41] That was true of church governments, pastors and communities as well as for the Evangelischer Kirchenausschuss or the Evangelischer Bund. Decisions here had already been taken in Dresden in autumn 1919 at the first Kirchentag after the War. There, after a short period of hesitation, conservatism had established itself in all important issues, thus foreshadowing the course that the church was to follow during the Republic. Otto Baumgarten remarked at the time: 'We could not avoid the impression that the nationalistic and patriotic emotions of the majority were even greater than those of the high church. We are therefore deeply concerned that our poor people may suffer the further misfortune of being unable to have a Protestantism free of the old alliance of throne and altar. Is the Evangelical Church really going to be a bastion of reaction?'[42]

The victory of conservatism which indeed made the church, as Baumgarten feared, a 'bastion of reaction', was no chance one. It matched the deep inner ties with which Protestantism had joined itself to the ideas of the 'old nationalism'. That made all the more urgent the question of the basis of the ties, the disastrous effects of which can still be seen in our time.

In the discussion of this question most of the references were

initially to Luther himself and to Lutheranism, which were said to
be the basis of the special relationship with the state, through
the concept of authority, in the doctrine of the two realms, the
relationship then having been given political expression in the
alliance of throne and altar. This argument is doubtless correct. But
in this context it also had decided limitations. It overlooked the fact
that as a concept and in substance 'throne and altar' are relatively
late:[43] their origin lies in the period of the French Revolution, and
throughout the nineteenth century they flourished essentially on the
solemnity of the counter-revolution. The argument also failed to
note that the German national confession of Protestantism generally
was in no way tied to confessional Lutheranism, but was proclaimed
by a great variety of theological camps. Both these things indicate
that here we have only secondarily to do with an originally dogmatic
problem. Nationalistic Protestant conservatism cannot be derived
directly either from Luther's theology or from Lutheranism, but is
rather the result of a historical development the beginnings of which
go back to the last decades of the eighteenth century.

In an interesting study Gerhard Kaiser has recently drawn attention to the connections between the offshoots of pietism and the
early forms of patriotism in Germany at the end of the eighteenth
century.[44] Kaiser shows how through intermediaries like Friedrich
Carl von Moser, Klopstock, Lavater, Herder, Novalis, Schleiermacher, Steffens and others a broad stream of religious feeling with a
pietistic colouring found its way into budding German patriotism.
This went so far that 'whole conceptual structures from pietism'
were transferred directly into patriotism (224). To single out a few
points: the natural-law idea of a state and social contract is replaced
'by the idea of patriotic revival' (226); the relationship between the
citizen and the state is interpreted as a 'community of love and faith',
and to enter completely into this is supreme fulfilment (ibid.); for
the religious patriots, freedom – in accordance with the pietistic
definition of the relationship between service and freedom – is not
freedom *from* the state but freedom *for* the state; death for the
Fatherland is decked out with the whole pietistic cult of blood and
wounds: 'Like the blood and wounds of Christ, the blood and
wounds of the patriot bring salvation and victory, and as the dying
Christ redeems Christianity, so the dying patriot redeems the
Fatherland' (228).

We cannot follow in detail all these connecting links and transferences, which Kaiser illustrates with a wealth of material (though this comes from within relatively narrow confines). What is decisive in this context is the result: 'Patriotism grew up as it were under the protection of religion' (231). Here it becomes clear how much Protestantism was involved in the rise of the German sense of nationalism, indeed how it could regard this nationalistic sense with some justification as its own creation. This young patriotism, which initially was still predominantly related to the natural culture, stood the test at the time of the wars of liberation. The year 1806 marked the turning point and at the same time saw the birth of Prussian-German nationalism in the narrower sense. The preachers of the wars of liberation, above all Arndt and Jahn, but also – with qualifications – Schleiermacher and Steffens, show the whole extent and depth of this secularization movement, the fruit of which appears at the end of this transitional period in nationalistic Protestantism.[45]

So far hardly any attention has been paid to this nationalistic Protestantism as the distinctive expression of the character of the Protestant church and piety in the nineteenth century. In fact it does not yield much for the history of theology. Nevertheless beyond question it made a deeper and more lasting impression on the form and substance of German Protestantism in the nineteenth century than theological discussion proper.

The characteristic feature of nationalistic Protestant piety lies in its transformation of the concept of God. In contrast to the *summum bonum* of the Enlightenment, God is first understood and experienced here as the Lord of history. God the Father, the Lord of peoples and kingdoms, the great God of battles, the omnipotent Avenger and Judge: this conception of God, strongly influenced by the Old Testament, forms the nucleus of the new piety. Dogmatic qualifications are almost completely lacking; there is no trace of a trinitarian conception, and the Apostles' Creed is reduced to the first article. The concept of 'his Volk' matches this concept of God. By being directly subordinated to God, Volk and Volkstum are given the status of the supreme order of creation. The battle over Volkstum (and its concrete political form, the nation) becomes the battle for God's order, for God itself. Service of Volk and Fatherland logically becomes the true service of God, and dedication to society the supreme moral demand.

Here lie the roots of those concepts which essentially shaped the picture of history and the self-understanding of the German bourgeoisie in the nineteenth century: the 'German God'; the Germans as his chosen people, chosen for their piety, honesty and loyalty; German history as the place of his revolution; political unity and freedom as the fulfilment of his will and his order. The Reformation preaching of the power of faith to justify was largely replaced by the proclamation of nationalism and its God, the modern, powerful, enormously effective gospel of the time. Throughout the nineteenth century Protestantism did not forget the fascination of this new message, its modernity, its dynamic, its capacity to move and enthuse masses.

Theological discussion remained remarkably untouched by all this. So these notions had all the deeper and more lasting an impact where education was disseminated, from the pulpits and cathedras of churches and schools.

Weymar's work on the 'spirit of history-teaching in upper schools in the nineteenth century' has also documented this situation from the sources for the first time.[46] On the basis of timetables and programmes, school books and books about teaching history, memoirs and accounts of teachers and pupils, this work outlines a picture of the foundations and tendencies of history-teaching in the nineteenth century – and here the sources which otherwise are hardly accessible even to the church historian are as interesting as a productive archaeological site.

There are in fact two reasons for the close connection between religion and history which can be noticed everywhere and which is in effect a characteristic of the teaching of history at this time. First the teaching of history still largely lay in the hands of theologians. For example, the famous Friedrich Kohlrausch, whose textbooks on German history appeared in a series of new editions down to the 1890s, and whose ideas on teaching and method 'for decades formed the basis of history teaching in many German states' (23),[47] was originally a theologian, as were a whole series of schoolmasters of a kindred spirit who followed in his footsteps. However, the substantive connection between religion and history was more important than this personal one. The alliance into which religion and history had entered in nationalist Protestantism showed religious and historical education to be two sides of the same coin. As we read in Kohlrausch: 'Next to religion, and in alliance with it, history will be the focal point of character formation' (27). The picture of world history which Kohlrausch outlines is accordingly both nationalistic and religious at the same time. It begins with the Old Testament stories, which are discussed from the perspective of 'faith in the one God' and the national unity of Israel. Kohlrausch hastens via the Greeks as the 'people of culture' and the Romans as the 'people of empire' to the early period of Germany in which he sees 'a primeval, pure, unmixed tribal people' at work. Because of their virtues, their excellencies and their piety the German peoples became 'the vessel which God had chosen for himself to keep his doctrine pure. For Jews and Greeks and Romans had already been debilitated by sensuality and vice: they could not grasp nor observe the new teaching...' This theme of the Christian Germanic mission, once struck up, could be pursued in Kohlrausch's account through the Middle Ages to more recent history. It was here that a 'distinctive feature' of the Germans emerged, namely their tendency to imitate alien culture. A picture of the Germans came into being which differed in its gentleness, seriousness, inwardness, depth and readiness to believe from the Western manner of thinking, which was characterized by critical understanding, dissection, demolition and a desire to destroy. Kohlrausch takes over Fichte's ideas about the German 'primal language', alongside which French appears as 'slight, alien chatter'. The account comes to a climax at the time of the wars of liberation, the threshold of a new period of the world, the centre of which will be Germany (Weymar, 27ff.). Despite individual critical voices, like the admirable Niemeyer or the former Tübingen Stift member Oscar Jäger, this view of history shaped the self-understanding of the German bourgeoisie in the nineteenth century and also found its way in a milder form into Catholic schools. It underwent many modifications and qualifications, now in a racist-biological direction, now in a conservative-romantic direction, and now in an imperialistic-political direction – but its basic features remained essentially the same: its sense of a Christian-Germanic mission, its picture of the German national character and of the way in which German history was shaped. The teaching of history had become, as Weymar puts it in the title of one of his chapters, 'The New Handmaid of Theology' (98ff.).[48]

The material which Weymar presents is so overwhelming that there can hardly be any doubt about the predominance of this picture of history, by whose cradle both nationalistic Protestantism and early historicism had stood together as sponsors. And this seems to shed new light on the question which I raised at the beginning. If the majority of those churchmen who represented the church in the Weimar Republic had grown up with this view of history, was it conceivable that they should decide for anything other than the 'old nationalism'? It still best represented the ideas of this picture of history – and did not the church have to hang on to it all the more firmly, since to a special degree it was its own property, a creation of the German Protestant spirit?

There is also much evidence of the ongoing spiritual power of this view of history after 1918. As at the Dresden Kirchentag in 1919, so too in the following years it opposed any 'democratic' reform of the church, any openness of Protestantism to its own concerns and the problems of the time. But the question takes us even further. At any rate it would be conceivable that this picture of history played a role not only in 1918 but also in 1933, and was a contributory cause to that remarkable uncertainty, indeed inability, to assess events which was characteristic of the Protestant church in these years and of the middle classes generally. For the self-understanding of 'Germanhood' which lay within it contained virtually no self-critical categories apart from the tendency to alienation and discord which has been cited so often. From this perspective the real significance of National Socialism must have been fundamentally unimaginable to large areas of the bourgeoisie and the church and thus have remained outside the sphere of critical reflection – not because people generally had abandoned illusions about human nature and its capacities for good and evil, but because on the basis of a particular self-understanding the Germans in particular were regarded as incapable of such consequences.

## II

Any attempt to reflect on what all this means for us today will have to begin from two presuppositions. Nationalistic Protestantism proved to be a great mistake for which we have paid dearly enough with a corrupted proclamation and depraved politics. That is one point. The other is the observation that in theory and in fact the year 1945 represented its irrevocable end.

Karl Barth was right when in 1945 he wrote to the German theologians in prisoner-of-war camps: 'The temptations, illusions and errors which obscured and weakened your preaching, as they already had that of your fathers, have been shown up for what they are and gone their way. The dreams are over, the constructions have been shattered, with which Christian Germans in particular have distorted and ultimately denied the gospel for so long.'[49]

Certainly 'the dreams are over, the constructions have been shattered'. But the great question now is: What will take their place? New dreams? New constructions?

In his letter Karl Barth continues: 'The Word of God really is no longer bound in Germany, on the basis of the harshest of facts.' This meant that the new task of theology and the church was: 'To believe in the free word of God himself, and with the free word of God on your lips to go among your poor people to raise them up, to comfort them, to call them to new responsibility, to arouse them to a new hope, to show them new ways, to point out and explain to them the miraculous nearness of their God, the Father and our Lord Jesus Christ... that is now the task that lies before you.'[50]

This passionate and moving appeal is profoundly and indubitably right where it calls the pastors away from all their old ties, away from all resignation and downheartedness, to the one Word of God, the proclamation of which is always the task of the church. But it must provoke a challenge where it gives the impression that with the year 1945 the freedom of the Word of God has now somehow become our possibility, as if at some point we could get a glimpse of freedom in itself and not always merely in the 'in, with and under' – even of a picture of history. We cannot live in an ahistorical realm; even the church cannot do that, far less theologies. They will continually develop their pictures of history, and the question cannot be whether they should or may do that; it can only be about the degree of critical awareness with which they do so. So particularly after the experiences of the last 150 years, reflection on the Word of God as the foundation and task of the church seems inseparably bound up with responsibility for the new conceptions of German history which are destined to replace the old outmoded ones.

In other words, we too must be involved in the bitter and laborious task of 'the revision of the traditional picture of history'[51] which is now taking place across the whole breadth of historical scholarship and is the presupposition for any future new outline.[52]

The contributions of German scholarship so far naturally relate above all to individual problems. Indeed it is impossible to conceive from what spiritual or political standpoint a new German history could be written at present, as long as Germany is divided and its further fate is so completely uncertain.

So it is no coincidence that two major attempts to reinterpret German history come to us from outside. It is all the more interesting to compare them, since the authors are almost pure representatives of the two great systematic world-views of our time. Hans Kohn[53] writes from the standpoint of Western, Anglo-Saxon pragmatic liberalism, while Georg Lukacs[54] represents historical materialism. Both authors have long had reputations as experts on modern German history and cultural history, and their works further confirm those reputations.

Kohn sees the fate of German history as lying in its aversion to the ideas of western, liberal democracy, characteristic of the nineteenth century, and its preference for a nationalism fed by irrational forces. For Kohn, in cultural terms the roots of this development lie in the Romantic movement, which particularly through its understanding of history gave German political thought that irrational trait which Anglo-Saxons find so hard to understand. Politically, for him Bismarck is the figure in whom this fate takes shape: 'Bismarck's triumph provided the occasion for justifying the ideal of the Prussian state and the traditionalism of German historical study over against the Western ideals of human rights and peace among the nations... With his contempt for humanitarian liberalism, Bismarck accentuated the dangerous tendencies which in the nineteenth century had begun to blind and confuse German thought' (178). Kohn is too wise to describe the way from Bismarck to Hitler as a straight-line development, but he sees the seeds of self-destruction at the heart of Bismarck's empire. From his basic approach, at the end of his account Kohn arrives at a clear evaluation of contemporary events: 'From the perspective not of Bismarckism but of the whole of Western civilization, the German Federal Republic is not a transitional makeshift; it is the first consolidated German democracy, the first German state for more than a century to be part and parcel of Western society...' (372).

Kohn's account is undoubtedly one-sided. Nevertheless, by virtue of the wealth of almost unknown voices to which he gives a hearing, by his Anglo-Saxon boldness of judgment and not least by the vividness of his account he seems to me to make an important contribution to the revision of our view of history – even if at the end one asks with some surprise whether history really is as simple as that.

Things are different in Lukacs and yet to some degree similar.

The 'destruction of reason' is not just, as the review in a daily newspaper recently thought, 'a giant compendium stuffed full of desolate, Stalinist platitudes'; it is the first comprehensive and consistent Marxist interpretation of nineteenth-century German philosophy and intellectual history, and that alone makes it worth noting.[55] Lukacs seeks 'to describe Germany's way to Hitler in the sphere of philosophy'. He sets himself the task of unmasking 'all the intellectual preliminaries to the "National Socialist world view", however far removed they may – apparently – be from Hitlerism and however little – subjectively – they may have such intentions'. For 'there is no such thing as an "innocent" world-view... the attitude for or against reason at the same time decides on the nature of a philosophy as philosophy, on its role in social development' (10ff.). In short, Lukacs' thesis is that in its socially conditioned fight against reason German philosophy increasingly fled into irrational-ism, which then reached its climax in the 'demagogic synthesis' of National Socialism. He begins with Schelling's concept of the 'intellectual approach' follows the line further through Schopen-hauer, Kierkegaard and Nietzsche to the representatives of the 'imperialist' (Dilthey, Simmel, Spengler) and 'pre-Fascist and Fas-cist' philosophy of life (Klages, Jünger, Baeumler, Rosenberg, etc.). Here – and this is the undiscussed premise of the whole book – reason means the 'materialistic shift to objective reality independent of our consciousness and its objective dialectic' (221 n.2), i.e. the philosophical principle of Marxism and Leninism. Therefore 'the fight against Marxism – seldom acknowledged openly and barely in the realm of consciousness' is the 'main tendency of irrationalism' since Nietzsche (483).

As with the best will in the world this can only rarely be demon-strated from the sources, Lukacs invents the theory of the two methods with which German philosophy fought against socialism and defended capitalism, one direct and the other indirect. 'While the direct apologetic is concerned to present capitalism as the best of all orders, the indirect method brings out the bad sides of capitalism, its atrocities, but declares them to be properties not of capitalism, but of human existence, indeed of existence generally' (181f.). What makes irrationalism for Lukacs most profoundly a way of thinking that is hostile to life and society is its rejection of 'rational progress', the 'denial of a single history of humankind' (here in connection with race theory) which at the same time implies 'the denial of the equality of human beings, the denial of progress and reason' (589).

Despite numerous quotations from Marx, Engels and Lenin distributed virtually throughout the book, one cannot avoid the feeling that Lukacs is in fact much closer to Hegel and the Enlightenment than to Marxism – albeit a Hegel who is interpreted completely in terms of an objective rationalistic dialectic.[56]

Lukacs also brings us right up to the present. For him the strongest indication of the change in world history after 1945 is the 'world peace movement', in which he sees the 'revolt of the masses for reason', for its restoration and defence (737).

I need not explain here why I would argue that to have the 'restoration of reason' in terms of Marxism-Leninism which Lukacs calls for would merely be to exchange a yellow devil for a green one (to alter a favourite quotation of Lukacs from a letter from Lenin to Gorki). Nevertheless, the basically Marxist approach of the work should not mislead us into failing here too to listen to the justified criticism of our more recent history which it contains.[57]

## III

Any attempt to draw some conclusions from all that has been said so far must, of course, be limited to a few points at which further consideration of this difficult and complex question might have to start.

I begin from the observation that despite their extremely different starting points, in one respect the views of Kohn and Lukacs virtually coincide. Both see the basic problem of modern German history in the predominance of irrationalism; for both, the immediate beginnings of this distinctive development in the German spirit lies in Romanticism.

We now know that however much at first aesthetic and literary motives seem to come to the fore in the Romantic movement, it was a comprehensive counter-movement to the Enlightenment with its Cartesian concept of reason. As such it was in no way limited to Germany, but nowhere else did it achieve such a predominant position. It seems as though here lie the roots of that hostility to reason which was in fact a peculiarity of the German development in the ninetenth century. We can find its traces everywhere, most impressively perhaps in the view of history that I have attempted to outline above. The broken relationship with the Enlightenment,

Germany's aversion to the West, the development of what Troeltsch in 1914 called the 'German spirit',[58] leading to the ideas of the 'nationalist opposition' in the Weimar period and its parallels in theology and philosophy, can hardly be explained in any other way. How unsatisfactory and problematic it is, however, to draw such a line is again shown by a comparison of Kohn with Lukacs. Whereas Lukacs reclaims Hegel entirely for reason, for Kohn he is basically on the side of irrationalism. Conversely, in Kohn, Wilhelm Dilthey is a representative of reason, while Lukacs puts him with Simmel and Spengler among irrationalist philosophies of life.

In fact names like Hegel and Dilthey, and indeed those of Schleiermacher or Ranke, make it clear how incapable the concept of irrationalism is of doing justice to the whole picture. For this irrationalism is matched on the other side by a position which is perhaps best described as 'historical thought'. Historicism, which is occasionally described as 'the second great enterprise of the German spirit after the Reformation', simply cannot be described as 'irrationalism'. Carlo Antoni sees the problem much more accurately when he regards this shift to history as an attempt 'to replace Cartesian mathematical reason... with a new historical reason.'[59]

This attempt, too, certainly has its problems. These do not just become clear at the beginning of historicism, which ultimately drew everything into the whirlpool of unlimited relativism, but equally in that remarkable hypostatization of history which we constantly encounter in this connection in German historical and political thought. For example, when we read in Spengler that 'world history has always justified those who are stronger and fuller of their self-assured life', and when Max Weber speaks of the 'rule of world history'; when there is a constant proclamation of 'responsibility before history', history seems to be an independent entity which is endowed with divine attributes. The links between this understanding of history and the concept of God in nationalistic Protestantism are obvious. That points once more towards the great question which all this raises for Protestant theology.

We cannot go back behind historicism. The experiences which it communicates to us, the possibilities which it has disclosed, are inalienable. And I would add that we do not want them to be lost. On the other hand, it is obvious that historical thought must be given new foundations and new limits. Here theology will above all have to see that no new hypostatization of history takes the place of the old and disputes the right of reason in all spheres of political action. Perhaps this is one of the tasks with which theology is entrusted in the wider context of the revision of our picture of history.

# Eugenio Pacelli and Karl Barth

## Politics, church politics and theology in the Weimar Republic*

Recent church history has so far been the domain of confessional historiography. There is perhaps no other sphere in academic theology in which right up to the present Protestant and Catholic scholars have gone such separate ways. In Old and New Testament study, in systematic and practical theology, at least since the Second Vatican Council it has been possible to see a growing exchange of views and results. Even in church history, collaboration has become closer in the sphere of the early church, the Middle Ages and even Reformation history. Only in more recent times and particularly in contemporary history do scholars still largely go their separate ways.

On the Catholic side there is the imposing work of the Commission for Contemporary History, which is involved in providing better sources for the period between 1932 and 1945 than for any other period in the whole of church history. And a large group of Catholic historians – secular historians and church historians – has clarified the history of German Catholicism with a wealth of thorough and careful accounts and investigations. This group has been almost exclusively concerned with Catholicism; German Protestantism and the Protestant churches hardly ever make an appearance.

A survey of the Protestant side is less informative. There are no comparable editions of source material; even the twenty-nine-volume series of works on the history of the church struggle and its supplementary volumes reflect not only the multiplicity but occcasionally also the narrowness resulting from the division of the

*This previously unpublished lecture was given in Vienna on 12 June 1980.

Protestant churches in Germany into Landeskirchen. However, in
this connection it is important to note that these works, in turn,
concentrate wholly on the problems of the Protestant churches. And
even the most recent works on contemporary church history from
the Protestant side hardly give any indication that there is also such
a thing as German Catholicism.

In its sections on contemporary history the only exception worth
mentioning – Kottje and Moeller's *Ökumenische Kirchengeschichte*
– is clearer about the divisions than the points of contact. I may say
that, since I was responsible with Erwin Iserloh for working on these
sections.

I regard this one-sided confessional approach – to put it briefly –
as inadequate. It is my conviction that the two great confessions in
Germany influenced each other more deeply and more lastingly
than they were aware of – even, indeed particularly, where they
confronted one another in hostility, whether this hostility was
expressed or not. Who can write a history of Germany in modern
times without constantly keeping the history of its European neighbours in view? And this example is still inadequate by itself, since
the two great confessions in Germany are very much more closely
connected, because they occupy the same territory and exist under
the same historical and political conditions.

My conviction of this connection does not derive, as the example
shows, from an ecumenical and systematic approach. Rather, it is
gained from my insights and work as a historian; not just in work
on the most recent period but also in work on the preceding three
centuries, where I have come up against the same problem. But
because at present I am intensively concerned with contemporary
history, it is worth developing this thesis in a contemporary context.

That is the explanation for my perhaps somewhat unusual topic:
Eugenio Pacelli and Karl Barth: Politics, Church Politics and
Theology in the Weimar Republic.

In May 1917 Eugenio Pacelli, who was forty-one at the time, was
nominated Apostolic Nuncio in Munich. This nomination is one of
the most important dates in twentieth-century German Catholicism.
For from this moment on the young and ambitious Roman diplomat
regarded the German church as his special task, which he did not
surrender until at the end of 1929 he was recalled to Rome to take
over the leadership of the world church as Cardinal Secretary of
State. There is a report by his closest collaborator, the German

Jesuit Robert Leiber, which says that German affairs occupied the Cardinal Secretary of State as much as, 'if not more than, all the rest put together'.[1] And even when ten years later, in 1939, Pacelli rose to become Pope Pius XII, things did not change. In fact probably no one in the first half of this century more persistently shaped the ecclesiastical and political destiny of German Catholicism than this true Roman, who in May 1917 approached the task of representing the interests of Rome in Germany with unbounded self-confidence and cool passion. I would just like to add in passing that over the same period German Protestantism, too, was subject to the most persistent influence from a foreigner – the Swiss theologian Karl Barth.

In order to understand Pacelli's significance for Catholic church policy in Germany we must begin from an event which was probably – for the second time I am choosing my words very carefully – the most important in the history of twentieth-century Catholicism: the publication of the *Codex Juris Canonici* in 1917. This new law book completed the development towards the centralization, unification and legal ordering of the Catholic church. The *Codex Juris Canonici* created a new and unified legislation for the church – canon law – in which all ministries, cultic actions and church legal definitions had a fixed role which applied throughout the church. The creation of this new law book from the two-thousand-year-old legal tradition of the church was an enormous, indeed amazing, achievement. It is associated above all with the name of Pietro Gasparri. And his closest collaborator was Pacelli.

Gasparri became Cardinal Secretary of State in 1914 and remained in this position until 1929, under two popes. Pacelli, in 1930, was his immediate successor. So for almost half a century – until Pacelli's death in 1958 – the leadership of the Catholic church lay in canonistic hands. Not least, this explains the enormous break represented by the pontificate of John XXIII in 1958; he was a patristic Catholic by origin and abruptly ended the canonistic orientation of the curial Pacelli.

But let us return to Pacelli's beginnings in Germany. Canon law was published, and a year later, in 1918, was also implemented. However, throughout Europe its implementation initially came to grief on the legal relationships in which the church was involved; these had grown up over history and were secured by treaty. One of the most important tasks of the new codex was to abolish the

many specific rights of the national churches in favour of a uniform
law which was exclusively determined by the pope. One important
issue here was the nomination of bishops. According to the new
*Codex Juris Canonici* (canon 329 §2) the Pope alone had this right.
However, in Germany – more accurately, in Prussia, Bavaria and
Baden, where the seats of the German bishops lay – for ages this
right had been shared by the respective cathedral chapters and the
state.[2] In all three Länder this legal situation had been solemnly
confirmed by treaties between state and church in the nineteenth
century, and the Curia had no chance of altering this legal situation
because the rulers carefully guarded their privileges, and any one-
sided abrogation of the treaties on the part of the church would have
endangered the state dotations. On the publication of the new law
in 1917 it looked as though the Curia would be faced with decades
of tough negotiations before the most important provisions of the
Codex could be implemented in Germany. Here the collapse of
November 1918 and its consequences created a completely new
situation virtually overnight.[3]

One of the first demands of the revolution was, of course, the
separation of church and state.

And so with the church articles of the Weimar Constitution there
fell into the bosom of the Catholic church something for which
otherwise it would have had to struggle laboriously, namely its
independence from the state and its autonomy in appointments to
church posts. As Article 137 of the Weimar Constitution had it, 'Any
religious association orders and governs its affairs independently
within the limits of the law, which is universally valid. It bestows its
offices without the involvement of the state or the civil community.'
However, these were only outline regulations, the details of which
still had to be filled in by the legislation of the Länder. So now the
whole policy of the Curia was aimed at achieving the widest possible
positive guarantees for canon law from individual Länder on the
basis of these regulations. This was the substance of the Holy See's
concordat policy from after the First World War until the conclusion
of the Reich concordat in 1933,[4] and its decisive advocate in Germany
was Eugenio Pacelli.

From a Catholic point of view this was a uniquely favourable
time. The Reich was weak, a plaything of its enemies, and concerned
to get all the support from abroad that it could, particularly through
the mediation of the Vatican. Moreover the Catholic party, the

Centre Party, held a key political position, and between 1919 and 1933 provided no less than five committed Catholic Chancellors in ten cabinets in the persons of Fehrenbach, Wirth, Marx, Brüning and – with qualifications – von Papen. Finally, through the wise policies of Benedict XV during and after the War the papacy had gained respect particularly in Germany, respect which was to the immediate advantage of the Papal Nuncio. The more fragmented German Protestantism seemed to be after 1918, the more impressive the Roman church appeared, with its unshakeable steadfastness and its supreme head.

[Pacelli began the first negotiations over the concordat as early as autumn 1919 in the area where the Curia hoped for the greatest co-operation, namely Bavaria. As early as the beginning of 1920 a compact collection of Roman demands lay on the table in Munich which left nothing to be desired in terms of clarity. In them Pacelli had planned a stance on the school question which would secure an almost unlimited right to supervision and intervention for the bishops. The Curia naturally also required the 'free and complete right to fill all church posts' and a guarantee in principle of state recognition of canon law to further its implementation, and if need be also state support for church rulings. The state right of supervision was again to be used in the service of the church.

At the same time Pacelli exploited his accreditation as Nuncio to the Reich, and when he presented his credentials to Reich President Ebert in summer 1920 he clearly made it known that the Curia was also interested in a treaty with the Reich – i.e. a Reich concordat.]

This is not the place to trace the devious ways of the Vatican concordat policy in the Weimar period. They are closely bound up with the political history of the unfortunate Republic and its special circumstances. At all events, here Pacelli used all the possibilities offered by the political situation to achieve a comprehensive recognition and guarantee for canon law. He achieved this most successfully in the Bavarian concordat of 1924.

This concordat was regarded in Rome as a kind of model concordat – a model not only for other concordats in Germany but also for concordats throughout the world. It ensured that the principles of canon law would be followed in appointments to church positions; in its articles relating to schools it gave the church wide-ranging influence throughout the educational system, particularly in the Volksschulen; and it laid obligations on the state of Bavaria to go on providing protection, recognition and support for the Catholic church and all its institutions.

By contrast, negotiations with the next treaty partner, Prussia, were more disappointing.

[Here Pacelli had more than met his match in the liberal Prussian Minister of Culture, Carl Becker. The Prussian ministerial bureaucracy yielded nothing in knowledge, skill and perseverance to the diplomacy of the Curia. So when after years of tough negotiations the Prussian concordat was signed in 1929, it did not cover the issue which was most important to the Curia, namely the schools question. The Prussian Prime Minister, the Social Democrat Otto Braun, then personally assured the Nuncio at a summit meeting[5] (here I am quoting from Braun's memoirs) 'that no regulation of any kind about schools could be incorporated in the concordat; the word school could not even appear in the text. The Nuncio,' Braun went on to report, 'declared in despair that he could not possibly go to the Holy Father in Rome with a draft concordat which made no mention of schools, and I reported that I could not go to parliament with a concordat which mentioned schools without courting certain defeat...' So Pacelli had no alternative but finally to yield. At any rate in the concordat with Prussia he gained the diocese of Berlin, as he had wanted, since this had quite extraordinary symbolic value for the Curia.]

The Baden concordat of 1932 again turned out favourably for the Vatican; because of the strong opposition in Karlsruhe it was not as successful as the Bavarian concordat, but it largely satisfied Rome. Moreover, this concordat also brought to light the particular problems of the whole concordat policy for the Catholic church in Germany. For Archbishop Fritz of Freiburg had made it known very clearly that he did not like the Roman centralism of the *Codex Juris Canonici* in the least and that he would have preferred to maintain the old freedoms of the church in Bavaria. Thus the negotiations only made real progress when Fritz died in 1931 and with Conrad Gröber the church appointed a bishop who was explicitly loyal to Rome and well disposed towards the concordat.

So while Pacelli could be well content with his successes in the German Länder, for all his efforts he failed in his great aim which was to be the crown and conclusion of the whole development, the Reich concordat. Between 1919 and 1932 more than half a dozen approaches got stuck, mainly through a clash of political interests.

[Regardless of the desperate situation of the Republic, Pacelli continually attempted to persuade above all the Centre chancellors make the moves he wanted. This led to a serious clash in Rome in summer 1931 between Pacelli and Brüning when Pacelli, who had meanwhile become Cardinal Secretary of State, categorically called for an initiative on the concordat from the German Reich Chancellor, and when this was refused – at that time the Reich was in the middle of a world economic crisis! – suggested that Brüning would have to form a coalition government with the right and make the conclusion of a concordat his condition.[6] Even in November 1932, only a few weeks before Hitler seized power, Pacelli attempted once again to make a start on the Reich concordat question with von Papen.]

So it was not at all surprising that when in March 1933 Hitler offered on his own initiative a concordat which contained everything for which Pacelli had been fighting in Germany since 1919 with a resolve as stubborn as it had been fruitless, the Curia should agree.

However, we should be clear that this concordat followed a different model from that of the previous three Länder concordats.[7] In substance it was concerned with the same questions: in particular the schools question was the decisive point. But its political status was different.

The earlier concordats had been negotiated with parliaments. This even led in Baden to a break-up of the coalition, and the vote in the Karlsruhe Landtag was the closest imaginable.

By contrast, the Reich concordat followed the model of the Lateran treaties. This was an authoritarian model. As early as 1929 Hitler had understood in a flash what this model could mean for his plans: the exclusion of the Catholic party and the winning over of the Catholics to the Third Reich. Hence his offer over the main demand of Article 32. In exchange the church got Article 23. The treaty was negotiated directly between Berlin and Rome. Hitler no longer needed any consent from Parliament, because the Enabling Act left the government a free hand.[8]

[Now we can, of course, ask what these Catholic developments meant for the Protestant churches in Germany. For anyone with even a slight knowledge of Reformation history will know what happened on 10 December 1520 at the Elstertor in Wittenberg: the burning by Luther and his students of the papal decretals, i.e. the collection of canon law. That was the public break with Rome: for

Rome stood and fell with canon law, and anyone who dissociated himself from this law dissociated himself from Rome. It was this act, in association with the great Reformation writings of 1520, which made it quite clear how serious Luther was and how consistently he was going forward step by step.

Since that time rejection of the idea of canon law as a specific spiritual law of the church has been one of the basic convictions of Reformation theology and the Reformation church. So what did the Vatican concordat policy and the *Codex Juris Canonici* signify for the Protestant churches?]

In 1918 the Protestant Landeskirchen were in a far more difficult position than German Catholicism. For the collapse of the local monarchies put them in a threefold crisis: legal, political and spiritual. Whereas the legal order of the Catholic church had been preserved, with the collapse of church government by local rulers the Protestant churches had lost the basic pattern of their constitutions, which had been valid for almost four hundred years. In political terms, they were homeless. The Catholic church could rely on a stable and tried party, the Centre Party, which moreover also in fact continued to represent the interests of the church in culture politics. The German churches in the Lutheran tradition could not contemplate anything comparable for theological reasons; the doctrine of two kingdoms and the lack of a framework of natural law prohibited the foundation of an exclusively Protestant party. Finally, the collapse of 1918 affected German Protestantism more deeply because the Kaiser's Reich had been to a particular degree its cause: it had been moulded by that Reich's picture of history and filled with its hopes. If we take all this together, we shall be able to understand how difficult it was for the Protestant Landeskirchen to find their place in the Republic. How could they understand themselves as churches? What was their new task? And how could all this be given a legal order?

The Weimar constitution had also liberated the Protestant churches, and in all the Länder constitutional church assemblies set to work to develop new forms of constitution. But even before theology and church law could really become clear about the relationship between the Protestant churches and state power, the efforts towards making concordats began on the Catholic side. And from this moment on two concepts dominated the Protestant Landeskirchen, first tacitly and then explicitly: equal status and simultaneous implementation. In all cases the Protestant side made its assent to the concordats dependent on the requirement that a treaty of equal value (not of the same kind!) should be concluded with them at the same time. And of course the government of the Länder, which were obliged to achieve parity, yielded to this demand. One need only note the dates of the treaties to understand the compelling logic of this development. The Bavarian concordat was signed on 29 March 1924, the Bavarian church treaty on 15 November 1924; the Prussian concordat on 14 July 1929, the Prussian church treaty on 15 November 1931 – an indication of how vigorous the objections to this treaty still were in the Prussian General Synod. The Baden concordat was signed on 12 October 1932, and the Baden church treaty on 14 November. And of course the conclusion of the Reich concordat in 1933 should also have been followed by a Reich Church treaty; this only came to grief because the Reich Church collapsed before this treaty could be negotiated.

A look at the comparative survey of the circumstances of the treaties which Werner Weber made in his exemplary 1962 edition of the German concordats of modern times shows how in fact they largely agree with one another:[9] the Protestant Landeskirchen were all given the same legal guarantees as were conceded to the Catholic church in the concordats. To mention just some of these items: they related, for example, to the principle of the free creation of and appointment to offices; the legal competence of church institutions in the state sphere (corporations under public law); the theological faculties; religious instruction in schools; church collaboration in the appointment of teachers of religion and so on (the concordats with the Länder and the church treaties are still valid today!).

Now what is the significance of the fact that the Protestant Landeskirchen, which *de facto* and for church-political reasons were in a weak position after 1918, largely found their legal position over against the state in connection with Catholic treaties? Of course it means that here the Protestant churches fell in much more fully with a Catholic concept of the church than was in keeping with the new theological beginning after 1918. The Catholic church knew what it had to demand; it had only to look in the *Codex Juris Canonici*. Protestant theology and the Protestant churches did not know so clearly. But they had no alternative to insisting on equal status and implementation of the agreements simultaneously.

[I say all this without making any criticisms. Moreover it seems to me that the historian has to deal particularly carefully with the judgment of history. After all, the mistakes and weaknesses of former generations which we are so fond of discovering and find it so easy to discover pose one particular question to us. What will be the verdict of our children on our time?]

I say all this without criticism, especially as I see no serious possibility that the Protestant church governments could have avoided this pressure, given the circumstances. But once this has been noted and said, certain tensions become clear which are characteristic of developments in theology and the church during the 1920s and 1930s; we also find it easier to understand the different courses that the two great German churches in Germany then took in the Third Reich.

Let us look at theology. In autumn 1919, at the very time when Pacelli was embarking on his concordat policy, Karl Barth presented his new theological approach in Germany for the first time. This was his famous Tambach lecture on 'The Christian's Place in Society'. With a bold phrase which as it were anticipated the whole of his theology, Barth interpreted the theme – which was meant to be a religious socialist one – in his own way: '*The Christian*: we must be agreed that we do *not* mean *the Christians*, not the multitude of the baptized, nor the chosen few who are concerned with religion and social relations, nor even the cream of the noblest and most devoted Christians we might think of: the Christian is *the Christ*.'[10]

The move from Christians to Christ; that was the move of theology away from human beings and towards God. It was a move towards the God revealed in Jesus Christ and thus to the God of the cross and the resurrection in that whole unlimited and undiminished abruptness and strangeness with which he stands over against the world. Now from this perspective all attempts to reclaim Christianity for society prove equally mistaken, whether they be conservative, liberal or religious socialist in origin. For, as Barth says, 'The Divine is something whole, complete in itself, a kind of new and different something in contrast to the world. It does not permit of being applied, stuck on and fitted in. It does not permiit of being divided and distributed, for the very reason that it is more than religion. It does not passively permit itself to be used: it overthrows and builds up as it wills. It is complete or it is nothing.'[11] And shortly after that, in his Aarau lecture of April 1920, Karl Barth also drew the consequence from this approach which most enraged his contemporaries: the consequence of the radical criticism of religion and the churches. As this lecture put it, religion 'forgets that she has a right to exist only when she continually does away with herself. Instead, she takes joy in her existence and considers herself indispensable... She is not satisfied with hinting at the *x* that is over the world *and* herself... She takes her place as a competitive power *over against* other powers in life, as an alleged superior world *over against* the world...'[12] I need not explain here that this approach went radically against any kind of church politics which on the basis of the Catholic understanding of the church required guarantees from the state for religious practices, i.e. any church policy which saw the church as one competing power alongside others and which in Pacelli's footsteps sought for and achieved state promises which provided equal status and simultaneous implementation. This was the nub of the arguments between Karl Barth and Otto Dibelius which found their best-known and most noted expression in Karl Barth's brief work *Quousque Tandem* of 1930.[13]

[However, before we turn to this argument, we should pause for reflection. At no moment and at no point in the 1920 did Barth engage in any polemic against Catholicism in the name of Protestantism. On the contrary, in explicit discussion he understood Roman Catholicism in a very serious sense 'as a question to the Protestant *church*',[14] indeed as a question 'whether and how far it is a church'[15] and further as a question 'whether and how far it is a *Protestant* church'.[16] For Barth was convinced that in many respects the Roman church knew more about what the church is than Protestantism did. It was church in its concept of God, its understanding of the sacrament and indeed also in its claim to authority, and if papal power, as Barth put it, 'had remained only churchly, spiritual power, and therefore a God-serving power, and had not become instead a power which displaces and replaces God, we, like Luther, should have no objection to kissing the Pope's feet'.[17] Though the picture of the true church of Christ might also have been distorted in Roman Catholicism, it harboured more Christian truth than neo-Protestantism, which dissolved the power of the divine claim into temperament, the will or history. Barth thought that if the interpretation of the Reformation along the famous Schleiermacher-Ritschl-Troeltsch line, or even along that of Seeberg or Holl, were really the one which Luther and Calvin had intended, he (Barth) would have been 'forced to make the choice between two evils... I should, in fact, prefer the Catholic.'[18] Roman Catholicism, he said, becomes a question for us, 'because in its presuppositions for the church, in spite of all contradictions, it is closer to the Reformers than is the church of the Reformation, so far as that has actually and finally the new Protestantism.'[19]

So there can be no question that Barth was convinced that one had already understood the nature of the Roman church when one had understood the central function of canon law as the new church law book for Catholic church politics. However, canon law had the effect on the Protestant churches, through the concordat policy, of making their claims, attitudes and self-understanding - again from the perspective of that radical theological approach - seem more Roman than the Roman church itself, precisely because they did not have the theological legitimation for these claims, attitudes and self-understanding which the Roman church could demonstrate in its concordat policy. In short, the Catholic church found it easier than did the Protestant church to accept guarantees from the state for the practice of religion because in its concept of God, understanding of the sacraments and claim to authority it preserved more of the tradition of religion within the Christian church than did neo-Protestantism.]

It was this which made Barth's criticism of developments in the church in *Quousque tandem* so sharp and bitter. It linked up with that general feeling of self-satisfaction in the church which began to spread at the end of the 1920s: 'The Protestant church has mightily overcome the tremendous threat to its existence.' This ran: 'The holy "nevertheless" has prevailed'; the 'church leadership of the past decade was a stroke of genius'.[20] This was because of the assurances and guarantees which had been given over the Christian religion in Germany; but as we have seen, these were less an achievement of Protestant church leadership than of Catholic church politics. And so Barth now declared, 'leaving aside all professorial ifs and buts, hindsight and foresight', this was a real 'scandal which cries out to heaven, that the German Evangelical Church keeps using this language'.[21] The scandal was that the church 'in such words and actions is only concerned about itself, is building itself up, vaunting itself, as unambiguously as could be...'[22] But a church which is thus concerned about itself, building itself up and vaunting itself, has long lost the promise and could not 'in any way be credible in its Christmas, Easter and Sunday preaching. When it says "Jesus

Christ", though it says it a thousand times, one can only hear its own satiation and security, and it would not be surprising if its "Jesus Christ" were not words thrown into the wind, ignoring the real need of real people...'[23]

Otto Dibelius, General Superintendent of Brandenburg, already rejected Barth's attacks on behalf of the German church governments at the Prussian General Synod in February 1930. The dispute between the two men then dragged on up to the threshold of the Third Reich. [Barth made his standpoint yet more precise in a lecture about the need of the Protestant church which he gave in Berlin in 1931.[24] Here, significantly, he went into the difference between the Catholic and the Protestant churches and the reciprocal relationship mentioned here. Where the church was not the church under the cross, renouncing all security, the 'question of the life of the church becomes a question of power, of rivalry with the Roman church, for which the question of power is significant and of decisive interest'.[25] Dibelius again replied by saying that Barth had no sense of the tasks of church government and that now was no time for theological criticism. 'We are forced into a battle more momentous than any that has been fought since the cross of Christ was borne on to German soil. In this battle no one sends their excuses because of theological hesitations.'[26]]

So these were the presuppositions on which the two great churches in Germany entered the Third Reich – I have only sketched them in outline because time is short. The Catholic, episcopal, church was influenced by a concordat policy orientated on canon law which made possible unified leadership and closed ranks; the Protestant church, made up of pastors and theologians, was determined by a clash between theology and institution which from the beginning virtually ruled out any common action on the part of the church. This will perhaps explain why the two churches in the Third Reich went such different ways. The Catholic church then retreated into the stronghold of the Reich concordat, which gave it security but at the same time also limited its social and political effectiveness to quite an extraordinary degree. By contrast, the Protestant church, to which Hitler had offered the same chance, broke up; and the Confessing Synods in Barmen and Dahlem in 1934 developed a new church order, the order of the Confessing Church, on the basis of the new theological approach.

I shall break off here, although of course it would be attractive to draw out the lines into the Third Reich and beyond. But rather than present a history of the church, I have wanted to give indications of particular circumstances and conditions which have shaped German church history in the twentieth century. So in conclusion I must say something about the significance of the whole development for our day. It would be natural for us, in retrospect, to take Barth's side and criticize that trend in church politics which I have seen embodied here in the figure of Pacelli, though of course it is also a Protestant trend. Nor do I want to conceal the fact that my own theological approach biasses me towards this evaluation. However, for the church historian that cannot be the last word. Rather, he has first to show what really happened; and in his account he has to put particular stress on those aspects which are perhaps not the most obvious ones to him and his time. So we must realize very clearly that the survival of the two churches in the Third Reich – and in this respect, too, the Protestant church was to some degree a beneficiary here – did not depend on the assurances which the Reich concordat had provided.

As I said at the beginning, it is my conviction that the two great confessions in Germany influenced each other much more deeply and lastingly than they realized. This brief survey of politics, church politics and theology in the Weimar period has, I hope, succeeded in making this clear.

# The Crisis of the 1930s as Questions to Christianity and the Churches[1]

Crisis and renewal, 'challenge and response', as the English historian and philosopher of culture Arnold Toynbee calls them, are the basic pattern of our historical understanding. That is also true of church history. Here too our attention is directed pre-eminently to the times of crises and their consequences: the crisis of the Roman empire and the move towards an imperial church in the fourth century; the dispute between imperial and papal power in the Middle Ages; reform and Reformation in the fifteenth and sixteenth centuries – these are famous examples of this basic pattern, examples of an epoch-making kind.

The topic which concerns us here lies closer to us in time. So we cannot as yet determine whether it has lasting significance for church history. But it seems to me to be beyond question that the crisis of the 1930s and the renewal which it has sparked off and introduced has changed German Protestantism deeply, at any rate in one respect – and in this respect it has changed it more deeply than any other event since the Reformation. For – by way of anticipation – this crisis and its consequences in fact marked the end of the government of Landeskirchen by local rulers, which for more than four centuries had determined the relationship between the German Reformation churches and the state. Legally, of course, as is well known, this institution faded out in 1918. But government of the Landeskirchen by local rulers was not just a legal figure. Its basic concept, namely the special, indeed unique, relationship between state and church which seemed to have been achieved in German Lutheranism, had not finally been done away with. Ultimately it was in fact the 1934 Synod of Barmen and its famous Theological

Declaration which ended this particular relationship between state and church as a theological idea – one consequence largely overlooked in the many articles on Barmen.[2]

Thus the prehistory and the significance of the Barmen Declaration should stand at the centre of this lecture, along with the consequences that this declaration had for the relationship betwen state and church described as church government by the local ruler. So this is not a further exegesis of Article 5 of the Barmen Declaration to determine its significance for the present or even future relationship between the Protestant church and the state in the Federal Republic of Germany but a historical theme – though one which at the same time is not untopical.

## I The outbreak of the crisis

The immediate crisis in German Protestantism for all to see began with the collapse of the Kaiser's Reich.[3] The November Revolution of 1918 and its consequences not only meant the end of its traditional legal order, church government by the local ruler, which bound the Protestant churches very closely to their respective territories by the supreme episcopate; the revolution also took away its political support, endangered its economic foundations and in spiritual terms was no less than a catastrophe.

Certainly thanks to the favourable situation in 1919, in the Weimar constitution it was possible to guarantee the legal and economic position of the church in a way which could hardly have been believed possible in the turbulence of the revolution, and this fact was recognized even by the conservative church governments. But this only apparently solved the spiritual crisis. That was the case not only for that critical theological movement which was associated with the name of Karl Barth and which bitterly attacked the new sense of satisfaction in the church; as will emerge, it was even more the case for the wider movement of German nationalistic Protestantism which, deeply discontented with the state of politics and the church in Germany, hoped for a national renewal of Lutheranism and a Lutheran renewal of the nation – a hope which was accompanied with a powerful dose of anti-Catholicism.

The extent and depth to which these nationalistic Protestant ideas were still widespread in German Protestantism emerged surprisingly clearly after Hitler's accession to power. The German-Christian notion of the great unity of Reich, Volk, Führer and Lutheran church spread with tremendous and apparently irresistible power in spring and summer 1933. The new government with its nationalistic concentration stirred up unprecedented new expectations in German Protestantism; much of what had been repressed since 1918 now came to the surface again and allied itself with the enthusiastic hope for the renewal of Germany and the completion of the Reformation in the form of a national Lutheran Reich Church.

For those who marched in this direction under the banners of church and nationalist movement, the basic principle of the separation of church and state to which the Weimar constitution held firm as representing liberal progress was understandably not very attractive. Granted, to begin with there were still no specific ideas in terms of church-state law as to what form the new relationship between church and state was to take in the future, but a fundamental change was expected everywhere: at least some inner co-ordination, even if the external form was preserved. Later, in autumn and winter 1933/1934, the young Protestant theoreticians of state-church law got together to find the appropriate formulations.[4]

The conservative resistance to the old church governments had already been overcome in summer 1933 – though not without powerful help from Party and state. In July a new Reich Church constitution was forced through; in September Hitler's personal representative was elected first Reich Bishop.

The victory of the German Christians seemed complete. However, resistance now began to form. A Pastors' Emergency League came into being as an alliance of pastors loyal to the confession; in January 1934 well over forty per cent of all Protestant pastors stood by the confession. The south German Landeskirchen of Bavaria and Württemberg, alongside Hanover the only ones to emerge reasonably 'intact' from the revolutionary events, fought for their independence, and up and down the country, for a variety of reasons, dissatisfaction with the new Reich Bishop grew. Nevertheless, the outcome of this unequal struggle could not be in doubt.

The fact that despite all this, six months later, in May 1934, with the first Reich Confessing Synod of Barmen the Protestant church in Germany had again found its voice, was primarily the work of one man, Karl Barth.

Anyone who wants to understand how it proved possible to oppose a church-political power which seemed almost overwhelming, to prevent the sought-after co-ordination of church and state and instead of this to make the church the independent guardian of the state – certainly the last thing that the German Christian movement had in mind – must begin with the theological work of Karl Barth.

## II  The significance of Karl Barth in early 1934

The draft for the 'Theological Declaration' of Barmen in which this whole development culminated was written in the week before Pentecost 1934 at the Hotel Baseler Hof in Frankfurt am Main. Three men were involved in working it out: Hans Asmussen, a young Lutheran from Schleswig-Holstein who had been removed from office at the beginning of the year and who from the end of 1932 had made a name as the author of the 'Altona Confession'; Thomas Breit, also a Lutheran and since 1933 Oberkirchenrat of Bavaria and representative of the Landesbischof of Bavaria; and the Reformed professor of theology Karl Barth, who had been teaching for some years in Bonn. There can be no doubt about Barth's decisive role in this group. On 21 May, i.e. only a few days after his return from Frankfurt, he wrote to a friend: 'The collaboration with Asmussen and Breit in which I was involved last Tuesday and Wednesday for the purpose that you know about was very enjoyable, and I believe that you and our friends in Wuppertal will also be satisfied with the result... Asmussen will report on the matter that we have prepared, while the text – with the exception of one sentence... is mine.'[5] This one sentence, which Asmussen contributed, was the second half of the second thesis ('in him we encounter a joyous liberation from the godless claims of this world to free and thankful services to his creatures').

So unlike, say, the Augsburg Confession with its somewhat complicated history, and unlike the Heidelberg Catechism with its many stages of revision, the Theological Declaration derived from one theological will. It is all of a piece.

That inevitably has consequences for understanding it. For while this declaration clearly became a confession of the church by the assent of the synod, when we consider its historical intent and significance we must begin by taking our bearings from the theological will which shaped it and determined it.

As will soon emerge, this is not the only possible historical orientation. But it is the most obvious and the most important one.

Among Barth's statements on church and theology at this time, two especially are of particular significance here.

The first is his public statement on the church struggle generally, the work with the title which is a famous as it is remarkable: Barth's *Theological Existence Today* of June 1933.[6] Many people nowadays overlook the fact that it was specially addressed to the German Protestant pastors and was one long plea to them 'in no circumstances'[7] now to forfeit their theological existence for anything that was regarded as a good cause. But what does this remarkable term mean? Karl Barth explains it very clearly: 'Our existence as theologians is our life within the church, and, of course, as appointed preachers and teachers within the church.' And that means, as he explains a little later, 'our attachment to God's word and plying our calling particularly to the ministry of the Word'.[8]

But what is the danger of forfeiting this theological existence? It consists in the possibility that we may 'no longer appreciate the intensity and exclusiveness of the demand which the Divine Word makes as such when looking at the force of other demands; so that in our anxiety in the face of existing dangers we no longer put our whole trust in the authority of God's word, but we think we ought to come to its aid with all sorts of contrivances.' 'That under the stormy assault of "principalities, powers, and rulers of this world's darkness", we seek for God elsewhere than in Jesus Christ and seek Christ elsewhere than in the Holy Scriptures.'[9]

Anyone who forfeited his theological existence in this way, Barth thought, was no longer a preacher and teacher of the church, but a politician or a church politician. This was nothing to be ashamed of, but 'it is something else to be a theologian'.[10]

This introduction is followed by a devastating criticism of the German Christians' church-political plans, but even more so of the plans of their opponents, the church opposition. Here Barth accuses them, i.e. the so-called Young Reformers Movement, his friends, of just meddling in church politics, namely 'tactics against tactics, tricks and counter-tricks, pronouncement against pronouncement', and thus, like the church politics of the German Christians, of having 'conceded a goodly portion of common politics'.[11]

Instead, Barth summons the pastors, where necessary, i.e. where the enemy comes into view, to 'repeat and affirm the church's confession by word and deed'. And he goes on: 'Where the confession is, the one, holy church is there present in the fight with error in which she will never lose the day. But, on the other hand, there is always error where there are "movements'" – here Barth was evidently thinking above all of the Faith Movement of German Christians and the Young Reformers Movement – 'and error and sectarianism is always at least close at hand. The Holy Spirit needs no "movements"; the devil has probably invented most of them.'[12]

What Karl Barth asserts here amounts to a complete change of fronts. He asserts that the dispute in and about the church is a *theological* theme and not a *church-political* theme, far less a *political* theme, and that therefore the battle has to be fought theologically – with the church confession in word and deed – and not church-politically or politically; if that happens it is irrevocably lost.

That was an amazing assertion then, and still is today. But it brought salvation. And here we can already recognize the original significance of the Barmen Theological Declaration. The fact that the Synod adopted this Declaration meant that for some weeks and months in spring and summer 1934 the church opposition took this theological line. It took it, having suffered the most shameful defeats wherever it had ventured into politics and church politics – most clearly at the devastating reception of church leaders by the Führer on 25 January 1934.[13] By contrast, wherever it had appealed to the confession, it had received unsuspected signs of the Spirit and of power.[14] As Pastor Graeber of Essen remarked vigorously enough in Barmen about these experiences, 'God has bashed our heads together and perhaps we need even more bashing'.[15]

So the historical significance of the Theological Declaration lay primarily in the fact that it did *not* make it necessary to raise the political questions which at that time were overpowering. Herein lay its liberating power, and also the mystery of its effect. And if I understand the Barmen message rightly in this respect, this is still an important point: that the church did not allow any political themes – whether appropriate or inappropriate – to be forced on it.

This basic position, which we already find in *Theological Existence Today*, is now repeated and developed in the second of Karl Barth's statements on theology and the church which I want to cite here; it is part of the immediate prehistory of Barmen. This is his 'Declaration on the Right Understanding of the Reformed Confessions in the German Evangelical Church of the Present' made at the first Free Reformed Synod in Barmen-Gemarke on 3 and 4 January 1934.[16]

Here we already find the form of thesis and repudiation; here we find the appeal to Lutherans, Reformed and United to speak as one; and here also we find for the first time in this form express mention of what Barth believed to lie at the heart of the church struggle.

At its heart were not political questions about oppression and deprivation of rights, nor church-political efforts at a co-ordination of church and state. As Barth said, and Asmussen later repeated almost word for word in Barmen, the struggle was over an error which had already been devastating the church for centuries, namely the view that 'alongside God's revelation, God's grace and God's honour men and women also have legitimate autonomy to determine the message and form of the church'.[17]

The declaration which the Reformed Synod then took over did not therefore adopt a political standpoint to counter that of the German Christians, but argued on a completely different level. It asserted that the error of the German Christians was in no way a political error but rather 'the error of the papal church and the enthusiasts', and that therefore the enemy was 'no new enemy, but an old enemy in a new form', namely the human claim that is always the same, the desire 'by referring to one's spirit, conscience and righteousness to be a second God alongside God'.[18]

And because despite all the differences of doctrine between Reformed and Lutherans, this front once faced a common opposition to Reformation teaching – papacy, heretics and humanists – Karl Barth could issue a summons for Lutheran, Reformed and United communities and churches to fight together once more against this heresy.[19]

Finally, making the church struggle a theological theme also led to the theses on the relationship between church and state. As Barth saw things, these had to be formulated in such a way that this relationship, too, was only to be defined in theological terms by the church, come what might. In no way could formulations with a political content appear here, since these would then make the whole declaration look like a statement with a political purpose which had slipped in through the back door.

Therefore here, in the January confession, Karl Barth distinguished as clearly as any Lutheran doctrine of the two realms between church and state, each of which had its own particular office. Here, as later in the Barmen Declaration, we read: 'The church cannot relieve the state of this its special office. Nor can it

allow the state to take away its own office; it cannot allow its message
and its form to be determined by the state.'[20]

So church and state are in a relationship of reciprocal independence and freedom. This is based on a distinction between their
offices. Just as the state does not possess a mandate for theology
and the church, so the church does not possess a mandate for politics
and the state. But – and this 'but' is very important – that does not
mean that the church leaves the state to itself and its so-called
autonomy and may 'offer it unqualified obedience'. That is explicitly
rejected. There is no mention of an unpolitical church averse to the
world which is interested only in human inwardness. Rather, the
distinction between the two offices means that the church can
respond to the demands of politics and the state only as church, and
that means theologically. In Karl Barth's words (and here we can
already hear the fifth thesis of Barmen) that means that the church
keeps company with the world, including the political world, 'in its
intercession, seriously recognizing its limited and bounded temporal
rights, but also recalling God's kingdom, law and judgment, in the
hope that the one who directs all things will make all things new'.
'That,' Barth explains, 'is the decisive action which the church can
perform for the world.' So the political means of the church are the
means of the church anywhere: intercession and preaching.[21]

I hope that it has become clear that the content of the 'Declaration
on the Right Understanding of the Reformation Confessions in the
German Evangelical Church' simply fills out and endorses the basic
decisions which had already been made in *Theological Existence
Today*. It was a matter of turning the church struggle (to alter a
famous quotation from Karl Marx) head over heels, i.e. of declaring
against all the appearances that the political and church-political
controversies were theological. Only when the church opposition
had understood this could it argue as church and thus become a
political factor. And that too is the nucleus of Barmen, as already
emerges from the affinity between the January text and the Theological Declaration. We can say with some certainty that without this
earthshaking insight there would have been no Confessing Church
in Germany.

To make that clearer, we must now look briefly at developments
in church politics in the first half of 1934.

## III Developments in church politics between January and May 1934

As Barth himself understood it, the acceptance of his declaration by the Free Reformed Synod on 4 January 1934 turned the opinion of an individual professor into a confession. But at first that meant almost nothing. For at that time there were dozens of confessions and confessional formulations. Moreover the Free Synod in Barmen did not even represent the whole of the numerically small Reformed minority in the church. So from Berlin, where the church-political dice were thrown, the whole event seemed marginal, and not just from a geographical point of view.

Here, in the Reich Church government in Berlin, marked changes had taken place at the end of 1933 which were hardly noted by the public. In the middle of December the young and ambitious Rhineland Bishop Dr Oberheid, a founder member of the German Christian movement, had transferred from Koblenz to Berlin and there had risen to become the first adviser of the Reich Bishop. Oberheid immediately made contact with the notorious erstwhile Church Commissioner August Jäger. And under the influence of Oberheid and above all with the support of the Prussian state government, a plan was now hatched to subvert the old Reich Church constitution, which was only a few months old, as it were in a 'revolution from above', and establish in its stead a unified German Lutheran National Reich Church. The underlying idea here was a modern revival of church government by local rulers (the end of which lay only fifteen years in the past) by handing over church authority *circa sacra* to the Reich leadership. As Hitler himself was unfortunately a Catholic, the Prussian Prime Minister Hermann Göring was envisaged as the first *summus episcopus* of the Lutheran Reich Church; he was to exercise his authority through a kind of ecclesiastical secretary of state. The Reich Bishop was entrusted with the so-called 'spiritual' leadership of the church. This structure was meant to ensure that in terms of personnel, form and content the Reich Church was in fact completely co-ordinated with the state of the Third Reich and remained so: the modern renewal of the old church government by local rulers and at the same time, as it was hoped and believed, the completion of the Reformation.[22]

Initially, at the beginning of 1934 the Reich Bishop still hoped for Hitler's direct assent to these plans. When that was not forthcoming,

August Jäger, who in April had replaced Oberheid, attempted to create *faits accomplis* within the Reich Church by the co-ordination of the Landeskirchen with a view to offering a united Reich Church to Hitler. And when the Synod of Barmen met at the end of May it almost seemed as though these plans would soon succeed. Almost all the political and church-political enterprises of the church opposition had either failed or had proved ineffective.

One of the reasons why the church opposition was operating so unsuccessfully was its disunity and the divisions within it. Undoubtedly the focal point of this opposition movement was the Pastors' Emergency League, though its effective intervention largely remained limited to the Old Prussian Church. According to its declaration of commitment the members were committed only to Holy Scripture and to the Reformation confessions, i.e. to a theological aim; but as Martin Niemöller led and organized the Emergency League, by early 1934 it had become primarily a church-political instrument.

The Pastors' Emergency League was joined in its opposition to the Reich Bishop by the two South German Landesbischöfe with their Landeskirchen – as it were the last pillars of the old church. Understandably, by virtue of their position and their interests they tended more towards continuity and thus towards compromise than towards a break.

And finally, in all the church territories dominated by the German Christians, in the Prussian provincial churches as in the other Landeskirchen, there were larger or smaller minorities in opposition, though at the beginning of 1934 their organization within the Landeskirchen was only a loose one, where there was any at all. The spokesman and leader of this motley opposition front was the Landesbischof of Bavaria, Hans Meiser, who also organized the church-political and political activities of the opposition in the period leading up to the reception of the Protestant church leaders by Hitler on 25 January.

The concern of the opposition was that this reception of the two parties in dispute should lead to the resignation of the Reich Bishop and a renewal of the Reich Church government. And politically the matter seemed already virtually to have been decided. By unceasing, intensive political work on almost half the Reich Cabinet, the Foreign Minister, the Minister of the Interior, the Finance Minister and the Vice-Chancellor had been won over to the cause of the church opposition. It was even more important that the Reich President had already declared that he would personally present the opposition case to Hitler. It was thought that the Reich Chancellor would hardly be able to withstand this united political pressure.

However, it then proved that Hitler and the Prussian Prime Minister Hermann Göring were far superior to the church leaders in the political game. With a simple but effective trick Göring succeeded in both intimidating and disheartening the representatives of the opposition to such an extent that two days later the bishops agreed to a declaration which gave unqualified support to the Reich Bishop and thus represented the precise opposite of what they had wanted.[23]

This church-political disaster had two immediate consequences. For the German Christian Reich Church government it was the occasion for going on to destroy the constitution, disable the Landeskirchen and incorporate them into the Reich Church without further ado. A beginning was made with the Evangelical Church of the Old Prussian Union, which was co-ordinated as early as 1 March 1934.

Not long afterwards, on 19 March, the German Christian church leaders of eleven Landeskirchen, including Nassau-Hessen, Saxony, Schleswig-Holstein, Hamburg and Mecklenburg, were called to Berlin to be told that over the next few weeks their Landeskirchen would similarly be incorporated into the Reich Church.[24] No resistance to these plans could be expected either from the church leaders or from the German-Christian synods of these Landeskirchen.

And so – as is all too easily forgotten – by the middle of May 1934 not only Thuringia and Hanover, where there was still considerable dispute over the issue, but also numerically about three-quarters of all Protestant Germans had been co-ordinated into the Reich Church. Only Bavaria and Württemberg remained as serious obstacles. All attempts by the church opposition groups in the various church provinces and Landeskirchen to avert the fate of co-ordination by political or church-political means had come to grief; in Nassau-Hessen and Saxony no less than in Hanover and even in Westphalia, where the opposition had by far the strongest position in Germany. And though in retrospect the purely formal and schematic aspect of these proceedings emerges clearly, their effect on contemporaries was deep and long-lasting. Given the speed and recklessness with which the Reich Church government and its allied

German Christian church governments were working, the demise of any German Evangelical Church worthy of the name seemed to be imminent.

Far more important for the future of the church than this apparently overpowering action, however, was another development which also began immediately after the Führer's reception.

We meet it quite clearly in a critical comment which two unknown pastors from the Province of Uckermark sent to the leaders of the Pastors' Emergency League at the beginning of February: 'The church-political actions have collapsed, not only as a result of the culpable reversal of course by the church leaders but also because the Pastors' Emergency League has allied its cause with theirs and has built on human dexterity in negotiations and human trustworthiness.' The authors went on to say that if a lesson was to be learned from experience the salvation of the church was not to be expected from political actions but from the faith of the community. They then outlined in a few simple sentences the difficult relationship between politics, church politics and proclamation at this time.

'True church politics in the Protestant Church is possible only as proclamation. True proclamation always has the effect of a political action in community, church and state. However, the proclamation may never be made to serve political or church-political ends.'[25]

It would have been hard to describe more precisely the theological course which Karl Barth and the Free Reformed Synod had already taken. And in fact this now became the course that was followed in the churches which had already been co-ordinated. A start was made with the provincial churches in the west of Prussia, chief among which was the church of the Rhineland.

As early as 12 February, barely three weeks after the Führer's reception, the Council of Brethren of the Rhineland Pastors' Brotherhood invited pastors and presbyters who supported the Pastors' Brotherhood to a Free Synod in Barmen to be held on 18 and 19 February. Despite the short notice, thirty out of thirty-three Rhineland district synods were represented by preachers and elders at this first Free Synod. The sermon by Friedrich Graeber from Essen with which this synod opened and the report by Joachim Beckmann showed what was now at stake, namely (in Beckmann's words), a church which 'understands itself in theological rather than anthropological or even sociological terms, i.e. in terms of God and not of human beings, the incarnation of God and not human ideas or human communities. This insight leads us to turn away with resolution and determination from all our previous ways and means towards a church which is obedient only to God.'[26]

What this new way looked like also emerged from the explicit adoption by the synod in its decision of the Theological Declaration of the Reformed Synod which had met in January.[27]

At the beginning of March, Berlin-Brandenburg followed this course; it was joined by Westphalia, in particularly dramatic circumstances, in the middle of March, and later also by Saxony.

The great question now was how to form a link between west and east and with the south German Landeskirchen.[28] On 11 April a joint action committee was formed in Nuremberg for this purpose. But here, too, progress was made only when in the middle of April the Reich Church government attempted to overcome the Württemberg church in a kind of coup. Although this first attack failed, the danger was recognized in both Stuttgart and Munich, and contacts with the other groups became even closer. This led on 22 April in Ulm to the so-called 'Ulm Declaration', which can rightly be called the birth of the Confessing Church.

In this document the 'assembled representatives of the Landeskirchen of Württemberg and Bavaria, the Free Synods in the Rhineland, Westphalia and Brandenburg, and many Confessing communities and Christians throughout Germany' declared that: 'Because of the lasting danger to the confession and the church, and also for the sake of the truth, we are establishing ourselves as a single body which by the power of God means to remain faithful to the confession, although we must expect this to cause us much distress. However, we are confident of God's Word, and joyfully take upon ourselves whatever God may lay on us, come what may, so that the cross of Christ really rules the life of the church.'[29]

With this declaration, Karl Barth's understanding of the church struggle as a *theological* decision had won through. Not all those who had gathered in Ulm understood this in the same way. But in principle here was a statement of what Karl Barth had always asserted: the issue was not one of political decisions, far less of church-political decisions, but rather of the church's confession, of 'theological existence today'. The way to the Synod of Barmen was open.

## IV The 'Theological Declaration'

It was in keeping with the way in which the struggle was made a theological theme that the obstacles on the way to the Synod and the passing of the Theological Declaration did not come from outside but from within, i.e. from theology and the church itself.

I shall leave aside all questions of church law, i.e. the problem of the relationship between the Synod of Barmen and the constitution of the German Evangelical Church, and the difficulties which arose as a result of the tension between the 'intact' churches of south Germany and the representatives of the 'destroyed' churches, and limit myself wholly to the theological problems.

There was a political reason why it was possible to limit oneself to the theological problems in this way. In this connection reference must be made to what in retrospect is the somewhat surprising circumstance that during the weeks of preparation the church authorities evidently did not worry about any police measures. And in fact, as we know, there was no reason for such concern. In the Reich Ministry of the Interior the announcement of the synod had been noted and apparently accepted; and the far more dangerous Prussian Gestapo counted on a split in the Confessing front which they did not want to jeopardize by police action.[30] So the church groups involved in the preparations made no attempt to keep them secret. The synod itself was held without interruptions and in full public view. Another reason for being clear about this is that the fact that the first Reich Confessing Synod in the Third Reich could meet in complete freedom also influenced the political judgment of its members. Even for Karl Barth, Hitler's state was not yet a totally unjust state as long as it left the church this freedom. We cannot understand the fifth thesis of Barmen which speaks about the relationship between church and state without understanding this experience, which was the experience of all members of the synod.

The resistance within the church caused the preparatory bodies far greater anxiety. This resistance to the whole enterprise of a Reich Confessing Synod and especially to a joint Theological Declaration came above all from the Lutheran camp. It was prompted by two factors.[31]

The first and at the time by far the most important resistance was prompted by fear of a 'unionism' which, it was believed, would in fact corrupt precisely that which was supposed to be being saved, namely the confession. This resistance was orientated on a historical concept of the confession which drew above all on the nineteenth-century Lutheran renewal movement and which regarded the Lutheran confessional writings as the church's foundation documents. Any involvement with, say, Reformed ideas, which was naturally suspected in a text drafted by Karl Barth, must therefore endanger the foundations of the Lutheran churches. So as early as the beginning of May the Landesbischof of Bavaria warned in the preparatory committee of the Synod against involvement with 'confessional questions' or a concern to 'draft a joint confession' – a somewhat curious restriction on the preparation of a joint Confessing Synod.[32]

Therefore the document which was passed jointly finally bore the title 'Theological Declaration on the Present Situation of the German Evangelical Church', in order to make it clear that this was not a 'confession' but a theological statement on a current issue. The introduction spoke of the German Evangelical Church as a 'federal union of confessional churches which grew out of the Reformation, of equal rights and parallel existence', and of a 'common word' which had now been placed in the mouths of the members of the Lutheran, Reformed and United churches. Finally, it explicitly commended to God 'what this may mean for the relationship of the Confessional Churches with one another'; all these formulations made clear what efforts had been made to enable the strict Lutherans also to give their assent.[33]

The second factor to prompt Lutheran resistance as it was expressed in the preliminaries and in the synod itself was in substance connected with the theology of the Declaration and primarily related to three questions: 'The question of natural theology, the question of the order of creation and the ethos of Christian action.'[34] The main suspicions here were removed by a reformulation of the fifth thesis, which Barth worked on far into the night after hours of discussion in committee; this put more stress on the office of the state. This did not, however, prevent the Erlangen Lutherans from censuring the Theological Declaration as soon as it appeared: they claimed that from a Lutheran perspective it was sheer heresy.

It is not easy now to explain the passion and stubbornness of the Lutheran resistance to Barmen at the time, because both the main factors which prompted it have meanwhile been countered by the course of history.

That is the case with the theological-political argument, where Barmen proved right. It is also the case with the confessional argument, where the 1973 Leuenberg Concord with its declaration that all Reformation churches are in communion has fulfilled the hopes of the Barmen Synod.

But what is the central substance of the Theological Declaration? I shall try to demonstrate that with some comments on the first, second and fifth theses.

As is well known, the text of the first thesis runs:

> Jesus Christ, as he is testified to us in the Holy Scripture, is the one Word of God, whom we are to hear, whom we are to trust and obey in life and in death.
>
> We repudiate the false teaching that the church can and must recognize yet other happenings and powers, images and truths as divine revelation alongside this one Word of God, as the source of her preaching.[35]

Without question this first thesis is the nucleus of the whole Declaration. Essentially, what it repeats is the powerful threefold *solus* of the Reformation: *solus Christus, sola scriptura, sola fide*. I would see the Barmen Declaration, with this repetition, as being far closer to the young Luther and his theology than to any other era of church history. By explicitly repeating the *solus Christus*, at the same time the Declaration demonstrated that the controversies with the German Christians were first and foremost a theological problem. This theological problem was not just a topical problem, produced say by the particularly offensive 'political theology' of the German Christians, but related to a much older question which had been discussed for centuries under the quite innocent concept of 'natural theology'.

Asmussen explicitly made this decisive point in his report at the synod, which was composed in collaboration with others.[36] If we protest against German Christian theology, he said – and this was not just meant as a tactical formula – 'then we are not protesting as members of the Volk against the recent history of the Volk nor as citizens against the new state nor as subjects against authority. We are protesting against that phenomenon which has already been slowly preparing the devastation of the church for more than two centuries.'[37]

Thus, by its own understanding, the Confessing Church which

emerged from Barmen had a theological, not a political, task. Its refusal to understand itself as a political resistance group in the Third Reich (quite apart from the question whether that would have been possible at all for external reasons) therefore derived not only from a universally criticized blindness, cowardice and readiness to adapt, but in essence from a theological decision.

On the other hand this refusal – and this is no less important – was in no way also a refusal to make political judgments and to influence politics. As we know, Luther too, despite the doctrine of the two kingdoms, did not hesitate to adopt a very specific political standpoint if need be, from the Peasants' War to the Counts of Mansfeld, provided that the distinction between the mandates remained clear. The same was also true of Barmen. The rejection of other 'happenings and powers, images and truths' as a source of proclamation already challenged the all-embracing claim of the new system. For no one at that time had to explain that what was meant by 'happenings' was the National Socialist Revolution, by 'powers' the Führer himself and by 'truths' the new world-view. No one could accuse the church of having meddled in an office which was not its own by making this statement. But anyone who was ready to hear could hear that the confession of Jesus Christ as the one Word of God set a clear, unmistakable limit to the divine aspirations of the totalitarian state, its supporters and its ideas.

And the original intention of the second thesis pointed in precisely that direction. Jesus Christ as (so the thesis put it), 'God's pledge of the forgiveness of all our sins...' and 'a claim on our whole life' was meant, according to Asmussen's explanation, as a warning against the temptation to seek God apart from Christ in the 'creatures of God and the events of history', i.e. to make one's own God. Moreover, this explanation by Asmussen said more about the Third Reich than he himself and the synod probably understood at that time. 'Wherever that happens,' Asmussen continued, 'other lords than Jesus Christ, other commands than his commands gain power over us. They offer themselves to us as redeemers, but they prove to be the torturers of an unredeemed world.'[38] The apparent redeemer as a torturer: Hitler's career could hardly be summed up more briefly and more evocatively! A church with this theological understanding of itself could also define its relationship to the state in a new and different way from that which had been possible for Lutheran tradition when the church was governed by local rulers.

In fact the fifth thesis contains definitions, distinctions and subordi-
nations which are characteristic of the young Luther, but from which
for various reasons the Lutheran churches in Germany had gradually
parted company.

The first half of this fifth thesis is about the state. It runs: 'The
Bible tells us that according to divine arrangement the state has the
responsibility to provide for justice and peace in the yet unredeemed
world, in which the church also stands, according to the measure of
human insight and human possibility, by the threat and rule of force.
The church recognizes with thanks and reverence towards God the
benevolence of this, his provision.'[39]

This was explicit confirmation of the value and sovereignty of the
state, and those involved in political action were given a good deal
of freedom in political responsibility – 'according to the measure of
human insight and human possibility' – which had to be free from
all intervention by the church. This first part of the fifth thesis is
miles away from any enthusiastic or anachronistic ideas about the
state. There is no mention of a 'sphere free from rule'. Rather, it
not only makes solemn recognition of the necessity of the state
but explictly confirms its 'monopoly of power' – not, however,
absolutely, but instrumentally, namely in the terms of its divinely
willed commission 'to see to justice and peace'. That is precisely the
insight that the young Dietrich Bonheoffer maintained in 1933 when
he argued that the church was aware of the 'absolute necessity of
the use of force in this world and also the "moral" injustice of certain
concrete acts of the state which are necessarily bound up with the
use of force'.[40] In this sense the Barmen Declaration also recognizes
the right and value of state action where such action is bound up
with the threat and use of force.

But the church has more to say to the state than to confirm it in
its action *qua* state and to give it grateful recognition. So the second
part of the thesis runs: 'The church reminds men of God's kingdom,
God's commandment and righteousness, and thereby the responsibility of rulers and ruled. She trusts and obeys the power of the
word, through which God maintains all things.'[41]

Thus at the same time the church also always reminds the state of
the limits to its power which are set by God's kingdom, God's
commandment and God's righteousness. Asmussen made this
unmistakably clear in his report to the synod when he said – and this
was still at the end of May 1934 (!): 'We believe that we are doing

nothing less than our duty before God, who alone is wise and alone is just, when in repudiating German Christian errors we point out that the wisdom of the state in its present form is nor God's wisdom, and that the criteria of justice which prevail in our state system are not the criteria of divine justice. And we must stress once and for all that we know no earthly law on the basis of which God's law could rightly be broken.'[42]

The church does not face the state in silence. By reminding the state of God's kingdom, God's commandment and God's righteousness, the church reminds it of its limits and at the same time tells the state what it simply cannot tell itself. The church reminds the state that there are criteria for its actions which it cannot set itself, but which are set by God's world. To these, rulers and ruled are subjected and to these they are responsible – whether they are prepared to perceive this or not.

The decisive factor here remains that the church understands that it cannot itself act politically, nor, if it sees the state failing, should it think that it can and should do better (except only in some extreme circumstances). Its task is to remind. If it keeps to that task and yet is not heard now, or later, or at all, 'It trust and obeys the power of the word, through which God maintains all things' (Barmen 5).

One certainly cannot say that German Protestantism at that time, or later, put these basic regulations of Barmen into practice particularly convincingly or impressively. Nevertheless - and here we come back to the opening thesis – the German Reformation churches have changed with and through the Declaration of Barmen. The traditional relationship of trust to the state, strikingly expressed in the centuries of the legal institution of church government by the local ruler, gave way to a critical solidarity. That has in fact become an ongoing feature of Protestant church history in the post-war period.

# The Church Struggle*

## I The term and its history

'Church struggle' is the term used to denote the varied history of the Christian churches in Germany at the time of National Socialist rule (1933-1945). The term has undergone various changes of meaning. It arose in an evocative sense at the end of 1933 when in the defensive struggle against the German Christian church government, awareness of the fundamental theological significance of the controversies began to gain ground in the Protestant church; previously these had been called either the church dispute or the church troubles. In the terminology of the Confessing Church, which was then taking shape, church struggle exclusively meant the struggle in the church over the church: the church struggle 'was and still is a struggle in our church for a stance in keeping with the confession and action in keeping with the gospel' (M.Niemöller, *Junge Kirche*, February 1934). With the collapse of the German Christian church government and the removal of the Reich Bishop from power the church struggle therefore at first seemed to be over. With the formation of the Church Committees in autumn 1935 (see II C 1 below) the term took on a different connotation. For the supporters of the Committee policy the church struggle now usually meant the struggles with the German Christians, which lay in the past. The opponents of the Committee policy transferred the term to the controversies over state intervention: 'Let the church order its affairs in real freedom... then the church struggle can be over in three months' (O.Dibelius to Reich Minister Kerrl at the end of February 1937). However, the term took on its most decisive political signifi-

*This article was originally published in *Evangelisches Staatslexikon*, Stuttgart and Berlin 1975, cols. 1177-1200.

cance where it was extended to the fundamental battle between Christianity and National Socialism: 'If we keep the image of a battlefield, then we must say that the German Christian movement in the sphere of the church and the spectacle which acts as the "German Faith Movement"... are being increasingly clearly recognized as the basically unimportant forward skirmishes behind which... has become visible the army of political religion which is purposefully advancing' (G.Jacob, Fourth Confessing Synod of the Old Prussian Union, December 1936). The term church struggle was also used in this sense in German-speaking countries abroad, namely as a designation for the struggle which 'the church in Germany is carrying on against paganism and the totalitarian claims of the National Socialist state' (A.Frey, *Der Kampf der evangelischen Kirche in Deutschland*, Zurich 1937). Until 1945 only the context showed what church struggle meant in any instance. After 1945 the term very soon became established as the description of a period of the history of both churches in the Third Reich. It is legitimate to use it in this way to denote a period, as long as this does not mean continuous political resistance by the churches against National Socialist rule, and the changes in meaning and the nuances of the term are clearly seen.

## II Historical focal points

### A. Prehistory

#### 1. Church and theology in the Weimar period

(*a*) *The new orientation in church politics*. There is no doubt that the leading groups in German Protestantism regarded the defeat and revolution of 1918 as also being a bitter loss for the Protestant Landeskirchen. The Landeskirchen took over their own church government and adapted their constitutions to the new political situation with some reluctance. A basically conservative trait which doomed all attempts at church reform to failure dominated the church and church politics in the first years of the Republic. However, around the middle of the 1920s this picture changed. The end of church government by local rulers was no longer regarded as a misfortune but as a gift and an obligation. The most impressive example of this new evaluation was Otto Dibelius's *Century of the*

*Church* (reprinted six times between 1926 and 1928), a unique confession of the new tasks and possibilities facing the church. The revolution and its consequences now appeared as the 'liberating storm' which at a stroke had created a free, independent Protestant church. 'The independence of the church is here... A church has come into being. An independent Protestant church!' This growing self-awareness is the most important feature of church developments betwen 1918 and 1933 and a decisive presupposition for any under-standing of the events which followed. In fact, until 1933 the independence of the church that had been forced on it by the revolution was one of its most important possessions, which it was resolved to defend against all state intervention. In substance church politics was increasingly orientated on the welfare and distress of the people. The church sought to be a Volkskirche, i.e. a spiritual and moral force which in solidarity with the national need gave the Volk a direction and goal. This claim to be a Volkskirche emerged increasingly in the later years of the Republic. The slogan was no longer 'Throne and Altar' but 'Church and Volk' (Königsberg Kirchentag, 1927).

(b) *The new theological beginning*. In contrast to the new orien-tation that had been forced on the church, a new theological approach developed which is above all associated with the name of Karl Barth, as a result of a direct encounter with the Bible. This was a theology which began from the 'otherness of God' – 'other than all that is human, including all human religion and culture' (Karl Barth, *The Epistle to the Romans*, 1919). In Barth's view the relationship between God and the world could only be expressed in paradoxical formulations. 'Man and his universe... a riddle, a question, nothing else. God confronts man as the impossible con-fronts the possible, as death confronts life, as eternity confronts time' ('The Word of God as the Task of Theology', 1922). This approach amounted to a radical break with almost all the traditions of the nineteenth century. For Karl Barth and his friends the liberal understanding of Christianity as a decisively important moral, spiritual and cultural factor became the great error of modern times. In challenging this error, at the same time they challenged culture-Protestantism and nationalistic Protestantism with all its ancillaries. At first Barth was not very involved in church politics, but he finally clashed with the new self-awareness of the church. In *Quousque tandem...?* (1930) Barth directly accused the official church of a scandalous betrayal of the gospel, a charge which Dibelius rejected with equal sharpness.

(c) *Political theology*. In contrast to dialectical theology, which did not adopt an explicitly political stance before 1930, from the beginning a group of young Lutheran theologians (E.Hirsch, P.Althaus) understood themselves in political terms. For them, divine and worldly political orders were very closely asosciated in the development of the first article of faith. In their view, a theology which could not expound law and gospel in concrete political terms was mere enthusiasm. So E.Hirsch interpreted 'Germany's Destiny'; P.Althaus spoke at the Fatherland Kirchentag, and together with their friends both represented the national values and orders of the time. They too clashed with dialectical theology in 1931 over remarks made by the Berlin pastor Günther Dehn who later became Professor of Theology in Halle (the Dehn affair).

## 2. The Hitler movement and the churches

(*a*) *Hitler's world-view*. In contrast to a view which was widely put forward above all after the Second World War, we must begin by assuming that Hitler's world-view shaped the NSDAP and the principles of its policy (J.C.Fest, 1973). The basis of this world-view was a pronounced Manichaeism. It posited a dualism in the world between a higher and a lower human race, the Aryans and the Jews. The fate of the world was decided in the struggle between the good principle and the evil principle. Hitler saw himself and his movement called to overcome evil in the world in the name of the good principle. Accordingly antisemitism had a decisive function in this world-view. It was not a means to an end, viz. rule; on the contrary, rule was itself a means to the end: the battle against the Jews. However much Hitler might adapt tactically to the situation in the years of his rise, rule and downfall, he never acted against his convictions on decisive questions. This is also a firm starting point for any understanding of his attitude to the churches.

(*b*) *The Party's church policy up to 1933*. The Party's policy towards the churches, which initially was largely tactical, must be distinguished from Hitler's world-view. On the basis of Article 24 of the Party programme ('The Party as such represents the standpoint of a positive Christianity'), which had 'positive' associations for many Christians, up to 1930 this policy pursued three aims: the avoidance of confessional controversies in the Party; dissociation from pseudo-religious sectarians (the expulsion of Artur Dinter in 1928); and a distinction between political and religious Catholicism. The important thing was therefore to avoid anything that might make the election of the NSDAP more difficult or even impossible in Christian circles. However, this strict neutrality could only be maintained as long as the Party itself was not challenged politically. So after its electoral victory in September 1930 the NSDAP tried increasingly hard to move from mere neutrality to an approach to the churches. On the Catholic side this proved difficult because a political confrontation with the Centre Party was unavoidable and the German episcopate had serious hesitations about the NSDAP world-view. On the Protestant side, Hitler's campaign not only ran parallel to the basic nationalistic tendency of Protestantism; here there was also the possibility of conquering the church by means of a church party and church elections. So at the end of 1932 for the first time 'German Christians (National Socialists)' appeared alongside Positives, Liberals and Religious Socialists in the Prussian church elections; they won around a third of all the seats ('German Christian Guidelines', 1932). Despite this electoral success in 1932/33 the NSDAP was still far from a 'conquest' of the Protestant church.

(c) *The political attitude of the churches on the eve of the seizure of power.* Despite the rapid growth of the Hitler movement, the Catholic church maintained its essentially negative attitude, above all for cultural and political reasons. There was a wide spectrum of opinion within the Protestant church. Contrary to common opinion, the extraordinarily lively debate over Hitler and the Party which had been carried on here since 1930 threw up remarkable differences. Not only Religious Socialists but also Liberals (like Martin Rade) maintained an attitude of critical detachment, as did representatives of dialectical theology (R.Karwehl) and determined Lutherans (H.Sasse). Clear-sighted analysis showed up the character of the movement as a 'political religion' with necessarily totalitarian consequences. However, this view was a minority one in the church. The view of the majority was represented by W.Künneth, who in 1931 formulated the Protestant church's 'Yes' and 'No' to National Socialism. It said 'no' to the racism, the cultural politics and the political praxis of the movement. A small minority – though increasingly supported above all by the youth – were Hitler's radical champions in the church. All in all, among the authorities in the church, restraint towards Hitler far exceeded assent.

B. The struggle over the confession, 1933/1934

*1. Hitler's triumph*

(a) *Hitler's aims*. Hitler's church policy pursued two aims. In the short term he was concerned to co-ordinate the churches with the nationalist revolutionary state; in the long term the question – which Hitler had probably not yet decided in 1933 – was whether the churches were to be counted among the 'Aryan' or the 'Jewish' forces and thus should be treated as allies or deadly enemies of his movement. With his distinctive political sense he understood that the different structures of the two churches called for different political tactics. So in early 1933 he pronounced the two slogans of his church policy: Reich concordat and Reich church. However, the presupposition of this policy – and Hitler had also understood this – was the churches' confidence in the new state. He provided this presupposition in the government declaration of 23 March which contained far-reaching guarantees for the churches. With these guarantees in their possession, allied in the fight against Bolshevism and borne up by the waves of national enthusiasm, within a few weeks the two churches had dropped their reservations about Hitler and began to give him increasing political support.

(b) *The Reich concordat*. Given the Holy See's traditional concordat policy and its vain negotiations with the Weimar Republic, Hitler's offer of a concordat seemed to represent a great opportunity for Rome, particularly as the new Reich was prepared to make far-reaching concessions, especially over the schools policy. In the meantime Hitler's purpose has become clear. Regardless of all later decisions of principle, at home he succeeded above all in excluding political Catholicism, which he rightly feared, and abroad secured recognition from an undisputed moral power, the Vatican. But at the same time this indicates the whole problem of this treaty. In church-political terms the Reich concordat very soon proved to be ambivalent. Its renunciation of political representation had bound the hands of the German episcopate politically; on the other hand, with its guarantees of status the treaty doubtless performed the important function of protecting the two churches as long as Hitler was bound to observe it for reasons of foreign policy.

(c) *The Reich Church.* Hitler also achieved his aim on the Protestant side equally quickly and surprisingly. This aim was the formation of the twenty-eight Protestant Landeskirchen into a German Evangelical Reich Church which was to be incorporated into the Reich under the leadership of a man who was devoted to him. The 'German Christians', who only became an important factor in church politics after the seizure of power, took the initiative at their first Reich conference in Berlin at the begining of April 1933. Here, with Party support, they called for a single Reich Church, the Führer principle, the dismissal of pastors of 'alien blood', and unconditional political and social collaboration with the new Reich. When the President of the German Evangelical Church Committee, H.Kapler, developed his own plans in opposition to this (a triumvirate), Hitler appointed a Königsberg army chaplain, Ludwig Müller, as his representative in church questions with the special task of doing all that was necessary for the creation of 'an Evangelical German Reich Church'. The attempt of the Protestant Landeskirchen to maintain their independence from the state (the choice of F.von Bodelschwingh as candidate for the office of Reich Bishop on 27 May 1933) failed for both internal and external reasons. Under the impact of the appointment of a state commissioner (A.Jäger) for the Protestant Landeskirchen of Prussia on 24 June 1933, the church leaders abandoned their resistance. In a short period Müller succeeded in preparing and passing a Reich Church constitution (Constitution of the German Evangelical Church of 11 July 1933, confirmed by the Reich Law of 14 July). The church elections which were then fixed for 23 July gave the German Christians, who received massive support from the Party and from Hitler himself, overwhelming majorities almost everywhere. On 27 September the new National Synod met in Wittenberg, and as expected unanimously elected Ludwig Müller Reich Bishop. Hitler's plan seemed to have succeeded.

## 2. The emergence of the Confessing Church

(a) *The resistance to Hitler's plans.* The surprising thing about the events of the years 1933 and 1934 is not the success of Hitler's plans but their ultimate failure. Particularly in the Protestant church, everything seemed in their favour: the broad nationalist tendency in German Protestantism, the traditional respect for authority, the old desire for a single German church, the understanding of the

Volkskirche and a theological pluralism which seemed to rule out a single assessment of the situation. Over against this, however, two new forces proved stronger. The *legal and institutional* attack on the Protestant church came up against the church's newly-won self-awareness and resolution to defend its independence from the state (see above A 1a). The *theological* demands for a radical political theology came up against dialectical theology, which challenged the links between German and Christian, kingdom of God and national revolution, as being false from the start (see above A 1b). Though initially the church governments seemed to be collapsing, the theological controversy entered a second phase in autumn 1933 and the German Christians – despite the support of Emanuel Hirsch - had nothing to match it. Church and theology, long since almost completely separated, allied themselves in common repudiation of a heresy that was destroying the church, to form a community with new theological and legal foundations: the Confessing Church. This is the most important result of the church struggle.

(b) *The hour of theology.* Karl Barth's *Theological Existence Today* appeared in the midst of the hectic activity of summer 1933. In it Barth declared that the issue was not one of church-political fronts but solely of holding firm to 'theological existence'. Martin Niemöller took up this theme when after the German Christian election victory he announced the withdrawal of the church opposition from church politics. The issue was now the confession. And this was not a matter of church politics but rather 'a practical task for the community and a theological task for the church' (*Junge Kirche*, August 1933). In fact, in view of the hopeless situation in church politics, intensive theological work began in many places (e.g. the Bethel Confession of August 1933). It was in keeping with this that at the end of September 1933 Niemöller announced the formation of a Pastors' Emergency League which required its members to be committed only to Holy Scripture and the Reformation confessions. The Pastors' Emergency League had a political focus through its statement that the application to the church of state legislation concerning the Jews (the Aryan paragraph) was a specific violation of the confession. By January 1934 more than 7000 members had joined the Pastors' Emergency League – almost half the active German pastors. At the beginning of 1934 the first Free Synods formed in opposition to the synods dominated by the German Christians; they included the Free Reformed Synod of

Barmen-Gemarke, which on 3/4 January 1934 endorsed a 'Declaration on the Right Understanding of the Reformation Confessions
in the German Evangelical Church of the Present' which had
been composed by Karl Barth. In Westphalia in March 1934 the
Evangelical Confessing Synod declared itself to be the 'legitimate
church synod of the province of Westphalia' and took over the
spiritual leadership of the community.

   (c) *The Reich Bishop's struggle for power.* The rise of the Pastors'
Emergency League was paralleled by a rapid collapse of the German
Christians. A speech by a radical German Christian at a rally in the
Berlin Sports Palace on 13 November 1933 calling for the abolition
of the Old Testament, the liquidation of Paul's Jewish theology and
allegiance to a heroic figure of Jesus led to a widespread dissolution
of the German Christian organization and the almost complete loss
of its foundations. Nevertheless the Reich Bishop maintained his
purpose. Hitler himself again committed the Landesbischöfe to
Müller in an audience on 25 January 1934. Thereupon with the
assent of the German Christian synods, Müller and his 'legal
adminstrator' August Jäger incorporated most of the Landeskirchen
into the Reich Church in the course of the summer. Only in Bavaria,
Württemberg and to some extent in Hanover did this fail because of
the resistance of the old church governments, who were tenaciously
supported by the communities.

   (d) *The Confessing synods of Barmen and Dahlem.* As early as
autumn 1933, in view of the hopeless theological devastation of the
Reich Church, the question had arisen whether people should not
separate themselves from this church and take the plunge into a
Free Church. However, the decision was made to move in another
direction. When the 'Representatives of the Lutheran, Reformed
and United Churches, Free Synods, Kirchentage and community
groups' met for the first Reich Confessing Synod in Barmen, they
had no doubt that they alone – not the Müller-Jäger regime and the
German Christian church governments – represented the German
Evangelical Church. At the Synod of Barmen a church had emerged
from the various Confessing groups, communities and synods: the
Confessing Church. The fact that this church could articulate a
common confession for the first time since the sixteenth cnetury
gave this synod a significance which extended far beyond the
immediate occasion. In this way it was one of the most important
church-historical events of the century. The Theological Declar-

ation, the 'Barmen Confession', which was passed there, gave the Confessing Church its foundation and direction for the whole period of the Third Reich. In six theses and six repudiations this confession established some simple basic truths of the gospel. It was unmistakably Karl Barth's theology which bore fruit here, namely in the first thesis. 'Jesus Christ, as he is testified to us in the Holy Scripture, is the one word of God whom we are to hear, whom we are to trust and obey in life and in death.' And in the repudiation: 'We repudiate the false teaching that the church can and must recognize yet other happenings and powers, images and truths as divine revelation alongside this one word of God, as a source of her preaching.' This was not only a demarcation from the German Christian false teachings, but – and this was far more important – it was immediately identified as the only ground of faith and the church. The approach was also followed in the other theses. Autumn 1934 brought still further decisions. At the beginning of October the second Reich Confessing Synod gathered in Dahlem, a suburb of Berlin, under the impact of the rigorous and violent measures taken by the Reich Church government against Württemberg and Bavaria. It drew the practical consequences of Barmen and refused allegiance to the German Christian church governments, rejected any further collaboration, appointed its own provisional church government and called on all the communities in future to observe only the instructions of the Confessing Church (the Church Emergency Law). Soon after that, at the end of October, Müller's church policy collapsed completely. Hitler, tired of the constant disputes in the Protestant Church and concerned about their consequences for foreign politics, summoned the rebel bishops Wurm and Meiser along with Bishop Marahrens of Hanover to Berlin and publicly rehabilitated them. The Reich Bishop's legal adminstrator faded into the background, the incorporation laws were repealed and Müller himself was removed from power. For a moment it looked as if the Confessing Church had won.

## 3. Evaluation

In 1933/34 the church struggle was exclusively concerned with the confession and church order. The Confessing Church had never left any doubt that otherwise it had unconditional political loyalty to Führer and Reich. In recent times (see IV C below) it has often been criticized for this – over one point certainly rightly. Despite its battle against the Aryan paragraph in the church, the Confessing Church which was in process of formation did not understand the significance and implications of National Socialist antisemitism. This guilt is irrefutable. However, the Confessing Church, in focussing on the confession, cannot be accused of having made the wrong issue its theme (M.Jacobs). The church could not have attacked National Socialism as a political religion more effectively than at the place where in God's name it denied the total claim of National Socialism on the whole of human life. In this sense the struggle for the freedom and purity of the proclamation of the gospel was at the same time a political battle against the forces which supported National Socialist rule.

## C. State policy over the church, 1935-1939

### 1. The establishment of the Church Committees

(a) *The appointment of the 'Reich Minister for Church Affairs'*. After the failure of the plans for the Reich Church, from the end of 1934 onwards Hitler considered two possibilities. One was a strict separation of state and church, and this was supported above all by the ideological rigorists in the Party like Rosenberg. The other was orientated on the model of a state church which was to accord the state far-reaching rights of supervision. This solution was supported above all on the state side. As there were beyond question considerable legal and material objections to a separation at this time – not least the Reich concordat – Hitler decided to attempt to solve the increasingly oppressive church question through Hanns Kerrl, a minister without portfolio, to whom he transferred for this purpose all the competence of Prussia and the Reich, new and old, in state-church law (Decree of 16 July 1935). This personal appointment was not only in keeping with Hitler's style of leadership but also left room for hope that through the new minister the state would in fact provide only that legal help for which the Provisional Church Government of the Confessing Church had already asked on 26 January 1935.

(b) *Kerrl's programme*. There is no doubt that Kerrl set out with good will to discharge his task. Officially his support *vis-à-vis* the Party derived from Article 24 of the Party programme (see II A 2b above), according to which 'protection of positive Christianity must be guaranteed' (thus on 8 August 1935 to the representatives of the

Länder). In addition he believed that Christianity and National
Socialism could be reconciled and that the churches had a task even
in the Third Reich. So he sought to unite the splintered Protestant
church by means of an amicable agreement. After thorough consul-
tations, on 24 September 1935 the 'Law for the Security of the
German Evangelical Church' appeared; this enabled Kerrl 'to
restore orderly conditions in the German Evangelical Church' and
'pass ordinances which are binding in law'. In the first of these
ordinances, dated 24 September 1935, he announced the formation
of a Reich Church Committee which would take over the leadership
of the German Evangelical Church. Here the minister saw himself
as a trustee appointing men in whom the church had confidence as
an independent leadership which would reorder the church. In fact
he succeeded in getting co-operation from the most varied groups
in the German Evangelical Church, with the former General Superintendent of Westphalia, Wilhelm Zöllner, who had always been
respected, at their head. However, the call with which the new Reich
Church Committee (which at the same time was the Landeskirche
Committee of the Evangelical Church of the Old Prussian Union)
introduced itself to the church public on 17 October 1935 already
showed how problematical this attempt was. This call spoke of the
gospel of Jesus Christ as 'the unassailable foundation of the German
Evangelical Church', but at the same time affirmed 'the formation
of the National Socialist Volk on the foundation of race, blood and
soil'.

(c) *The success of the Committee policy*. Despite all the difficulties,
by the end of 1935 it had proved possible to set up Church
Committees in a whole series of so-called 'destroyed' Landeskirchen
in which hitherto an emergency government of the Confessing
Church had functioned alongside the German Christian church
government. This stripped the German Christian church governments of their power and brought the abolition of disciplinary
measures and arbitrary actions, but of course it also disputed
the legitimacy of the organs of the Confessing Church in church
government. Thus in his enactment of the fifth ordinance of 20
December 1935 the minister prohibited 'the exercising of any
functions in church government and church authority' by the 'Provisional Church Government' of the German Evangelical Church
and the 'Councils of Brethren' for the Old Prussian Union, Saxony,
Nassau-Hessen and Kurhessen-Waldeck.

## 2. The split in the Confessing Church

(a) *The compromise made by the First Provisional Church Govern-ment.* Soon after the Synod of Dahlem it proved that the Confessing Church could no longer be said to be a unity. On the one hand were the so-called intact Landeskirchen of Bavaria, Württemberg and Hanover, the prime concern of whose leaders was inevitably the preservation of their churches; on the other side, in the so-called destroyed Landeskirchen, above all in Prussia, there were the Councils of Brethren, who had constantly to implement the resolutions of Dahlem in the face of the German Christian church leaders who were still in office. Both trends together made up the Confessing Church; however, it was evident that the different conditions under which they lived and the different decisions which were made as a result would hardly allow them to take a common line in the long run. Still, on 20/21 November 1934 it proved possible to form a joint 'Provisional Church Leadership of the German Evangelical Church' under the presidency of Marahrens; however, this already bore clear signs of a compromise (Barth, Niemöller and others resigned from the Reich Council of Brethren).

(b) *The dispute over the Church Committees.* In the face of the state's Committee policy, the latent tensions in the Confessing Church developed into an open break. Whereas the intact Landes-kirchen, which did not have any Church Committees, and some Councils of Brethren of the Confessing Church in the Länder were inclined to co-operate with the Committees, the Prussian Council of Brethren in particular said a clear no. On 3 January 1936 the Reich Council of Brethren decided in favour of the uncompromising Prussian course, whereupon the Provisional Church Government rejected its decision. That in fact amounted to a split in the Confessing Church. The attempt to overcome this split at the Fourth (and last) Reich Confessing Synod in Oeynhausen in February 1936 came to grief. From then on, the Confessing Church split into two groups: the moderate group of the intact Landeskirchen and some Lutheran Councils of Brethren who at a very early stage secured their own leadership (formation of the 'Council of the Evangelical Lutheran Church of Germany' on 18 March 1936) and the 'radical' group made up predominantly of the Prussian Councils of Brethren, who elected a new 'Provisional Church Government' (Second Provisional Church Government of 12 March 1936).

(*c*) *Theological problems*. These decisions were only superficially concerned with questions of organization and with political and church-political calculations. In truth what was under discussion was the nature of the church. Because Kerrl and the Church Committees started from the assumption that the Confessing Church was one church group among many, all of which had to be reconciled with one another (leaving aside the radical German Christians), they challenged the claim made by the Confessing Church at Barmen and Dahlem to be the one true Evangelical Church in Germany. Was the church merely a pluralistic association for particular ends, or was it a community committed to the confession and proclaiming the confession? Those were the alternatives. Dietrich Bonhoeffer made a stand in a highly controversial article 'On the Question of Church Community', in which he declared: 'Anyone who knowingly separates from the Confessing Church in Germany separates from salvation. That is the knowledge that the true church has always been compelled to recognize.' In view of these basic theological differences, despite all the attempts it was impossible to conceive of any mediation between the two groups. And in fact they only managed to come together again in the last years of the war.

## 3. The failure of the Committee policy

The split in the Confessing Church at the same time sealed the fate of the Church Committees. In any case their work had come under growing pressure from groups within the Party which were hostile to the churches and which were less and less concerned about a 'pacification' of the Protestant church. But the Church Minister himself lost interest in the Committees when he saw that they were not the way to achieve the union which he sought. So when in December 1936 the Reich Church Committee found in favour of nine Confessing pastors against the German Christian church government in Lübeck, Kerrl refused to support it. The result was the resignation of the Reich Church Committee in February 1937.

## 4. New plans

(*a*) *Hitler's electoral decree*. As early as the end of 1936 Kerrl was planning a new ordinance with the aim of considerably extending state supervision of the churches. Instead of this, Hitler ruled in a decree dated 15 February 1937, issued without Kerrl's knowledge, that now the church should 'be completely free to give itself a new constitution and thus a new order'. The Reich Church Minister was thus authorized to prepare for 'the election of a General Synod'. We still do not know the cause and purpose of this surprising step. The decree prompted lively activity in the Protestant church. Kerrl, who was in any case sick, resigned and put his Secretary of State Muhs in charge of affairs. Muhs managed to get things under control by administrative measures (the system of finance departments, Ordinance 15 of 25 June 1937; the transference of church leadership to the legal heads of the church administrative bodies, Ordinance 17 of 10 December 1937) and by dealing harshly with the Confessing Church of the Old Prussian Union. Under the impact of this tough policy the divided Confessing Church once again undertook to establish a unitary leadership (the Kassel Group, 6 July 1937). The attempt misfired; nor was Hitler's election decree implemented.

(*b*) *Kerrl's last attempts.* In this quite desperate situation, from summer 1938 on Kerrl made yet another attempt to achieve a 'pacification' of the church. However, like all state authorities, he had lost a great deal of influence in the general shift in power within the Reich in favour of the Party. His conception continued to be that of a loyal, centralist state church, which he now wanted to build on a Volkskirche centre and with the help of the laity. In October 1938 he succeeded in persuading the most important Landesbischöfe to issue a sharp statement against the Confessing Church. This success encouraged him to go on working to create a 'United Front', which was to be composed of German Christian and non-German Christian church governments simultaneously; the Confessing Church was to be forcibly excluded (the 'Five Principles' of 26 May 1939). However, all these attempts proved to be increasingly illusory. At the beginning of the war the Reich Church Ministry was reduced to its purely adminstrative functions. Kerrl died in 1941.

D. The resistance to the National Socialist ideology

*1. The problem of the double church policy*

In the church struggle confusion was caused for contemporaries, as it is for historians, by the two faces of the National Socialist church policy. Whereas the Third Reich as a state – at first through the Reich Ministry of the Interior and then through the Reich Church Minister – publicly strove for the 'pacification' and preservation of the Evangelical Church as a force loyal to the state, powerful forces in the Party very soon made it known that their aim was the annihilation of the Christian churches and Christianity in Germany generally. This contradiction, as the records of the supreme Reich authorities have meanwhile shown, was not just apparent, but a political reality. Many of the problems of the church struggle after 1935 can be derived from it. In the state sphere a *modus vivendi* certainly could not be completely ruled out. That, at any rate, is how things looked to the Reich Church Committee and later the so-called Church Leaders' Conference, which after 1937 became the Reich Church Minister's most important partner. But even the radical wing of the Confessing Church never at any point contemplated the apparently obvious step of a complete separation from the state; on the contrary, it still fought for state recognition. The refusal of the (Second) Provisional Church Government to co-operate in the Church Committees was not a rejection of collaboration with the state generally, but related only to the form of state procedures. On the other hand the churches found themselves faced increasingly with public hostility which was backed by the Party and was expressed in numerous measures of oppression and persecution. Because the churches opposed these, initially they seemed only to be defending themselves, especially as they were anxious to stress the distinction between their loyalty to nation and state and their ideological opposition. However, the more the Third Reich became an ideological state, the more the ideological resistance in fact turned out to be political resistance, since it put Hitler's rule in question at a decisive point, namely its total claim on the whole person. The great majority of the churches peristently refused to see these consequences, and instead attempted to play down the conflict by effusive declarations of national solidarity. The Party, for which since 1938 the annihilation of Christianity and the churches in Germany had become a vital question, was far more clear-sighted. The reason why this fact could largely remain hidden was that Hitler continued to pursue his twofold church policy, probably deliberately. Whereas up to 1938 he supported the state direction, though without restraining the Party, from 1938 onwards he tended increasingly to take a hard line, but again without completely dropping the state church policy. So the whole matter remained in a kind of twilight, and decisions were more difficult than they seem

110 *A Requiem for Hitler*

to have been in retrospect – as will be evident from even a glance at comparable situations in the present.

## 2. The battle against 'neopaganism'

(a) *The enthusiasts.* In summer and autumn 1933 the enthusiasm for National Socialism and the new Reich reached a climax in both churches. Among other things, this enthusiasm was also a response to the religious fervour and enthusiasm which were doubtless present in the Hitler movement, and which seemed to open up quite new possibilites for mission among the Volk. The 'Third Reich' was in part understood as the fulfilment of the ages (Joachim of Fiore) and seen as in enthusiastic terms as a new combination of politics and faith. In particular the Thuringian trend among the German Christians and later Bishop Weidemann of Bremen's 'Coming Church' put forward these convictions and maintained them – with growing support – until the collapse of the Third Reich.

(b) *The controversies with Rosenberg.* After the Sports Palace scandal (see above B 2 c), the general enthusiasm suffered a further setback through the appointment of Alfred Rosenberg to be responsible for 'the whole spiritual and ideological training and education of the Party' (24 January 1934). The author of the *Myth of the Twentieth Century* (1930, [24]1934, etc.) was rightly regarded in both churches as an exponent of the radical forces in the NSDAP which were hostile to the churches. In fact since the beginning of 1935 Rosenberg, supported by strong forces in the Party, had been running a propaganda campaign against the church and Christianity. At the same time the völkisch religious 'German Faith Movement' (J.W.Hauer, von Reventlow) became very active. This led to the first, official clash through a 'Word from the Provisional Leadership of the German Evangelical Church to the Communities', dated 21 February 1935. The declaration resolved on by the Confessing Synod of the Evangelical Church of the Old Prussian Union dated 5 March 1936 was much clearer. After a condemnation of the 'racist-völkisch world-view' it stated: 'Earthly law fails to recognize its heavenly judge and protector, and the state itself loses its authority, when it allows itself to be clad in the regalia of an eternal kingdom and makes itself the supreme and ultimate authority in all spheres of life.' The Reich Ministry of the Interior, which up to the end of 1934 recognized and sometimes even represented some of the interests of the Confessing Church, then radically changed direction and had the announcement banned by the police as an attack on state and Party. Failure to observe the ban led to the temporary imprisonment of more than 700 pastors. However, the great confrontation which might immediately have taken place was – as in subsequent periods – avoided by both sides. In his further attacks ('To the Obscurantists of Our Time', 1935; 'Protestant Pilgrims to Rome', 1937), Rosenberg explicitly referred to the 'private character' of his views, and indeed this was not completely false, in that Hitler did not in fact think much of a new völkisch religion of this dilettante style. On the other hand the churches again stressed 'obedience to the authorities', which was to be shown even in the face of persecution and oppression (Third Reich Confessing Synod in Augsburg, 4-6 June 1935).

(c) *The struggle gets fiercer*. The ideological controversies were continued with differing emphases down to the end of the Third Reich. The move from ideological opposition to direct political criticism was made for the first time in the Memorandum of the (Second) Provisional Government and the Council of the German Evangelical Church to Hitler on 28 May 1936. Here, too, primarily opposition to the National Socialist world-view was expressed; but then, in a section on 'Morality and Justice', clear mention was made of the burden laid on consciences by hatred of the Jews and antisemitism, by the misuse of the oath, by the manipulation of the electorate, the concentration camps and the lack of rights in the face of attacks by the Gestapo. Although this memorandum probably never reached Hitler himself, it caused a considerable stir abroad as a result of its publication – which initially was probably unintentional. On 10 July 1936 the Reich Church Committee also decided on a statement, but it was a very moderate one. G.Jacob presented the clearest and most perceptive analysis of the situation at the Fourth Confessing Synod of the Evangelical Church of the Old Prussian Union in Breslau on 16 December 1936. In a lecture on 'Church or Sect', he declared: 'Today's state, as a state bound to dogma, cannot content itself with the loyalty of its citizens. It must call for religious decision, enthusiasm and fanaticism. And Christian restraint *must* seem to it to be political opposition and a violation of its sacral foundations...'

(d) *Mit brennender Sorge*. After the Catholic bishops had presented their objections on many occasions, lastly in an extensive memorandum dated 20 August 1936, at the beginning of 1937 the

Curia also decided to make a public statement on the situation of
the Catholic church in Germany. On the basis of an outline by
Cardinal Faulhaber, Cardinal Secretary of State Pacelli drafted the
papal encyclical 'With burning concern', which arrived in Germany
in the beginning of March, being printed and distributed in secret.
It was read aloud from the pulpits of all Catholic churches on Palm
Sunday, 21 March. Although it was formulated as a word of comfort
and encouragement for German Catholics, the encyclical contained
such clear criticism of National Socialist religious policy and thus of
National Socialism itself that its impact extended far beyond those
to whom it was addressed. The mention of a 'war of annihilation'
and the 'more or less public violation of the treaty' which had been
made 'the unwritten law of action' 'by the other side', made it clear
that this accusation could not remain limited to the Reich concordat.
The condemnation of the National Socialist world-view, the charge
of oppressing Catholic believers and the recognition of natural law
as an absolute legal norm were clear enough. Nevertheless the
encyclical also allowed the possibility of a distinction between the
Reich government and the National Socialist measures hostile to
the church, because despite all the objections Pius XI was resolved
to hold fast to the concordat. Hitler was completely taken by surprise
by the publication of the encyclical. The Gestapo was unable to
prevent its circulation. The Reich Church Minister was particularly
bitter. His position between the rebellious churches and an increasingly hostile Party was difficult enough in any case, and this step by
the Curia had made it even weaker. So it was not surprising that in
line with his plans to strengthen state supervision of the Evangelical
Church he toyed with the idea of abrogating the Reich concordat
and thus strengthening his position over against the Catholic church.
But here too Hitler wanted to avoid a final break, and as his desire
coincided with that of the Curia, the Reich concordat remained
officially intact. However, for the clear-sighted on both sides, even
less doubt was possible that the enmity between National Socialism
and Christianity was implacable.

E. The way towards the 'final solution' of the church question

*1. The Niemöller affair*

It is hard to judge the significance of the churches' resistance to
National Socialist ideology for the history of the Third Reich. In

more recent accounts it is generally given little space or even omitted altogether. However, if we begin from the reaction of the Party, the church question seems to have been quite important. There were several reasons for this. The Party saw quite rightly that in fact the churches were becoming the focal point of an ideological opposition. This development was all the easier, as on the whole there was hardly any doubt about the reliability of the churches within the nation and their loyalty to the state. However far the laws were stretched, they were hardly sufficient to make ideological resistance a punishable offence. Moreover, the Party had no doubts about how far and how deep church membership really went among the people. All this became clear in the trial of Martin Niemöller in February 1938. The extraordinary attention paid to this trial at home and abroad and the significant character references for the defendant from the state, the military and the academic world indicate the great significance that the church question generally had acquired in the estimation of the Third Reich. The judgment on 2 March 1938 virtually amounted to an acquittal. Thereupon Hitler intervened personally and ordered Niemöller's imprisonment in a concentration camp. There he remained to the end of the war as the Führer's personal prisoner. This was doubtless a reaction to the persistent ideological rebellion of the churches and marked a change in National Socialist church policy. Whereas Himmler and Heydrich argued increasingly strongly for supervision and suppression of the churches as direct ideological opponents (in 1936 an office was established at the security police headquarters for 'Churches, Sects, Emigrants, Jews and Lodges' – later to become Office IV B, 'Political Churches, Sects, Freemasons and Jews' in the Reich Security Head Office), Martin Bormann began the systematic liquidation of the churches by state-church law. Although Kerrl still kept to his state-church model and attempted to bring the churches round with every means at his disposal, the increasing weight of the Party now began to make itself clearly felt.

## 2. The new church policy in Austria

In strict opposition to Kerrl, Bormann advocated a separation of state and church with the aim of transforming the churches by the removal of all state privileges. By decentralization and privatization he sought to change the churches into a special kind of association under private law which would be easy to control and could be liquidated at a given time. Bormann had the opportunity of an initiative in this direction for the first time with the occupation of Austria in March 1938. While the Austrian bishops were still welcoming the Anschluss and praising the pre-eminent merits of the National Socialist movement 'in the sphere of völkisch and economic reconstruction' and the defence it provided against 'all-destructive godless Bolshevism', and the Protestant churches were also making similar comments, Bormann was already working towards a completely new legal status for both churches in the Ostmark, which was not covered by the concordat. Once he had succeeded in limiting Kerrl's sphere of responsiblity to the old Reich, after a good deal of argument, the 'Law on the Levying of Church Contributions in the Land of Austria' appeared. It was dated 28 April 1939, and largely realized Bormann's ideas. This law gave the 'Catholic church, the Protestant church of the Augsburg and Helvetic Confessions, and the Old Catholic Church in the Ostmark' the right to raise contributions for the churches. Only those who were full members were liable to pay contributions. The organization of the contributions and their level were subject to state approval, as was the use to which the revenue was put. At the same time, all state contributions to the churches were abolished. Bormann explained the significance of the new regulation to the Reichleiters and Gauleiters in a secret circular. For the first time this made a complete division between state and church, but not in the traditional sense, by creating two parallel entities with equal rights. Rather, the church was made subject to the state by the regulation of its resources, and had a degree of independence only within its own sphere of responsibility. However – and this shows how obscure the situation was – despite constant pressure Bormann did not succeed in winning Hitler over completely to his radical line. When in May 1939, along with the Gauleiter of Baden, he tried to apply the Austrian regulation to Baden also, the Reich Church Minister managed to thwart him by pointing out possibly serious complications because of the concordats and church treaties. In fact the constitutional status of the two churches was never attacked in principle in the old Reich right up to its collapse.

## 3. The Reich Gau of Wartheland

As Bormann was initially prevented from implementing his programme in the old Reich, he concentrated his interest on areas which lay outside the concordat, above all the Reich Gau of Wartheland which was created in 1939; it had been made up of the territory of the former Prussian province of Posen. Its Gauleiter and governor, A.Greiser, was ready to run his Gau in every respect – and particularly in church politics – as a model Gau along the lines of the Party chancellery policy. The civil representative was the former 'Legal Administrator' of the Reich Church, August Jäger, who had been responsible for the 1934 incorporation policy. The new Gau was regarded not only as being outside concordats and treaties, but also as being a 'sphere outside the law'. Accordingly the Reich governor began to apply the new National Socialist law in all areas. Now the real intentions of Bormann's church policy clearly emerged. First of all the new Gau took over the Ostmark law on church contributions which had come into force on 14 March 1940 – though clearly already in a tougher form. But as early as July new guidelines for church politics were published (the 'thirteen points'). Among other things they ruled: '1. There will no longer be any churches in the state sense but only religious societies in the sense of organizations... 4. There will no longer be any relations with groups outside the Gau... 5. Full membership can only be had after a written declaration... 6. All subordinate confessional groups and auxiliary organizations (youth groups) are abolished and prohibited... 12. The associations may not take part in welfare work; this is solely the responsibility of the NSV. 13. Only clergy from the Warthegau may be involved in the associations. They will not be not full-time clergy, but must have other employment.' From the start there could be no doubt about the significance of these 'thirteen points'. By means of special legislation similar to that which had already been applied to the Jews since 1933, they were meant to lead to the liquidation of the Christian churches in the Warthegau. The thirteen points were given legal form in the 'Ordinance on Religious Associations and Religious Societies in the Reichsgau Wartheland' of 13 September 1941. In it, the new status of 'legal entity with private rights' was provided for the 'Posen Evangelical Church of German Nationality', as also for the other Protestant churches and the 'Roman Catholic Church of German Nationality in the Reichsgau Wartheland': this legal description delivered the church over completely to the will of the National Socialist state.

### 4. The postponement of the 'final solution'

At the latest after 1941 the National Socialist leaders were clear about the need to annihilate Christianity in Germany because of the ideological rebellion of the churches. In a circular letter from Bormann dated 9 June 1941 which was sent to all Gauleiters in the Reich but which had to be withdrawn on Hitler's orders, the head of the Party chancellery, who meanwhile had become the most powerful man in the Party, declared that Christianity and National Socialism were utterly incompatible. Only when the possibilities for church influence had been completely removed would the National Socialist leadership have complete influence on all the Volk. 'Only then will Volk and Reich be assured of their existence for the future.' It is certainly no coincidence that Hitler used quite similar wording in his numerous comments on these questions in his table talk of 1941/1942. Thus on 13 December 1941 he said: 'The war will come to an end. The last great task of our time will then be to clear up the church problem. Only then will the German nation be completely safe.' The SS also prepared for a final settling of accounts. At a working conference of all church specialists in the Reich Security Head Office on 22 and 23 December 1941, SS Brigadier Müller declared that it was now necessary for the specialists to confront the churches with closed ranks. 'The Gruppenführer has therefore finally decided that in future there must be a united fight by state police offices against the most dangerous of all dangerous opponents. The political church is now taking on the role of the Spartacists and Marxists of 1918. The political churches must now be presented with the bill for this attitude. We must therefore bring together this material with all the means at our disposal...' These comments leave no doubt about the Third Reich's concern to destroy the churches. However, tactical considerations meant that this aim had to be kept back until the end of the war. So the great confrontation was once again prevented by the war, with the agreement of both sides.

### F. The effects of the war

The war affected the church struggle in three ways. First of all Hitler's 'truce' and the need for national solidarity seemed to open up a new possibility of a positive relationship between state and church. On the other hand, it was the war in particular which made the claim of the National Socialist régime and its criminal character so clear that opposition and resistance grew in both churches. Finally, the pressure of events in the Protestant church led to a consolidation which created the basis for church developnents in the post-war period.

## 1. The 'truce'

(a) *Hitler's orders for a cease fire.* At the beginning of the war Hitler prohibited 'any action against the Catholic and Protestant churches for the duration of the war'. As was evident from the church policy in the Warthegau (see E 3 above), this prohibition related only to the so-called old Reich, and here in fact it worked against great spectacular actions but did not prevent a consistent policy of paralysis and suppression of church activities on the pretext of the demands of the war.

(b) *Under the banner of national solidarity.* The 'truce' made it possible for leading groups in both churches to call for national solidarity, laying all reservations aside. Moral support for the war was a demand of the hour and was accepted as such, even by many of the the opposition groups in the churches. Thus not only did the official representatives of the churches – the German episcopate and the newly created Clergy Council of the German Evangelical Church – join in the admonition to 'Obedience towards the Führer' and in the 'Prayers for Führer and Reich'; for example, even Bishop Sproll, who had been expelled from his diocese of Rottenburg in 1936, asked for God's blessing on all those who had followed the Führer's call, and from his concentration camp Martin Niemöller announced his readiness to serve in the navy. When the campaign against Russia began, church leaders of both confessions issued appeals to fight against Bolshevism; the Clergy Council of the German Evangelical Church published a message which expressed the hope that 'throughout Europe under your [Hitler's] leadership a new order will arise and an end will be put to all inner disturbances, all profanation of what is most holy, all violation of the freedom of conscience'. It was not surprising that the German Christian church governments should have maintained this tone to the end. But it was shameful that the Clergy Council, of which Bishop Marahrens of Hanover was a member, should have send a telegram to Hitler after the 20 July 1944 attempt on his life which said: 'Thanksgiving is being offered in all the Protestant Churches of Germany for God's gracius protection and his manifest preservation...' Landesbischof

Wurm of Württemberg, by contrast, was very much more critical, and he increasingly became the *de facto* spokesman of the German Evangelical Church against the state.

(*c*) *The advance of the Party*. Despite the truce and declarations of national solidarity, Bormann above all continued his battle against the churches. As early as 1941 oppressive measures reached a new peak, though from then on they declined under the demands of the war. The 'thirteen points', which also became known in the old Reich very quickly (see E 3 above), left no illusions about the fate planned for the churches. This strengthened both the resolve to resist and the will to unite.

### 2. Conflict and resistance

(*a*) *Preaching in the war*. There was no nationalist preaching in the Second World War as there was in the First. Rather, the reports of the Security Service show that above all in the second half of the war many sermons were notably restrained in their endorsement of National Socialist propaganda. Even if open opposition was expressed relatively rarely, this restraint was probably rightly seen as a sign of ideological rebellion which the National Socialist leadership wanted to get rid of sooner or later (see above D 2c, d). One could take Wurm's pastoral letters, which speak emphatically of guilt and atonement, as instructions on preaching: our people 'has also drawn great guilt upon itself by the way in which the struggle has been carried on against the members of other races and peoples... Can we be surprised when we too now feel that? Even if we did not endorse the actions, we have often kept silent when we should have spoken out! That is how many people feel today, and especially Christians among our people...' (1 October 1943).

(*b*) *The resistance to the euthanasia programme*. One of the issues over which the church for the first time made public accusations was the murder of the mentally ill which Hitler had ordered in October 1939 and which by 1941 had already claimed more than 70,000 victims. Since many of the mentally ill had been accommodated in church institutions, the church governments had reliable knowledge of these plans at a relatively early stage. After July 1940, Wurm among others protested in numerous letters to state and Party officials at the 'deliberate extermination of weak and infirm fellow-countrymen'. The Bishop of Münster, Graf Galen, told his congregation from the pulpit in 1941 that he had laid charges of murder against the authorities under section 211 of the Criminal Code. These protests and charges were in fact successful. At the end of 1941 the so-called euthanasia programme was considerably restricted and finally came completely to an end.

(*c*) *Failure over the Jewish question.* Active attempts to oppose the mass murder of the Jews and those unfit for labour in the occupied zone, in the East, are so few as to be hardly worth mentioning, measured by the extent of the crime. Skilful hushing up of the facts and rigorous persecution by the state combined with the churches' concern to see and hear as little as possible, especially as they could hardly count on support from their congregations over the Jewish question, let alone from the wider public. So all the attempts at aid basically remained individual enterprises, which often enough had to combat misunderstanding and enmity not only at home but also abroad. By 1940 all the members of the aid organizations were in concentration camps, and very few survived to the end of the war. When the 'final solution' of the Jewish question was decided at the end of July 1941, and soon afterwards Jews in the old Reich, too, were ordered to wear the Star of David, the church chancellery of the German Evangelical Church reacted with a circular letter to the supreme church authorities 'to make appropriate provisions for baptized non-Aryans to be kept apart from the church life of German congregations'. Cardinal Bertram advised the episcopate 'to consider the holding of special services for Catholic non-Aryans only if great difficulties should arise over church attendance by non-Aryan Catholics'. Only in September 1943 did the German episcopate dare to condemn the killing of innocent people in a pastoral letter, and four weeks later the Twelfth Confessing Synod of the Evangelical Church of the Old Prussian Union followed this with a 'Message to Pastors and Elders on the Fifth Commandment' in almost the same wording (16/17 October 1943).

(*d*) *The political resistance.* Neither church took part in political resistance in the strict sense, though there were numerous personal links with it. Here the conviction that the church had no mandate for conspiracy was associated with the practical limitations imposed by the Volkskirche situation and the church-political measures. So conspirators like the Protestant pastor Dietrich Bonhoeffer and the Jesuit Father Alfred Delp were outsiders in the two churches. Nowadays this failure to offer resistance is often regarded as a decided fault on the part of the churches. However, precisely because of the complex history of the church struggle, the question which H.Rothfels formulated as early as 1948 still remains: 'Did the churches not, by defending themselves within their very own realm, provide the forces of opposition with a firmer nucleus and a sharper cutting edge than any external revolt could have done?' The Christian convictions which finally led conspirators from a great variety of resistance groups to offer active resistance could confirm this assumption.

## 3. The work of union

Under the growing pressure to which the Protestant church found itself exposed, from November 1941 Landesbischof Wurm made a new attempt to unite the splintered trends within the church. With the assent of the church leaders' conference, the councils of brethren and the Lutheran Council, there were tedious negotiations, at the end of which, in Easter 1943, thirteen statements on the 'Task and Service of the Church' were published. Taking up the insights of Barmen (see B 2 d above), and on the basis of scripture and confession, they were meant externally to provide guidelines for an 'attitude towards further interventions by the state' and internally to secure 'united spiritual leadership of ministry and the church' (Wurm). The 'thirteen statements' commanded astonishingly wide assent. Even if for external and internal reasons there was hardly any further collaboration on this basis before the end of the war, there is no doubt that the 'work of union' took on decisive significance for the new church order after the war. That was true both in the take-over of church government in the 'destroyed' Landeskirchen, where representatives of the Councils of Brethren worked with men from the church government which had existed before 1933, and in the formation of the Evangelical Church in Germany, which similarly was conceived and ultimately also brought into being on the broad basis of the 'work of union'.

## III  The Beginnings of the Evangelical Church in Germany

The fronts and questions of the church struggle remained a living issue in the Evangelical Church of Germany down to the end of the 1960s. The main dispute was over the theological and political consequences of the church struggle. But even the basic decisions about the reordering of the Evangelical Church after the war were for a long time subjected to lively criticism because it was felt that exclusively conservative forces had come out on top (this was the view of H.Diem, H.J.Iwand, E.Wolf and others). In fact, however, the alternative 'restoration or new beginning' (to recall the title of H.Diem's 1938 book) was never a viable one. It could not be denied that the developments had an inner consistency, even where the Confessing Church was involved.

A. The Treysa conference

At the invitation of Landesbischof Wurm, representatives of most of the Protestant Landeskirchen and the most important church groups met at Treysa in Hessen from 27 to 31 August 1945 to consider the future course of the Protestant church. The situation was an extraordinarily complicated one, especially as the difficult external circumstances had made a previous understanding almost impossible. The members of the Lutheran Council (see C 2 b above) had travelled in the hope and with the intention of founding the 'Evangelical Lutheran Church of Germany' at a preliminary conference and thus at the same time influencing the future form of the Evangelical Church in Germany towards a confessional confederation (the 'three pillars' theory). This plan failed at the last moment because of Wurm's objections to it. In complete opposition to this, Martin Niemöller put forward the conviction in the name of the newly-constituted 'Council of Brethren of the Evangelical Church of Germany' that there must now be a completely new structure along the lines of Barmen and Dahlem; 'We want a church made up of living comunities, and the fact that the church is community should also be expressed in its structure and its organiz-ation.' However, there was no going back to the beginnings of the church struggle. Rather, it proved that with the 'work of union' a preliminary decision had been made, and no group could any longer set itself above that. In fact the 'work of union' meant that even during the war and with the explicit assent of the Confessing Church, the strict Confessing Church position of the first years of the church struggle had been abandoned. By signing the 'thirteen statements', the councils of brethren had returned to a central position which was once again firmly focussed on the Volkskirche. It was this decision which made it possible for them to join the church governments after 1945. The claim that after the war the Confessing Church succumbed in battle to an overwhelming conservative tendency does not accord with the truth. The most important decisions of Treysa had already been made in 1943. The 'Provisional Order for the Evangelical Church of Germany' presented to the conference was also in line with the work of union: on the one hand it guaranteed the independence of the Landeskirchen and on the other it expressed a concern for unity among the Councils of Brethren by the formation of a council as the supreme governing body. The composition of the twelve-person body reflected confessional and church-political forces. The basic order of the Evangelical Church of Germany in 1948 did not make any fundamental changes to these decisions.

B. The Stuttgart Declaration of Guilt

Whereas the decisions of Treysa doubtless did not fulfil the expectations of the future legal form of the church associated with Barmen and Dahlem, at its second session in Stuttgart on 18/19 October 1945 the new council showed that the spirit of the Evangelical Church had fundamentally changed as a result of the church struggle. The council declared to a delegation of representatives of the World Council of Churches, in a formula which has become famous: 'Through us infinite sorrow has been brought upon many lands and peoples. What we have often witnessed to our communities we now say in the name of the whole church: Indeed for long years we have fought in the name of Jesus Christ against the Spirit which found its fearful expression in the National Socialist rule of violence; but we accuse ourselves of not having confessed more boldly, prayed more faithfully, believed more joyfully and loved more ardently.' This declaration of guilt, over which there was at once lively controversy, had a threefold significance inside and outside the church. 1. It provided the common basis for the work of the council and unmistakably indicated a resolution within the church to make a new beginning. 2. The Stuttgart Declaration of Guilt was the first in a long series of statements in which the Evangelical Church accepted its special responsibility for political events in Germany. It was not a political statement, even it that was what it was often wrongly understood to be, but it was a statement with political consequences. 3. The Stuttgart Declaration of Guilt built a bridge to the ecumenical world and thus – four months after the collapse –

opened up possibilities of encounter which would serve to break down hatred in the world - as they did. The Stuttgart Declaration of Guilt is a direct consequence of the church struggle. Although it was certainly not undisputed, it shaped the spirit of the Evangelical Church of Germany in post-war history and was subsequently repeated in numerous statements, most directly perhaps in the memorandum 'The Situation of the Exiles and the Relationship of the German People to its Eastern Neighbours', dated 1 October 1965.

## C. The Darmstadt statement of the Council of Brethren

Despite the joint Stuttgart declaration, the political consequences of the church struggle were disputed in the Evangelical Church. On the one side were the Lutheran churches with a more conservative orientation, which saw the church struggle above all as a renewal and revival of the significance of the confession, and on the other side the Council of Brethren argued its conviction that the failure of the church in the church struggle called for far-reaching penitence and change which had only begun with the Stuttgart declaration. It expressed this conviction in a 'Statement by the Council of Brethren of the Evangelical Church of Germany on the Political Course of our People', dated 8 August 1947 (the Darmstadt statement). Its starting point was the 'message of the reconciliation of the world with God in Christ', but that could be neither heard nor delivered 'unless we allow ourselves to be called home by Jesus Christ, the good shepherd, from all the false and evil ways on which we went astray as Germans with our common will and actions'. In particular the statement mentioned 'the dream of a special German mission', the alliance of the church with the powers of conservatism, the false formation of social and ideological fronts and the refusal to understand the admonitions of Marxism and to make the 'cause of the poor and those without rights the cause of Christianity'. In clear opposition to the formation of fronts in the 'cold war', the statement warned against the slogan 'Christianity and Western culture' and instead called for a return to God and dedication to one's neighbour in the power of the death and resurrection of Jesus Christ. The statement led to lively arguments not only in public but also in the Council of Brethren itself: these were incorporated into a commentary written to provide an explanation and clarification

(J.Beckmann, H.Diem, M.Niemöller and E.Wolf). The Darmstadt Statement marked out a position within the Evangelical Church which was new, and which was rightly regarded as a legacy of the church struggle. However, the fact that key members of the Confessing Church (H.Ehlers, H.Asmussen, E.Osterloh, etc.) thought another course to be the correct one prevents it from being claimed as the only legitimate legacy of the church struggle.

D. Theology of law and legal practice

For a long time new insights into legal status and legal form in the Evangelical Church in Germany have been particularly stressed as an important result of the church struggle (*Die Religion in Geschichte und Gegenwart*[3] (= *RGG*, col.1452; cf. also *Evangelisches Staatslexikon*[1], cols.948f.). The contribution of the church struggle to the theology of law is indeed significant for the basis of Protestant church law. In particular, with the church struggle, the fundamental connection between church order and the confession, and freedom for the church from all ties to the state, have become undisputed principles of the Protestant theology of law. However, we have to recognize that the legal practice of the new Landeskirche constitutions has been barely affected by these principles. Despite new approaches in constitutional law in individual cases (Hessen, Rhineland), the structures of the 'authoritarian church' which were generally condemned at Treysa very quickly re-established themselves in the Landeskirchen as these were established in law. Here the weight of the legal traditions and the unchanged pressures to be a Volkskirche worked together. This development can also be noted in the basic 1948 order of the Evangelical Church of Germany. In its first article the traditional and the new understandings of the Evangelical Church in Germany were set side by side. According to para.1, the Evangelical Church of Germany is 'a federation of Lutheran, Reformed and United churches'; according to para.2, it makes visible 'the existing communion of German Evangelical Christianity', which is aware of its obligation 'as the Confessing Church to implement the insights of the church struggle in the nature, task and order of the church'. In terms of constitutional law, para.1 was implemented; para.2 was realized only in individual decisions made by the Council and the Synod.

IV  The history of research

A. Protestant research into the church struggle after 1945

Whereas there was hardly any Catholic research into the church struggle worth mentioning before the end of the 1950s, on the Protestant side a very intensive concern with the church struggle began very soon. From the beginning it was also self-critical. This self-criticism, however, never related to the fundamental decisions of Barmen and Dahlem, but depending on the standpoint of the authors related to the political susceptibilities of the Protestant churches in general and their Lutheran wing in particular, and also to inconsistencies and mistakes within the Confessing Church itself. There was an awareness of having failed, as the Stuttgart Declaration of Guilt (see III B above) had stated. However, people felt equally that the basic theological decisions had been correct. So the works on the church struggle focussed above all on two questions: whether and to what degree the Confessing Church had remained faithful to these decisions or where it had departed from then; and what significance these decisions had for the new understanding of the church. In particular the last aspect was developed many times: in christology, social ethics (the kingly rule of Christ, the right to resist), church law and practical matters. The history of the church struggle was understood essentially as a problem of the church and theology. The article on the church struggle by E.Wolf ('Kirchen-kampf', *RGG*[3], cols.1443-1453, 1959) is an evocative account of this understanding. According to it, the history of the church struggle 'in the sphere of German Protestantism is the history of constantly new attempts and repeated setbacks on the course of the Evangelical Church towards a theological understanding of itself...' The questions of the political and social circumstances of the church struggle and the political actions of the church in the Third Reich were largely left out of account by this approach. In terms of research the result was a concentration on theological and church themes and an almost complete lack of historical and political investigations into the history of the church struggle (Arbeiten zur Geschichte des Kirchen-kampfes, 28 vols, 1958-1974). There was hardly any interaction between research by church historians and research by secular historians. Only in recent years has there been a change here. In principle it has to be said that this understanding of the church struggle largely corresponded to the self-understanding of the Confessing Church, whose representatives dominated the research (J.Beckmann, H.Brunotte, G.Harder, W.Niemöller, K.D.Schmidt, E. Wolf, etc, 'Commission of the Evangelical Church in Germany for the History of the Church Struggle', since 1955).

B. Catholic research into the church struggle

In the meantime, the question of political action by the church had been vigorously taken up by scholars on the Catholic side. For more than a decade the apologetic account by J.Neuhäusler (*Kreuz und Hakenkreuz*, 1946) had held the field, but with the Reich Church trial before the Federal Constitutional Court (verdict on the concordat, 1957), critical questions began to be asked about the politics and practice of the Catholic Church in the Third Reich. In 1961 E.W.Böckenförde published a programmatic article on German Catholicism in 1933 in the journal *Hochland*, in which he called for 'a rethinking both of the question of the sphere of competence of the pastoral ministry in political affairs and also of the formation of political judgments and political self-understanding in German Catholicism'. In 1963 Hochhuth's play *The Representative* raised the question of the attitude of the papacy: in the same year C.Amery declared; 'It is clear... that at least up until 1939 German Catholicism was not committed to the freedom either of the Jews or of the victims of concentration camps.' It was in accordance with this situtation that the 'Commission for Contemporary History in the Catholic Academy in Bavaria', in contrast to the Evangelical Church in Germany's Commission for the Church Struggle, decided to 'lay special emphasis on the political and social aspects of the church struggle' (K.Repgen). In the meanwhile this programme has been achieved by a large number of editions of sources and other accounts. However, here too – as on the Protestant side – there is no comprehensive modern summary.

C. New approaches in criticism since 1966

As early as 1966 Heinz Zahrnt took up the problem of an understanding of the church struggle which was predominantly orientated on theology and the church. Even the Confessing Church had not 'in the first place fought for the purity of doctrine and the independence of the church and only in second place, if not in third or fourth, offered resistance against the general injustice...' M.Jacobs then adopted a radical standpoint. He rightly saw that criticism of the political praxis of the Confessing Church was at the same time criticism of its basic theological decisions and thus of the theology of Karl Barth. 'Was Karl Barth right,' he asked, 'to interpret the church struggle in terms of the struggle of natural theology against a theology of revelation? Was this really the decisive point in the face of National Socialism? Could it really have been then and can it again be now just a matter of church and confession? Would this not be, and was it not then, a case of introversion in the church, i.e. the expectoration of its pneumatic experience of presence, its faith in kergyma and confession? That was perhaps understandable in the historical situation, but it is nevertheless the substance of the matter.' Jacobs was convinced that the dialectical theological approach lay at the root of the wrong decisions: 'With theological liberalism the theme of the *humanum* has become known outside the church.' Jacobs and others feel that Karl Barth played a fateful role. By contrast, E.Bethge attempted to distinguish between the correct basic theological decisions of the Confessing Church and the inadequate political consequences which followed from them. Whereas Barth went on to develop a political theology on the basis of Barmen, with very few exceptions the Confessing Church in Germany did not follow him here and lived 'until 1945 in a kind of schizophrenia' between church resistance and political loyalty to the state. F.W.Marquardt then drew a radical line from Barth the political theologian (*Theologie und Socialismus*, 1972). This discussion reflects the questions raised by contemporary 'political theology', but what significance it has for research into the church struggle has yet to be seen. It has doubtless brought liberation from the constraints of past years and directed the attention of research more firmly to the political, social and ideological aspects of the church struggle.

## V The church struggle in the history of the twentieth century

Given the situation described above, a summary evaluation of the church struggle is difficult. Therefore to end with I shall simply stress three important aspects.

1. Church historiography so far has largely discussed the church

struggle as a singular and distinctively German phenomenon. However, though we must appreciate the special circumstances in
Germany, it needs to be stressed more than hitherto that the German
church struggle belongs in a series of controversies which have
developed in the course of the twentieth century between totalitarian
forms of government and the Christian churches. During the church
struggle this was noted clearly with respect to Russia, as when in
January 1937 Karl Barth declared 'that it is no longer possible to
distinguish in principle between the cause [the church struggle] and
a battle fought against the church as such and its substance, as
this has been and is being fought with other methods in Russia'
(*Theologische Existenz heute*, NF 49). In fact the church struggle
confirms the experience that in the long run totalitarian rule and
Christian proclamation inevitably clash, no matter how long and
how successfully this may be denied by both sides. That is true of
the totalitarian systems deriving from any ideology. The possibility
and necessity of compromise on both sides is not excluded but
implied by this, as is characteristically made clear by the way in
which the great confrontation in Germany was constantly put off.

2. More than any previous era, the church struggle demonstrated
the difficulties confronting political pronouncements and actions
by the church in the twentieth century. To make scripture and
confession its theme was the only way, the only legitimate way, for
the church to arrive at a consensus over a false political theology in
a revolutionary political situation; this procedure can already be
noted in the resistance of the revivalist movement to nationalistic
Protestantism at the beginning of the nineteenth century. The insight
that this theme was not totally unpolitical but led to particular
political consequences was more one forced on the church than one
that developed out of it. However, to conclude from this that the
church must be brought to a direct insight into what is politically
right and called for in any situation is to repeat the mistake of the
German Christians and to discard Bonhoeffer's fundamental insight:
'The church cannot primarily engage in direct political action, since
the church has no knowledge of the necessary course of history.'

3. The hope that it would be possible to retain the basic insights
of the church struggle into the nature, task and order of the church
in the future has not been fulfilled. The Protestant church, at least
in the Federal Republic of Germany, now once again presents the
picture of a pluralistic Volkskirche, the tensions in which are hardly

less than in 1933. The reason for this is a failure to pay sufficient attention in the post-war period to the basic theological distinction between times of persecution and times of peace. There is perhaps confirmation here of what was already decided in Article 10 of the 1577 Formula of Concord about adiaphora.

# Political Resistance or Self-Assertion as a
# Problem for Church Governments*

## I The question

Separate treatment of the church governments in connection with
the problem of resistance seems justified, since the church governments of the two great churches were in a different situation from
pastors and believers. Thus as a rule bishops and church governments
had more possibilities of getting information (where they made use
of them) and exerting influence. Not a few pastors and faithful
therefore expected them to make a decisive statement on the
growing oppression of the churches and the illegal measures of the
régime. On the other hand the bishops bore the responsibility for
their dioceses or Landeskirchen: for the existence of these as
institutions as well as for the orderly continuation of preaching,
pastoral work and other activities. The thesis of the following
remarks is that when we weigh up these various elements, the
dominant feature was in principle a concern to safeguard and assert
the *status quo* in the face of political or church-political actions which
could endanger it or even put it at risk. In individual instances this
did not exclude other decisions.

The question arises for the Catholic Church more sharply than
for the Protestant Landeskirchen because of the special significance
of the episcopate: in the Landeskirchen, the church government
had comparable authority only in exceptional cases. Nevertheless,

*This article was originally published in J.Schmädeke and P.Steinbach (eds.),
*Widerstand gegen den Nationalsozialismus. Die deutsche Gesellschaft und der
Widerstand gegen Hitler*, Munich and Zurich 1985, 254-63.

very similar patterns of reaction can be noted in both churches. So we must first look at the conduct of the Catholic episcopate.

## II  The Catholic episcopate

The main lines of Catholic church policy in the Third Reich were largely laid down on the church side by the Holy See. That was a consequence of Roman centralism, and the tendency was strengthened by the man responsible for Vatican policy, Cardinal Secretary of State Pacelli, who had long associations with Germany as nuncio in Munich and Berlin. Just as the Reich concordat was prepared and signed in Rome as a *causa major* under church law,[1] so too the basic decisions on all questions connected with the Reich concordat were made there. These decisions followed the line already laid down by the conclusion of this treaty. That meant that the Holy See and the episcopate sought together above all to secure their rights under the treaty. As a result of numerous diplomatic steps by the Holy See,[2] but also of countless petitions at lower and middle levels,[3] breaches of the law by the state were identified, and pressure was exerted – not always in vain during the first years – to put a stop to them. However, this church-political line could only be successful if the church for its part carefully avoided any situation which could be interpreted as a breach of its duty of loyalty to the concordat. This duty of loyalty followed not only from individual articles of the concordat (e.g. Article 16, the bishops' oath of loyalty; and Article 30, a prayer for the prosperity of the German Reich and Volk), but even more from the content of the concordat as a whole, which guaranteed a 'depoliticizing of the clergy and the associations' in exchange for concessions by the state.[4] So while the concordat bound the state, given the unequal balance of power it bound the church even more.

This remained the official course of Catholic church politics up to the end of the war. It excluded any direct political resistance on the part of the episcopate or any individual bishop. So 'there was no Catholic resistance in Germany, there were only Catholics who resisted'.[5]

The main advocates of this course in the German episcopate were the President of the German Conference of Bishops, Cardinal Bertram of Breslau, Bishops Berning and Wienken, and the apostolic nuncio Orsenigo.[6]

Although this course determined Catholic church policy up to the end of the Third Reich, it was by no means undisputed. First more at the periphery and then increasingly in the episcopate itself, resistance grew against a policy of surrender and compromise which, while attempting to rescue the institutions of the church, instead endangered its credibility. We can see this development from three examples.

The first is the well known fact of the murder of one of the most prominent German Catholics, the President of Catholic Action in the diocese of Berlin, Ministerial Director Dr Erich Klausener, in connection with the so-called Röhm Putsch on 30 June 1934. According to the detailed report on events which the Berlin ordinariat sent to all bishops on 13 July,[7] no member of the episcopate could doubt that this was a political murder which was intended to hit Catholicism as a political force.

So presumably a good many people were waiting for a public protest from the bishops. Waldemar Gurian, the Catholic journalist, who had emigrated to Switzerland shortly beforehand, made himself their spokesman. His book *St Ambrose and the German Bishops*, which appeared in Lucerne, presented the problem in an impressive way. As Gurian implored Pope and bishops: 'The church is not an association which adapts itself to particular circumstances of power; it is the guardian and protector of the moral order for all mankind and all peoples. The church must speak out when worldly power endangers and breaks up this order.'[8] So he felt that 'The silence of the bishops is perhaps even more fearful than everything that happened on 30 June. For the silence destroys the last moral authority in Germany, brings uncertainty into the ranks of the faithful, and threatens to lead to estrangement between the bishops and the people, who can no longer understand this silence.'[9]

Despite these entreaties, the German episcopate never made public statements on these events. Rather, Bishop Bares of Berlin, doubtless in accord with Cardinal Bertram of Breslau, attempted to dampen down the stir over the murder as far as possible. The pulpit proclamation for the diocese of Berlin on 8 July in which Klausener's death was reported was limited to the bare essentials. In addition, the clergy were explicitly told to 'observe due restraint' over the events 'and not to lose sight of the general good of the church'.[10] This formula without doubt contained the key to understanding this attitude.

After due consideration, for the general good of the church silence evidently seemed more advisable than a risky and useless protest. It would be too simple in retrospect to interpret this silence merely as a sign of opportunism and cowardice. Those familiar with this time will be aware that there were reasons for making such a decision. Nevertheless the question here remains open.

The second example shows that doubt about the legitimacy and sense of following a course of compromise had meanwhile also found its way into the episcopate. After the crisis between state and church sparked off by the encylical *Mit brennender Sorge*, in autumn 1937 Cardinal Bertram offered the state further negotiations. Bishop Preysing, who meanwhile had succeeded Baring in Berlin, declined to collaborate in such negotiations. In a letter dated 18 October 1937 he said, among other things, that he felt it 'pointless, if not fatal, to carry on peace negotiations when the enemy has not offered any cease-fire. The church is paralysed in its defensive war. The state is continuing its war of annihilation.'[11] A memorandum sent at the same time also said that the church-political situation made it necessary 'finally to bid farewell to as-if politics and call spiritual forces and actual events by their true names'; it was also necessary to depart from 'the rules of subtle diplomacy observed hitherto' and finally to get as much publicity as possible and 'to enlighten Catholic people... through brief, topical pastoral letters'.[12] This proposal would have marked a transition from a more passive policy of negotiation and compromise to a policy of active, public protest. However, Bertram emphatically rejected it and announced his resolve to keep to the previous line.[13] From this moment the bridges between Berlin and Breslau were down. Only the loyalty and discipline of the hierarchy prevented an open break. In 1937/38 Bertram knew that the great majority of the German episcopate and the Holy See were behind him in this decision.

In the third case, the dispute over the pastoral letter in 1941, this was no longer the case – at least as far as the German episcopate was concerned. A small group within the Conference of Bishops, including Bishops Gröber, Berning and Preysing, had worked out a new pastoral letter in the summer and autumn of 1941.[14] The situation had been deteriorating seriously. The measures taken to murder the mentally ill, reports about persecutions in the occupied territories, especially in Poland, a devastating action against monasteries and the houses of religious orders, and not least the invasion of Russia on 22 July 1941, had changed the mood even in the Conference of Bishops. In addition, it was evident that clear and open speaking, as had been practised by the Bishop von Galen of Münster in his famous sermons, was successful.

All this led the committee which had originally been appointed to take responsibility for matters relating to the orders to draft a joint pastoral letter which was finally to identify things in Germany for what they were. In fact the language of the draft produced in November 1941 had an unparalleled openness and boldness. With the exception of the Jewish question, which had been deliberately omitted, hardly a critical theme was absent.[15] The explanation why the pastoral letter was necessary, which had been added, said that the question of success or failure was unimportant. The one decisive question was: 'What is our duty in the present moment? What does conscience require? What does God, what do German believers expect of their bishops?'[16]

It was a significant sign of the change within the episcopate that by the end of November twenty bishops had already assented to the joint publication of this pastoral letter. Then first a plan intervened to join with the Protestant church in making a last attempt to persuade the Reich government to put an end to its increasing persecution of the churches. When this attempt, too, as usual got nowhere, at the beginning of 1942 the question of publication was again debated. But now Bertram firmly declared that he could not agree to publication 'in principle and for practical reasons'.[17] The President of the Conference sensed that his decision had put him in a minority. Just as for a long time Preysing had stood alone, so now Bertram complained that 'though a member of the conference since 1906', he was 'feeling increasingly isolated'.[18]

Nevertheless the old cardinal unswervingly kept to his line, and discipline in the episcopate was still so great that the pastoral letter was not agreed jointly or issued publicly, though several bishops nevertheless brought it to the attention of the faithful, But this meant the failure of the great joint move which alone could have had real political significance. That individual bishops like Graf Galen preached extraordinarly bold sermons against injustice which found a wide hearing was no substitute for this joint move.

## III The Protestant church governments

On the Protestant side things were different in many ways. According to the Lutheran and even more the Reformed understanding, church order is not hierarchical but based on the communities. In contrast to the Catholic episcopate, here the role of church government is a ministry which is bestowed for a time and which in principle can be revoked. During 1933 extensive use had been made of this principle – though in a way which had not been foreseen.[19] The German Christian movement had gained majorities in most elected church bodies during the first stormy months of its rise, and almost everywhere this had led to the dissolution of the old consistorial church governments. They had been replaced by young, German Christian bishops, whose authority was undisputed. After the failure of the plans for a Reich Church at the end of the 1934 only three Landesbischöfe in the whole of the German Evangelical Church had survived the storm: Meiser in Munich, Wurm in Stuttgart and Marahrens in Hanover. So within the Confessing Church their Landeskirchen were described as 'intact churches'. In the other major Landeskirchen, above all in the Old Prussian Union, there were two church governments: an official, German Christian, government under a bishop, and alongside it a free church government headed by a council of brethren. So these churches were called 'destroyed churches'. It was left to pastors and communities in them to decide which church government they obeyed.

We can leave aside the German Christian bishops in connection with the problem with which we are concerned, as they did not claim any independence from the state. It is all the more interesting to observe that within the Confessing Church the church governments in the 'intact' church areas did not act in the same way as those in the 'destroyed' church areas. The church-political course adopted in the 'intact churches' was more like that practised by the Catholic episcopate, and accordingly was more concerned with the preservation and safeguarding of church functions – with all the readiness for compromise which that seemed to entail. By contrast the councils of brethren in the 'destroyed churches', where in any case there was nothing to be lost, became more independent of the state and therefore dared to make more critical public statements. However, this cannot in any way be understood as 'resistance', but simply as the openness required by the church because of its task.

The fundamental conflict intensified in 1935 after the appointment of a Reich Church Minister. The dispute as to whether he and his authority – the manifest expression of which was the so-called Church Committees – should be recognized broke the Confessing Church apart in February 1936. From then on there were two major wings: the 'moderates' under the leadership of the 'intact churches' and the 'Council of the Evangelical Lutheran Church of Germany', and the 'radicals' under the leadership of the so-called '(Second) Provisional Church Government'. Only during the war did Landes-bischof Wurm of Württemberg succeed in bringing both wings together again by his great personal authority in the so-called 'work of union'.

Two events will make clear the different ways in which the authorities in the 'intact' and the 'destroyed' churches judged the situation.

On 4 June 1936 a memorandum was handed over 'to the Führer and Reich Chancellor' in the Reich Chancellery on behalf of the 'Provisional Church Government'. For the first time in the history of the Confessing Church this made a direct attack not only on National Socialist ideology but also on the political practices of the Third Reich. Thus under the heading 'Morality and law' it attacked the 'völkisch morality of expediency', of which it gave numerous examples: the inflation of the political oath; the rigging of the Reichstag election of 29 March 1936; the continued existence of concentration camps and the fact that Gestapo measures were outside the supervision of the law.[20]

This memorandum, which bore ten signatures, was at first to be kept strictly secret, in order to make it possible for Hitler to give a personal answer. Its publication in the foreign press in the middle of July as the result of a deliberate leak on the part of one of those involved put the 'Provisional Church Government' in a very difficult situation and compelled it to disown the authors of the memor-andum.[21] At the same time, however, it endorsed their resolution 'to stand publicly by this word' and it drafted a pulpit declaration to be read out by all Confessing pastors on 23 August.[22] This declaration was politically muted; nevertheless, in addition to its call for loyalty to the state it contained the statement that loyalty was being shown 'when the Christian resists a command which is against the Word of God and in so doing reminds the authorities of the need for obedience to God' – this was the Lutheran justification for political resistance in a nutshell.[23]

As far as one can see, the declaration was read out by many of the Confessing pastors in the destroyed churches. Moreover an estimated million copies of it were circulated as a pamphlet.

However, the bishops of the 'intact' churches refused to have the declaration read aloud in their Landeskirchen, although they agreed with its content. Marahrens explained this refusal in September 1936 with a reference which Bertram could have put in a very similar way. The Bishop of Hanover wrote that he could not approve of the attempt 'to bring about change in the indisputable facts which have been observed and the distresses associated with them by proclamation from the pulpits. It would thwart other very serious efforts and negotiations.'[24]

The most serious crisis between the Landesbischöfe and the 'Provisional Government' came about in autumn 1938. In view of the tense political situation the 'Provisional Government' had ordered a 'Service of prayer in the face of the threatening danger of war' for 30 September 1938. Among other things the opening liturgy stated: 'We confess before thee the sins of our people. Thy name is blasphemed among it, thy Word is fought against, thy Truth is suppressed. Much injustice is done publicly and in secret.'[25] This litany only takes on its full weight when we remember that the leaders of the Wehrmacht had planned a coup d'état in the case of war – war for which Hitler would then have been made responsible.[26] Here there was beyond doubt a kind of legitimation of these plans by the church.

Although the service was never held because of the Munich agreement, the SS paper *Das Schwarze Korps* used the liturgy as the occasion for serious charges against the Confessing Church, which was accused of 'betrayal of Land and Volk'.[27] Under the impact of these charges the Reich Church Minister succeeded in persuading the bishops of the 'intact' churches to make a statement in which they publicly dissociated themselves from the 'provisional government'. 'We condemn most strongly,' the statement said, 'the attitude expressed [in the liturgy of prayer] and dissociate ourselves from the persons responsible for this demonstration.'[28] 'No event in the changing history of the Confessing Church in Germany... stirred up painful division between the councils of brethren and the Lutheran bishops more deeply than this.'[29] In fact it was only possible

to resume the broken relations during the course of 1940, when
Bishops Wurm and Meiser had withdrawn their statement. The
Bishop of Württemberg was largely responsible for this move; in
July 1940 he had already been the first German bishop to protest to
the Reich Minister of the Interior against the 'euthanasia measures',[30] and in subsequent years became increasingly prominent
through his urgent warnings.


## IV Concluding reflections

There is no doubt that there was a potential for resistance against
the theory and practice of National Socialism in the two great
churches (as Hitler rightly saw from the beginning). But at no time
was this potential for resistance activated to any great extent by the
church governments in the two churches (in principle this also
applies to the councils of brethren in the Confessing Church). There
are various reasons for this restraint - theological, national, personal
– and in the Protestant church confessional as well. However, a
similar pattern of behaviour in both churches leads one to the
conclusion that the decisive motivation for the church governments
was their concern to preserve the church and the tasks of the church,
even in a totalitarian state.

In fact, right up to the end of the war no German bishop on either
the Catholic or the Protestant side was arrested for political reasons.
This was less the consequence of a kind of 'agreement' than an effect
of Hitler's skilful church policy, which sought to avoid direct
confrontation with the churches during the war.

What actual resistance was offered to the régime by the churches
always came from below: from pastors, communities and individual
Christians. As the lists of victims show, they also had to bear the
full burden of the persecution. Quite often, for political reasons,
church governments even refused to show solidarity with those who
had been arrested and condemned.[31]

In retrospect we must try to understand the burden and the
particular problems of church leaders in a state with a totalitarian
ideology. The historian has no simple answer to questions about
what would have been the 'right' behaviour in this situation. Perhaps
two remarks from the immediate post-war period will make the
whole extent of the problem clear.

On 15 April 1947 the highly controversial Landesbischof Ludwig

Marahrens stated in his report to the Landessynode of Hanover: 'For me the decisive thing was this: I achieved my aim of bringing the church through the threats uttered by the state and maintained the preaching of the gospel in the communities, peace in the manses and tranquillity at work.'[32]

By contrast, on 23 February 1946 Konrad Adenauer wrote to a Bonn pastor: 'I believe that if all the bishops had together made public statements from the pulpits on a particular day, they could have prevented a great deal. That did not happen, and there is no excuse for it. It would have been no bad thing if the bishops had all been put in prison or in concentration camp as a result. Quite the contrary. But none of that happened and therefore it is best to keep quiet.'[33]

# Politics and Church Politics in the Third Reich
## The shift in church politics in Germany, 1936-7*

Fifteen years ago, in October 1967, I gave a lecture at the Historians' Conference in Freiburg under the title 'How the National Socialist Leadership saw the Evangelical Church up to the Outbreak of War'; it was published in the *Vierteljahrshefte für Zeitgeschichte* in January 1968.[1] At that time it was the first attempt to depict the history of the Protestant Church in the Third Reich in connection with the political decisions of the National Socialist leadership. My contribution today takes up that first attempt and thus also gives me an opportunity to consider developments in contemporary church history since then. Here two points are particularly striking.

First, where church historians previously considered political decisions at all, as a rule they only examined events directly connected with the church, like the political and police measures which were aimed at restricting and curtailing church activities. Meanwhile it has become clear that the history of the churches in the Third Reich can only be understood in connection with all the fundamental political decisions of this time. Hitler subordinated church policy, like all the realms of political life – foreign policy, internal policy, defence policy, economics and culture – to his particular goals. The church policy of the Third Reich was at no point a policy in its own right, but always had a function to fulfil. That means that one can write the history of the churches in the Third Reich meaningfully only as part of a wider history. Often the

*Originally published in D.Oberndörfer and K.Schmitt (eds.), *Kirche und Demokratie*, Paderborn 1983, 107-21.

explanations for surprising shifts in Hitler's church policy are to be found in quite different political areas from those one might expect.

The explanation of church history in terms of the overall history of the Third Reich, not just in general terms, but also in specific details, is one recent development which stands out clearly. Incidentally, it follows from this, conversely, that church history, given its importance in connection with the Third Reich, can make an important contribution to an understanding of the history of the Third Reich as a whole.

Secondly: the further point which is particularly striking in the development of contemporary church historiography in recent years is the question of confessionalism. We have gained the insight that we can understand the history of the two great Volkskirchen in Germany in this period only if we keep their two very different situations in mind simultaneously. The usual practice in confessional historiography – Protestant church historians writing the history of the Protestant church and Catholic church historians writing the history of the Catholic church – has produced a wealth of significant monographs in our time, but it has hardly furthered our understanding of the overall relationship between the Christian churches and the Third Reich. The need for an approach which covers the two churches and a recognition of its fruitfulness arises from the fact that both churches were subject to the same political conditions, and the same questions and problems arising out of these conditions. From the beginning Hitler quite deliberately implemented his policy for the two churches simultaneously and in the same way, and in the view of the National Socialist leaders the two churches increasingly became one and the same ideological opponent, the more time went on. This necessarily raised the same questions and problems: the conflict between self-assertion and national solidarity, the clashes with the excesses of the National Socialist world-view, the relationship with Bolshevism and anti-Bolshevism, and above all attitudes to the Jewish question, because this affected their history to a particular degree. So a treatment of the two churches together not only leads to new results in the sphere of church policy; this approach opens up new perspectives on the basic Christian questions of the time, how far Christianity failed at this time and how far it stood the test.

The following remarks are an attempt to apply the approach sketched out here to a particular period of history, that between the outbreak of the Spanish Civil War in summer 1936 and the end of 1937. During this period there was a shift in the politics and the church politics of the Reich the causes and context of which we shall go on to investigate.

## 1. Germany and the Spanish Civil War

25 July 1936 was a date of extraordinary significance for German and European history, and its effects can hardly be underestimated even in retrospect. A week earlier the expected military revolt had broken out in Spain.[2] The situation of the rebels soon proved difficult everywhere. Thereupon one of their leaders, General Franco, decided to send an urgent, improvised plea for help to Mussolini and Hitler. The two emissaries bound for Berlin reached the German Führer and Reich Chancellor at Bayreuth on the late evening of 25 July. Hitler made his decision without delay. That same night Göring and Blomberg were instructed to do everything necessary for the immediate support of Franco.[3] From 29 July, twenty Junkers 52 transports supplied Franco's Moroccan troops in the Spanish homeland and thus gave the rebellion decisive military support.[4]

There is much discussion today as to what led Hitler to make this decision, which was quite risky in view of the uncertain state of Germany. Initially neither military nor economic motives stood in the foreground, however important they became later. Rather, Hitler's decision was guided by the conviction that a defeat of Franco would mean the victory of Bolshevism in Spain and France.[5] Hitler's estimation of the situation in this respect clearly coincides with the analysis made by the German embassy in Madrid, which ended a situation report on 23 July with the sentences: 'Consequences of government victory would be very damaging for domestic and foreign policy. Within Spain it would guarantee Marxist rule for a long period with the danger of a Spanish Soviet regime. Abroad, Spain would firmly attach itself ideologically and materially to the Franco-Russian bloc... There would be an opposite development if there were a victory of the monarchist Fascist rebels.'[6]

There is no reason to assume that Hitler saw things otherwise. So a decision in favour of German intervention came as it were right fom the centre of his political thought. The fight against Bolshevism, one of the unshakeable basic ideological orientations of his policy, evidently entered a new stage with events in Spain. As so often in

Hitler's important political decisions, here too matters of principle were bound up with the needs of the moment. The fight against Communism and Bolshevism had always been crucial for him, but now, in that hasty nocturnal decision, for the first time it took concrete form in foreign policy.

There have many descriptions of the way in which the Spanish Civil War lastingly influenced and changed the constellation of European powers. Special attention has rightly been paid to the rapprochement of Germany and Italy, which was also given visible form with the proclamation of the Berlin-Rome Axis on 1 November 1936, because it was here that the future fronts were prepared.

By contrast, so far little attention has been paid to the effects of the 25 July decision on policy within Germany, although these were hardly less significant.

Hitler's memorandum on the political and economic situation in Germany which he drafted at the Obersalzberg in August 1936 shows how deeply he himself was disturbed by developments in Spain. In this memorandum he expressed his conviction that since the outbreak of the French Revolution the world had been moving 'with increasing rapidity to a new conflict, the most extreme solution of which is called Bolshevism', but the content and aim of which was 'merely the removal and replacement by internationally disseminated Jewry of the social classes which hitherto have been the leaders of mankind'. At that time Europe had 'only two states which can be seen as standing firm against Bolshevism: Germany and Italy'. Even if Hitler did not want to prophesy the time 'when the untenable situation in Europe becomes an open crisis', it was nevertheless already necessary to prepare for this unavoidable conflict with all possible means. 'In the face of the need to repel this danger,' Hitler declared, 'all other considerations have to fade into the background as being quite insignificant'. According to this memorandum political leadership, solidarity in ideology, military preparation and the mobilization of all economic forces were the vital means for solving the task which Hitler ended by formulating like this: 'I. The German army must be ready to fight in four years. II The German economy must be on a war footing in four years.'[7]

In fact, from the end of August 1936, in connection with the Spanish Civil War a mobilization of public opinion can be noted which was unusual even for the Third Reich. On an enormous scale, with leading articles, news reports, features and pictures, the events in Spain were exploited for an unprecedented campaign against the growing danger posed to the world by Bolshevism.

Unfortunately the Republican side made it easy for the propagandists of the Third Reich to identify the term Bolshevism with an unbroken series of murders, lootings, rapes and other atrocities. In fact what happened behind the Republican lines exceeded all open cruelty previously known, and the simple trick of keeping quiet about the same kind of atrocities on the Spanish Nationalist side gave the 'red danger' superhuman proportions.[8]

This campaign reached a climax at the Reich Party conference held between 8 and 15 September 1936. From beginning to end, from Hitler's opening remarks through the speeches by Goebbels and Rosenberg to Hitler's closing speech, which lasted for several hours, this Party Conference was dominated by the alleged Bolshevik danger and the need to repel it. 'The brutal mass slaughter of Nationalist officers,' Hitler claimed, 'pouring petrol over the wives of Nationalist officers and setting light to them, the killing of children and babies of Nationalist parents e.g. in Spain, is meant to deter those with similar views in other lands from resistance in a similar situation.' But no one, he went on to declare, 'will have any doubt that National Socialism will oppose the attack of Bolshevism everywhere and in all circumstances, and will smite it and destroy it.'[9]

Even if it is very difficult to provide detailed evidence, there can be virtually no doubt that this campaign largely succeeded. Even those who in no way counted themselves Hitler's supporters could identify with his stance against Bolshevism. The events in Spain became proof of Hitler's constantly repeated assertions that Bolshevism represented the greatest danger for Europe and that only one Germany with closed ranks could cope with this danger. That produced an effect of solidarity which could often be detected and seen, above all in the second half of 1936.

## 2. The reactions of Catholicism

The way in which Spanish events were treated in Germany could not fail to have an effect on the two great churches. Indeed, we can take the reaction of the churches as an indication of how far public opinion and the general mood in fact was influenced by this development.

We look at Catholicism first. In summer 1936 the Catholic church in Germany was in a very oppressive situation. Under the slogan 'Deconfessionalization of public life', which the Reich Minister of the Interior had proclaimed in 1935, Party and state had consistently and systematically attempted to force the Catholic church out of public view. The main points of attack were the Catholic associations, which were hit by the ban on dual membership of confessional and National Socialist associations; the Catholic press, which was hampered by increasing restrictions and bans; and the campaign against the confessional schools, which by the use of every kind of threat and allurement had brought about considerable decline in them. Developments in the schools in particular were being followed with especial bitterness by the German episcopate and the Holy See, because the safeguarding of confessional schools throughout the Reich had been the decisive church gain in the Reich concordat and had been the most important reason for signing this treaty.

Hand in hand with these restrictive measures went a carefully targeted campaign which slandered Catholicism and made it seem criminal; this campaign found unmistakable expression above all in the waves of trials of priests and members of religious orders for currency offences and above all for moral offences.[10]

No Catholic with any awareness, far less any priest or bishop in Germany, could have failed to sense this growing pressure. On the other hand, however, it had to be noted that church life in the narrower sense was continuing almost uninterrupted. No church was closed; no believers who did their Sunday duty, no priest who kept inside the church – both literally and metaphorically – was attacked or hindered. There were exceptions, but they were not typical. Conflicts always arose only where the state and Party thought that the Catholic church was engaged in politics – and that included everything outside the sphere of the church.

This was the situation, and it is not surprising that it was assessed quite differently within Catholicism. There were optimists in the episcopate, among the clergy and church people, who in the long run believed in the possibility of a reconciliation; and there were pessimists who regarded the oppression so far as merely the herald of far more rigorous measures. However, both were agreed that the present situation of the church was oppressive and difficult.

This was the situation when news of the outbreak of the Spanish Civil War reached German Catholicism. There was no doubt that in this conflict the Catholic church was on Franco's side and had to be. Even if there had been no other reason, it would have been enough that in its fight against the rebels the Republican side was at the same time carrrying on a merciless campaign of revenge against the Catholic church in Spain. By the end of the war twelve bishops, hundreds of nuns and thousands of priests and monks had been murdered,[11] and countless churches and monasteries plundered and burned.

The truth was terrible enough, but the way in which it was disseminated in Germany made it even more effective. For here the only apparent cause for the atrocities was Bolshevik hate of Christianity and the churches, and naturally the critical voices within Spanish Catholicism – not just among the Basques – were not heard at all.[12]

When the German bishops met for their annual plenary conference in Fulda between 18 and 20 August 1936, they found themselves in a complicated situation. On the one hand there was unanimity over the oppression of the church in Germany, but on the other hand the danger of world Bolshevism loomed very large, and Europe – here the bishops agreed with Hitler's view of things – had hardly any other bulwark against it than Germany. Weighing things up, the bishops felt that while the situation of the church in Germany was painful, it was incomparably better than in Spain or Soviet Russia. All this led almost inevitably to the pastoral message of the German bishops on 19 August 1936. It was wholly dominated by the theme of the Civil War and combined an offer to share in the fight against Bolshevism with the call for a 'restoration of the religious peace guaranteed by the concordat'.[13] The pastoral letter – in accord with the official view of things – spoke of the 'diabolical purpose and tenacity' with which Bolshevism was advancing 'from east and west against Germany as the heart of Europe, to take it as it were in a fateful pincer movement'. Unmistakable features of the message were the appeal to the task of the Führer, the call to unity and solidarity, but also criticism of the National Socialist ideology: 'Here there can be no help from world views which merely arise from blood and the character of the time, but only from convictions which stand firm in all weathers, because they are grounded in God, the Holy and Eternal One...'[14]

The situation was as complicated for Hitler as it was for the German bishops. There is no doubt that since the conclusion of the Reich concordat he had joined in and supported the general tendency to fight againt the Catholic church, even if others – like Rosenberg, Bormann and a series of Gauleiters – seem to have been the real instigators. On the other hand he was convinced of the need for a war against world Bolshevism, and in his memorandum had explicitly declared that in the face of this emergency 'all other considerations had to be put in the background as being quite unimportant'. Now the bishops' offer was on the table, and Hitler had to decide what it meant for his aims.

This was the situation when Hitler invited Cardinal Faulhaber of Munich to the Berghof on 4 November for a three-hour conversation. Here too Spain was the dominant theme and – as Faulhaber's notes put it – 'the danger of Bolshevism in foreign politics'. Hitler warned the Cardinal that the Catholic church 'should not deceive itself: unless National Socialism gets the better of Bolshevism, all is up in Europe for Christianity and the church'.[15] In the light of this conviction he made what must have seemed to him to be a generous offer which could not be refused, using a similar phrase to those in his memorandum: ' "Just think, my Lord Cardinal," ' Hitler said, ' "and discuss with the other church leaders how you want to support the great task of National Socialism in preventing Bolshevism from getting the upper hand and how you want to establish friendly relations with the state. Either National Socialism and the church will win together or they will both go under. I tell you, I will do away with all the little things that disrupt peaceful co-operation, like the trials of monks and the German Faith Movement. I do not want to engage in any horse-trading. You know that I am opposed to compromises, but a last attempt should be made." '[16]

'The bishops,' Faulhaber added to this memorandum for his colleagues, 'will therefore have to make specific proposals, either in the form of a new pastoral letter or a new address...'

If we follow things to this point, they seem to confirm a thesis which was put forward e.g. by Karlheinz Deschner in his book *Mit Gott und den Faschisten* (With God and the Fascists). In his view, the Catholic church collaborated with the Fascist dictators Mussolini, Franco and Hitler from the beginning and systematically supported their aims.[17] This theory certainly applies more to Mussolini and Franco. It would also apply in Hitler's case had Hitler been a Fascist. But Hitler was not a Fascist. He seemed to be, and for a while probably thought that he was. But at two central points his decisions increasingly went against the Fascist pattern: in his policy over the Jews and in the church question.

Five years later, in his table talk during the Russian war in 1941/ 42, Hitler could even make this distinction himself. In February 1942, after one of his usual outbursts against the clergy, he declared: 'Had there been no danger that Bolshevism would overrun Europe, I would not have supported the revolution in Spain: the clergy would have been exterminated!'[18] And in June 1942 he similarly observed in connection with the Catholic church in Spain: 'I would not be surprised if one day there were not a new Civil War in which the Falangists had to join forces with the Reds in order to overcome the alliance of clergy and monarchists.'[19]

In November 1936, as his conversation with Faulhaber showed, Hitler was still a long way from such decisiveness. He was still evidently attracted by the idea of an anti-Bolshevik alliance with the church, just as the episcopate hoped despite all its bad experiences that it would be able to arrive to an agreement on the same basis. At the same time the nagging mistrust which Hitler had of the Christian churches from the beginning had grown to such a degree that he evidently could only be happy with an unconditional capitulation by the church. That is clear from his reaction to the 'specific' proposals from the German episcopate announced by Faulhaber, which appeared as a 'Pastoral Message from the German Bishops on Defence against Bolshevism' at Christmas 1936.

This pastoral letter repeated unconditional support for Hitler in his battle against Bolshevism; but it also repeated the questions which the bishops had about the ongoing oppression of the church.[20] This criticism endorsed Hitler's mistrust. Although Faulhaber pointed out in a personal letter to the Führer and Reich Chancellor that abroad, too, 'this unanimous commitment of the German bishops to the Führer and his role in world history, the repelling of Bolshevism', would not go unheard,[21] this last step by the episcopate met with no response from the state side. Hitler did not acknowledge the letter, though he did not reject it either.[22] Possibly he hoped that with time there might still be a shift in the Catholic attitude.

Thus the situation of the Catholic church in its relationship to the Third Reich at the end of 1936 was just as difficult as before the outbreak of the Spanish Civil War, though in the battle against Bolshevism it seemed to have found a great common interest.

## 3. Fronts and plans in Protestantism

Whereas Hitler as a Catholic made the basic decisions relating to the Catholic church himself, from the beginning he left Protestant church policy to Protestant colleagues.[23] One after the other, first the German Christians, then the Reich Minister and finally the Reich Minister of the Interior had the task of consolidating German Protestantism in a single Reich Church with a National Socialist stamp. Frustration with the Protestants gave Hanns Kerrl, who had been appointed Reich Church Minister in early 1935, mainly in order to unify and pacify the Protestant church, a heart attack: he did not return to work until that November.[24] In fact the Minister's attempt to unify the splintered groups with the help of the Church Committees which he had appointed could be written off as early as spring 1936. Although he had the broad consent of the church centre, the Prussian council of brethren and the Provisional Government of the Confessing Church refused to compromise or collaborate, and thus put the Reich Church Committee in an untenable position within the church. On the other hand the need for the Committees to dissociate themselves from the radical wing of the German Christians inevitably led to growing difficulties with some of the Party. And finally it became increasingly obvious to all thinking members of the Protestant church that the Reich Church Minister was either unwilling or unable to prevent the growing persecution and oppression of the Christian churches by the state and the Party. This quickly weakened his own position with the Church Committees, so that here too things fell apart.

The situation of the two great churches in Germany in summer and autumn 1936 thus seemed quite extraordinarily different. On the one side was the Catholic church, which was fighting with closed ranks for the preservation of its rights under the concordat and felt that in anti-Bolshevism it had found a new common interest with the Third Reich; on the other was the Protestant church which was at war with itself, and quite different groups, trends and church governments claimed that they had made the right decision in a hopeless situation.

This difference in situations, which indeed was only an expression of the fundamental difference between Protestant and Catholic theology, the Protestant and the Catholic understanding of the church, has been emphasized by the way it has been treated in confessional research, which has always only considered either one church or the other.

Consequently previous accounts have failed to note that the political challenges were the same for both churches and led to the same reactions, for all the difference in the situations.

For the Protestant church, too, the outbreak of the Spanish civil war was also a signal. Certainly Protestantism was not directly involved with the Spanish church, as was German Catholicism, but in principle it too was firmly opposed to Bolshevism. And so here too an attempt was made by means of this common interest to arrive at some understanding with the state which would at the same time make it possible to discuss the critical points.

One expression of this attempt was a 'statement on the church situation' which was approved at a conference of all the important representatives of the central church on 20 November 1936. This said that particularly in view of the overall situation, it was of decisive significance for 'the status of the church within the Volk' to be clarified as 'a matter of principle'.

And just like the Catholic episcopate, the Protestant bishops and church leaders made quite plain the basis on which such a clarification could be made.

As they unequivocally stated: 'We stand with the Reich Church Committee behind the Führer in the German Volk's life-and-death fight against Bolshevism.' But the way in which their statement went on was no less clear: 'We expect a complete end to be put to the anti-Christian propaganda which in recent times has become increasingly blatant, and which disparages the church and all it counts holy in an intolerable way.' 'The Protestant church,' it ended, 'which seeks to be nothing less than the Christian church for the German Volk, needs internal freedom to deliver its proclamation if it is to do its work.'[25]

However, it was precisely this 'internal freedom to deliver its proclamation' which the Reich Church Minister was either unwilling or unable to grant the Protestant church. So he dropped the Reich Church Committee, which thereupon offered its resignation on 12 February 1937. With this step the third attempt to unite the Protestant church from the state side had failed. The way out of this situation sought by the Reich Church Minister was an obvious one. Even before the resignation of the Reich Church Committee his ministry had worked out a draft decree, the content of which was to 'extend the rights of state supervision to the Protestant churches'. This was no less than unlimited state control of the Protestant church, its laws and ordinances, its finances and all its officials.[26]

The Reich Church Minister was so sure of his case that on Saturday 13 February he announced his plans to a group of church representatives with the explicit comment that no debate was 'necessary, as the laws are already in print and will appear on Monday'.[27] And in fact news to this effect appeared throughout the German press.

But that very Monday the minister was disowned and a quite surprising shift in church politics took place.

In the collection of information made by Martin Bormann in 1943 'from old notebooks', under 15 February 1937 there is the entry: 'Führer discusses church questions with Kerrl, Goebbels, Frick, Hess, Himmler, Heydrich, Muhs, Stuckart at the Obersalzberg.'[28] So Hitler had made a new decision, not by himself, but evidently after a lengthy discussion with his most important colleagues concerned with internal and Party politics, which was published that same day. According to the statement the Protestant church was now 'to give itself a new constitution and a new order in complete freedom, in accordance with the wishes of the church Volk'. The Reich Church Minister was empowered to make all necessary prepaations for the election of a general synod.

As in many comparable instances, we know nothing about any motives which led to Hitler's surprising decision.

There are no minutes of this session, and as far as I can see the records do not give the slightest indication of what might have moved Hitler to such a change of course. The mere announcement of an election 'in complete freedom' involving around two-thirds of all Germans was a sensation in February 1937 and evidently went against all that church circles in particular expected from Hitler. Given the situation, one can hardly find an explanation simply in the development of Protestant church affairs. One is more reminded of Hitler's conversation with Faulhaber, which lay only a year in the past, and his offer to make a 'last attempt' at peaceful collaboration. This new decision, too, was something like a 'last attempt' before the state throttled the church, an attempt moreover which, given the universal assent among church people of which Hitler felt sure, could bring the voluntary co-ordination of the Protestant church that he wanted. If nothing but argument and controversy could be expected in the state-church solution, here all those involved in the struggle against Bolshevism evidently saw possibilities for pacifying the church along National Socialist lines which could not fail to make an impression at home and abroad.[29]

In fact, to begin with the preparations for the election were made with great care. On 22 February the same group met again in Berlin to discuss the church question, and agreed to hold a further meeting at the beginning of March. Meanwhile Kerrl prepared a variety of letters and the order for the election, which involved a lively exchange of views between the Reich Church Ministry and the Reich Chancellery. On 17 March the head of the Reich Chancellery, Heinrich Lammers, suggested to the Reich Church Minister on Hitler's instructions that he should discuss questions connected with the election with the Führer's Representative and the Reich Minister of the Interior. Surprisingly, however, this is the last record of any substance on this matter. After it there is a draft date of 22 March and yet other dates at increasingly long intervals until the matter finally disappears into the archives on 24 May 1940.

When I described this development in my lecture on October 1967, I observed that with the 17 March suggestions 'Hitler's interest in church questions seemed suddenly and quite inexplicably to have died'.[30]

However, this development was not quite so inexplicable if one takes the Catholic church into account. For on 21 March, Palm Sunday 1937, the encyclical *Mit brennender Sorge* was read out from Catholic pulpits in Germany.

## 4. The break in early 1937

In his conversation with Faulhaber, Hitler had reduced the relationship between the church and the Third Reich to this formula: 'Either National Socialism and the church win together or they both go under.' With this he linked the unspoken expectation that the churches would give unconditional support to the Third Reich and its ideology. As we have seen, both churches were prepared to join in a common front against Bolshevism. But they were not ready to support National Socialism as an ideology in the process. This finally became clear in February and March 1937, and led to a break which both sides sought to conceal. However, it emerged increasingly clearly as time went on.

The Protestant church reacted first. Challenged by Kerrl's plans and Hitler's electoral decree, at the end of February Otto Dibelius sent an open letter to the Reich Church Minister, tens of thousands of copies of which were circulated inside and outside Prussia. In clarity it left nothing to be desired. 'Herr Reichminister,' Dibelius wrote, 'when children are told in their morning religious instruction that the Bible is the Word of God which speaks to us in the Old and New Testament, and when in the afternoon they have to learn by heart "What is our Bible? Our Bible is Hitler's *Mein Kampf*" – who has to change his teaching?' If the state were aware of its limits, Dibelius continued, it could rely 'on the readiness of the Protestant Christians of Germany for sacrifice'. But if it wanted to take upon itself 'power over the souls of men and the preaching of the church, we are,' Dibelius wrote, 'bound by Luther's words to offer resistance in God's name. And we shall do that!'[31]

Soon after that, on 9 March, the Reich Council of Brethren of the Confessing Church sent a message to the communities which said, in keeping with Dibelius' words: 'Today the church is called on to allow the Word of God and a human world-view to stand side by side and to combine them in its preaching. The church must reject this demand.' The office of the authorities and the office of the church were not to be confused and mixed: 'The freedom of the church lies in the sole rule of Jesus Christ alone.'[32]

True, the Reich Council of Brethren spoke only for some of the Protestant communities and pastors, but its voice was heard far outside the Confessing Church. So as early as the beginning of March the Reich Church Minister could already reckon that the general synod elections would not produce the unanimous acknowledgment of Führer and Volk by the Protestant church which was sought, but on the contrary would provoke controversy in the church and deepen still further the gulf between it and the state.

Presumably the Reich Church Minister would have begun by implementing Hitler's plan nevertheless, had not an event taken place on the Catholic side which in Hitler's eyes changed the whole political situation.

This event began with the Holy See. Pius XI, at first happy about the success achieved with the Reich concordat,[33] had followed the oppression of the Catholic church in the Third Reich since 1934 with growing anger. It was only with difficulty that Cardinal Secretary of State Pacelli succeeded in preventing a public condemnation of

Hitler's breaking of the treaty, which had already been planned several times. Now, at the end of 1936, the Pope was at the end of his patience.

So at this time the three German cardinals Bertram, Schulte and Faulhaber, and the Bishops of Münster and Berlin, Galen and Preysing, were invited to Rome to discuss 'considerations and decisions in this area'.[34] At a series of discussions with the Pope and the Cardinal Secretary of State in the middle of January the decision was made to voice the complaints of the church in a public papal encyclical addressed to German Catholics.

Here the situation was just as complicated for the Holy See as it was for the German episcopate. The Pope, who was even more concerned about events in Spain than the German bishops were, could not and would not overlook the fact that German and Italian troops were supporting Franco and thus the Catholic cause in Spain. Moreover, attention had to be paid to the Reich concordat, which despite all the breaches was still better than no treaty at all. On the other hand, the self-respect of the church could no longer tolerate a lengthy silence. And Pius XI possibly saw more clearly than his Secretary of State and the German bishops that Hitler was a very different figure from the Fascists Mussolini and Franco. Be this as it may, as he bade farewell to Bishops Preysing and Galen he remarked: 'In its aims and methods National Socialism is just the same as Bolshevism. I would like to say that to Herr Hitler.'[35]

For this reason the Holy See decided in two simultaneous encyclicals to condemn Communism and accuse the Third Reich of oppressing the church and perverting justice. However, whereas the encyclical *Divini Redemptoris* mentioned Communism in Russia, Mexico and Spain directly by name,[36] at the suggestion of Faulhaber the formulation of the encyclical *Mit brennender Sorge* was not polemical,[37] but accused National Socialism above all indirectly, by a description of the foundations of the Catholic church.

Nevertheless, it was an amazing piece of organization and at the same time an extraordinary challenge to the National Socialist régime when on Palm Sunday, 21 March 1937, the papal encyclical was read aloud from all Catholic pulpits to German Catholics. As things were, every hearer knew what was meant when it mentioned 'public persecution' of the faithful, 'a thousand forms of organized impediments to religion' and a 'lack of teaching which is loyal to the truth and of the normal possibilities of defence'. Even if National

Socialism was not mentioned by name, it was condemned clearly and unequivocally as an ideology when the encyclical stated: 'Anyone who makes race or Volk or state or form of state or state authorities or other basic values of the human shaping of society into the highest of all norms, even of religious values... perverts and falsifies the divinely created and divinely commanded order of things.'[38]

Whereas the reading of the encyclical was widely felt in German Catholicism to be a liberation, state officials and the Party reacted with anger and disapproval.[39] Nevertheless the great reprisal that was feared did not come. The concordat remained in force and despite everything the intensification of the battle against the two churches which then began remained within ordinary limits. However, these events represented a shift in Hitler's church policy.

The Reich Church Minister noted in a memorandum in March 1941 that with the decree for the election of a general synod dated 13 February 1936 'my authorization as Reich Minister for Church Affairs comes to an end: I no longer carry out church policy on my own responsiblity to my best of my knowledge and conscience.'[40] In fact since March 1937 there had been nothing else for the Church Minister to do. The reason for this was that since the events of February and March Hitler had finished with the churches. His hope to win both churches over to his aims had been shattered. That removed the need for him to have any kind of constructive church policy. Only tactical considerations remained.

However, this too was not just the decision of a day. Rather, throughout 1937 we can see hesitation as to whether a solution of the church question might not be found in one form or another. But by October 1937 at the latest Hitler had made up his mind, both personally and politically.

On 5 November 1937 he communicated to the innermost leadership group in the Reich his decision to solve the question of German Lebensraum as soon as possible, by the use of force.[41] Shortly before this, on 31 October, he had made similar comments in a speech to propaganda leaders, observing that 'after inner struggles he had freed himself from the childish religious ideas which are still around: "I feel that I am now as fresh as a foal in the pastures"'.[42]

It is clear that here a development had come to an end, a development which we can also observe in many other areas, but which takes on a remarkable and distinctive accent from the

perspective of church politics. It looks as though the end of Hitler's
church policy at the same time represented for him the final end of
all the shadowy ties which may still have held him back during these
years. Now he stood by himself, and the world was soon to experience
what that meant.

# A Requiem for Hitler

## Cardinal Bertram, Hitler and the German Episcopate in the Third Reich*

For a long time Catholic historiography has held to the picture of a church which was almost solid in its opposition to National Socialism. This picture has changed in recent years in an almost dramatic way. Certainly it had long been known that there were tensions between the president of the German Bishops' Conference, Archbishop Adolf Cardinal Bertram, and Bishop Konrad Graf Preysing of Berlin. And anyone who knew the publications of Walter Adolph,[1] a close collaborator of Preysing in church politics, which appeared in the 1960s, and above all the excellent contributions by Ludwig Volk to the history of the Fulda Bishops' Conference,[2] was already aware that these tensions were far more than a mere difference of opinion about what was going on in the church. Nevertheless, for a long time the theme continued to be more of peripheral interest and was discussed under the unexciting heading 'Differences of Opinion in the Episcopacy over the Right Tactics'.[3] It has taken a series of more recent publications to make people generally aware of the fundamental significance of the conflict between Bertram and Preysing, works like the second large volume of the Acts of Cardinal Faulhaber of Munich, edited by Ludwig Volk,[4] and the memoranda produced by Walter Adolph between 1935 and 1943, a complete collection of which has for the first time been published, edited posthumously, by the Catholic Commission for Contemporary History.[5] So this conflict has become a central theme in the most

---

*Part of this article was published in *Frankfurter Allgemeine Zeitung* 249, 25 October 1980.

recent surveys of the Catholic church struggle by Klaus Gotto, Hans Günter Hockert and Konrad Repgen.[6] They indicate that the differences in the episcopate over the correct tactics deepened after 1937 to become 'serious differences over the best form of resistance' and finally to 'very fundamental problems'.[7]

In fact, after 1937 there was a split in the German episcopate which grew deeper and deeper as time went on, and which in the end largely paralysed the capacity of the German bishops to act in politics and in church politics. How did that come about?

## Before 1937

Graf Preysing, at that time still Bishop of Eichstätt, was one of the very few people who from the beginning saw the Third Reich as a corrupt and pernicious régime. He held to this conviction, evidently without the least hesitation and doubt, even in the days of Hitler's great successes.[8] As early as May 1933, when the German bishops were consulting over the draft concordat from the Vatican, he was the only one to call for an explicit and public repudiation of National Socialist ideology with the noteworthy comment that the bishops should have been 'able to refer in this pastoral letter to a conflict which would probably come'.[9]

As is well known, the Vatican and the majority of German bishops thought otherwise, and as a result first the Reich concordat was concluded, to be followed for years by that remarkable intermediate stage in which despite the almost unlimited calumniations and repressive actions against Catholicism, representatives of both church and state felt almost month by month that a peace treaty would be possible.[10] At this intermediate stage both the Vatican and Cardinal Bertram, the President of the German Conference of Bishops, used tactics which seemed thoroughly in keeping with the situation. In a stream of petitions and complaints, both pointed out the infringements of the law by the régime and pressed for the concordat to be observed. In doing this they carefully avoided any statement which could be interpreted as a fundamental criticism of the Third Reich. The basic intention of this procedure was clear: only those who recognized the legitimacy of the government could keep it to its obligations under the concordat.

For many people at that time this intermediate stage seemed to have come to an end in March 1937 with the publication of the famous encyclical *Mit brennender Sorge*. The time of open confrontation seemed to have arrived. However, it very soon emerged that the encyclical was open to different interpretations. It could be understood as a last and extreme way by which the church might maintain its rights and its truth within the framework of the concordat; but it could also be interpreted as the first step towards open confrontation, a step which could be and had to be followed by further steps.[11]

## The outbreak of the conflict

Cardinal Bertram, who by inclination and conviction was a strict supporter of the course of loyalty, stood by the first possibility. One might even conjecture that he felt that the encyclical was fundamentally more a disruption of his own line in church politics. At any rate, he received the news of its appearance without any enthusiasm. When Walter Adolph reported to the Cardinal on Preysing's instructions 'that the Holy Father has published an encyclical on the church situation in the German Reich', Bertram merely retorted: 'So it's out; but I haven't seen it yet.'[12] It is hard to imagine less enthusiasm for such an event. Similarly, Bertram also attempted to blunt the effect of the papal letter by ruling that the critical passages were not to be read out. His view was that 'the introductory thoughts about the failure of the Reich government to observe the treaty are meant more for the leaders, not for the great mass of believers'.[13]

Of course the Cardinal presented and defended the encyclical to the Reich government without any qualifications. But at the same time he attempted to avoid any further exacerbation of the situation and to prevent the open break between church and state which threatened.

Preysing saw things quite differently. For the Bishop of Berlin, the encyclical meant that the time for hard and open talking had come. So he reacted with deep disappointment to the Cardinal's continued readiness for negotiation: after the crisis seemed to have been overcome Bertram was resolved to offer the Reich government new negotiations, initally over school questions. In a letter to Bertram dated 18 October 1937 Preysing therefore refused to be involved in such negotiations and among other things also stated that he felt it was 'hopeless, if not fatal, to carry on peace negotiations when our opponents do not guarantee any truce. The church is paralysed in its defensive war. The state is continuing to wage its war of annihilation.'[14] A memorandum sent by Adolph at the same time also said that the church-political situation called 'finally for a dissociation from as-if politics; it is time to call spiritual powers and actual events by their right names. The concordat has become a farce';[15] furthermore, it was time to drop 'the rules of the subtle diplomacy which have been observed hitherto'; and finally, it was important to seek publicity wherever possible and 'inform the Catholic people...by short, topical... pastoral letters'.

Bertram's tetchy answer shows no understanding of Preysing's position. Rather, the Cardinal defended his line in church politics at length and at the same time made clear his resolve to continue to maintain it in the future.

From this moment on the bridges between Berlin and Breslau were down. Over the following period Bertram only made mocking or sarcastic comments about the Bishop of Berlin ('Now the Bishop of Berlin is beginning to pontificate'), while Cardinal Bertram was described in Adolph's notes as a 'seventy-nine year old greybeard, autocratic and mistrustful', who was no longer capable of leading the church.[16] Only the loyalty and discipline of the hierarchy prevented an open break.

### The balance of power in the episcopate

It is not easy to assess the balance of power in the episcopate. For the period of this conflict, however, the years 1937/1938, we may begin by assuming that the great majority of German bishops were on Bertram's side, though for different reasons. That is of course true of the leadership group in the narrower sense, the Papal Nuncio Orsenigo and Bishops Berning and Wienken. It is also certainly true of Cardinal Schulte of Cologne,[17] and with reservations also of Cardinal Faulhaber of Munich.[18] It was evidently difficult for Preysing to assess Archbishop Gröber of Freiburg and Graf Galen, the Bishop of Münster, who were both also influential men in the episcopate. At all events, in Februrary 1938 Adolph noted a comment by Preysing 'that things were really desperate. Only Kaller (the Bishop of Ermland) and he saw things clearly.'[19] The attitude of the Vatican in this context was decisive. It says much for the skill of Pacelli that both parties felt that he was on their side.[20] But if we look at the politics of the Cardinal Secretary of State as a whole, there can be no doubt that at this time he too still decisively favoured Bertram's line. The urgency of the desire in Rome, too, to come to an understanding with the Reich after the 1937 crisis is clear simply from the fact that in March 1938 Pacelli indicated in strict secrecy to the Reich government that he would 'come to Berlin for negotiations if that is desirable'.[21]

### The congragulations on Hitler's birthday

Since Pacelli had so many links with Germany, his election as Pope in March 1939 in fact seemed to mark an improvement in relations. Hitler sent his ambassador to give the newly-elected Pope 'the warmest congratulations of the Führer and the government'.[22] Pius XII expressed his thanks in an unusually friendly letter which he had discussed beforehand with the German cardinals.[23] A few weeks later, at the express wish of the Pope, the Nuncio opened the great congratulatory court for Hitler's fiftieth birthday on 20 April 1939.[24] This all happened in the hope, also shared by the German cardinals, that the new Pope would also provide a new opportunity for an understanding with the Reich.[25]

Thus Cardinal Bertram could feel that he was acting in line with general church policy when the next year he sent 'warmest congratulations' to the Reich Chancellor and Führer in the name of the bishops of all the dioceses in Germany.[26] However, he was doing more than engaging in an astute piece of church politics when he went on to say that the congratulations were 'associated with the fervent prayers which the Catholics of Germany are sending to heaven on their altars on 20 April for Volk, army and Fatherland, for state and Führer'. At the same time the Cardinal reminded the Führer of the concerns and complaints of German Catholics and asked for his understanding 'of our dutiful and constant concern to preserve the Christian character of our people in the fullest sense'.

It has been thought that this was essentially a desperate attempt 'to bring the complaints of the Catholic part of the population to the attention of the supreme authority'.[27] However, this explanation fails to recognize the earnestness and the depth of loyalty which the German Cardinal thought due to the Catholic German head of state, particularly in a time of war.

In retrospect we may find this loyalty inexplicable and indeed intolerable. But there is much in the history of German Catholicism which makes it understandable, and in reality here the Cardinal stood with countless other Germans who believed that they were fighting in the war for Führer, Volk and Fatherland, and only recognized after the collapse what they had really been fighting for.

For Preysing, however, this was the last straw. When he was sent a copy of the letter, he responded by resigning from the press responsibilities which had been entrusted to him in 1935 by the Conference of Bishops and which were important in church law.[28] To the Cardinal who, whether deliberately or unintentionally, misunderstood, he finally explained quite clearly that the reason for this step was 'the fundamental divergence of our views over the church-political situation' as it had now emerged once again in connection with the programmatic statements in the letter to the Reich Chancellor and Führer. In addition to this, he contemplated leaving the Conference of Bishops and resigning his see. Only the urgent request of the Pope restrained him from doing both these things.[29]

However, the hope often expressed by Rome that an open statement at the next conference of bishops in August 1940 would mitigate the clash came to nothing.[30] Rather, there was a sensation at the session when after Preysing's introductory comments Bertram rose with the observation that 'their lordships might have a conversation if they wished, but he himself was leaving the room'.[31] As a break between the President and the assembly was quite unthinkable, the session was closed forthwith by Cardinal Schulte of Cologne. The next day Bertram resumed the presidency of the conference without any further comment, and despite all objections formally continued to hold it until his death.[32]

## The blocked pastoral letter

The whole complex of problems caused by Bertram's continuation in office became clear in the arguments over a pastoral letter which a small group within the Conference of Bishops, including Bishops Gröber, Berning and Preysing, had worked out in the summer and autumn of 1941.[33] Through the Faulhaber archives we can now follow the history of this document in detail.

The situation leading up to it had become substantially worse. The measures taken to the murder the mentally ill, reports about persecutions in the occupied territories, especially in Poland, a devastating action against monasteries and the houses of religious orders, and not least the invasion of Russia on 22 July 1941, had changed the mood even in the Conference of Bishops. In addition, it was evident that clear and open speaking, as it had been practised by the Bishop of Münster in his famous sermons, was successful.

All this led the committee which had originally been appointed to take responsibility for matters relating to the orders to draft a joint pastoral letter which was finally to identify things in Germany for what they were. In fact the language of the draft produced in November 1941 had an unparalleled openness and boldness. With the exception of the Jewish question, which had been deliberately omitted, hardly a critical theme was absent.[34] In the letter the church complained about the persecution that was being directed against it, but 'with even greater sorrow' it complained about the violation of the basic rights given by natural law. It made explicit mention not only of the right to the protection of property, truth and honour but also of the right to personal freedom and the right to life. It explained unequivocally what it meant by this: 'Just as in Germany anyone can be deprived of his freedom without being found guilty and appearing before a judge, so anyone can be deprived of health and life without being found guilty and appearing before a judge. No one can supervise the violent measures of the Gestapo and no one prevents them from dispensing life or death at will.'

The explanation why the pastoral letter was necessary, which was added, said that the question of success or failure was insignificant.[35] The one decisive question was: 'What is our duty in the present moment? What does conscience require? What does God, what do German believers expect of their bishops?'

It was a significant sign of the change within the episcopate that by the end of November twenty bishops had already assented to the publication of this pastoral letter.[36] Then first a plan intervened to join with the Protestant church in making a last attempt to persuade the Reich government to put an end to its increasing perseuction of the churches.[37] When this attempt, too, as usual got nowhere, at the beginning of 1942 the question of publication was again debated. Now Bertram firmly declared that he could not agree to publication 'in principle and for practical reasons'.[38] So the great joint appeal to the public which the Bishop of Berlin had been calling for since 1937 was never made.[39]

The President of the Conference sensed that his decision had put him in a minority. Just as for a long time Preysing had stood alone, so now Bertram complained that 'though a member of the conference since 1906, he was feeling increasingly isolated'.[40] Nevertheless the old cardinal unswervingly kept to his line. What moved him to do so?

## Bertram and Hitler

The key to understanding Bertram's behaviour lies in a small collection of papers which is kept in what used to be the Archbishop's archive in Breslau under the title 'On the Situation in 1942/43'.[41] It contains part of a correspondence which the Cardinal had with Hitler between 1940 and 1944.

Despite the difficulties which his congratulatory letter of 1940 had caused, the President of the Conference of Bishops evidently felt it his duty to continue to congratulate the Führer and Reich Chancellor every year on 20 April. However, he no longer used his presidential letterhead, but wrote as Archbishop of Breslau and 'Senior of the German Episcopate' – i.e. formally in his own name but in fact still with the claim to be the spokesman for the whole of German Catholicism.

As in 1940, after sending his congratulations, all the Cardinal's letters began by expressing the close bond of German Catholics with Führer and Volk, army and fatherland, and then went on to repeat the urgent request for the Führer to turn 'an open eye' (as the 1942 letter put it) 'to the severe afflictions which are being prepared for the Catholic church by influential circles and even by state institutions'. Here it became clear – and this was evidently the heart of the argument – that Bertram was making a deliberate distinction between these 'influential circles' and Hitler himself. So the request in 1943 was that 'in the midst of all the tasks which come together in the Führer's headquarters the Führer would not close his eyes to the efforts within Greater Germany, supported by influential officials in the Party and the state, to destroy the holy bond which binds pastor and flock in the Catholic church...' That could only have been written by someone whose basic assumption was that the persecution of the churches in Germany basically went against Hitler's knowledge and will and that the time would come when the Führer and Reich Chancellor would return to the principles invoked in the Reich concordat. In fact it was only on this presupposition that the understanding between the Cardinal and the Head of State reflected in these letters was possible.

What is surprising about this correspondence, however, is not only what Bertram said, but just as much what Hitler said. As early as 1940 Hitler's reply to Bertram had already been unusually detailed and cordial, and year by year the Führer was concerned to show the Cardinal trust and understanding from his side. For example in 1942 he stressed 'that where the supposed interventions in church affairs are not occasioned by the conduct of individuals, they are unavoidably connected with the needs of wartime... I have no other interest,' he continued, 'than that state and church, in the best possible mutual understanding, should do everything possible to overcome the difficulties of wartime and thus contribute to the final victory.' In 1943 he assured Bertram: 'You may be certain, my Lord Cardinal, that your concerns will always be examined with particular urgency.' And the last letter of 13 July 1944 ended with the sentence: 'You may be sure, my Lord Cardinal, that I know the rectitude and integrity of your aims and fully accept them.' And a final greeting was added in manuscript: 'In sincere respect, Yours sincerely, Adolf Hitler.'

It is not easy to interpret these letters. Conversations in the Führer's headquarters in 1941 and 1942 provide so much indubitable evidence of Hitler's growing hatred of Christianity and the churches and his desire to annihilate them that initially one must understand the letters as delaying tactics, as one of those lying deceptions at which Hitler was a master.[42] And if in this way he in fact intended to avoid an immediate confrontation with the Catholic church at least during the war, these tactics indeed proved to be a great success. On the other hand it is hardly imaginable that at this period Hitler would have sent a similar letter – indeed any letter at all – to a Protestant church leader. So perhaps there were also distant recollections of the years when to be a priest seemed to the young Hitler to be 'the embodiment of all humanly attainable heights';[43] perhaps a last relic of a Catholic's respect, of which Hitler himself was hardly aware, for the church and its hierarchy moved Hitler in these letters. At all events, that is the way in which Bertram must have read and understood them.

A requiem for Hitler

On 21 January 1945, now eighty-six and bearing all the signs of old age, Cardinal Bertram had left Breslau on medical advice shortly before the encirclement of the city by Russian troops, and moved to Schloss Johannesberg near Lauering, an old residence of the Prince Bishops of Breslau.[44] It is here that news of Hitler's death must have reached him on the late evening of 1 May or the morning of 2 May. It ran: 'From the Führer's headquarters it is reported that our Führer Adolf Hitler fell today for Germany at his command post in the Reich Chancellery, fighting against Bolshevism to his last breath.'[45] It was probably while the Cardinal was still under the immediate impact of this news, which there was no possibility of verifying, that he took up his pen. In his own hand he gave all the parish priests of the archdiocese instructions 'to hold a solemn requiem in memory of the Führer and all those members of the Wehrmacht who have fallen in the struggle for our German Father-land, along with the sincerest prayers for Volk and Fatherland and for the future of the Catholic church in Germany'.[46]

The letter with these instructions in the Breslau archives bears neither date nor signature. But the Cardinal's handwriting is unmis-takable, and we can also be certain that it is dated after 1 May, after all the days of uncertainty (see front cover for a facsimile).

We do not know whether the instructions were followed anywhere in Silesia or indeed whether it was possible for them to be handed on. But this question, too, is not important. The important thing is that in these instructions the Cardinal once again confirmed the basic significance of his line in church politics. For according to Catholic church law a solemn requiem may be held only for an important reason and for a public concern of the church (*pro re gravi et publica simul causa*).[47] So the paper shows that all down the years the Cardinal was not in fact acting out of tactical considerations, but that despite all the insults to the church, the threats and the persecutions, he continued to see and respect Hitler as the Catholic state head of the Reich. He did not have to live to realize how wrong he was in this.

Adolf Cardinal Bertram, the last Prince Bishop of Breslau, died on 6 July 1945.

The letter with his instructions was struck through by another hand.

## Retrospect

Throughout the period of the Third Reich, the President of the German Bishops Conference unwearyingly and tenaciously defended the rights of the Catholic church in countless letters, petitions, plans and memoranda against all attacks from state and Party. He would make no concessions to the National Socialist world-view. At the same time, however, Bertram had exerted all his influence to avoid any direct and public criticism of Hitler and the Third Reich by the Catholic church. In this respect he was no less nationalistic and trustful of the authorities than any German Lutheran. His understanding of his office, his historical experience, which was deeply rooted in the Kaiser's empire, and the location of his diocese near the Eastern frontier contributed to this. At the same time, however, one can see in his attitude the tenacious effect of the Reich concordat. Although today it may be described as 'the form of a legal treaty preventing the assimilation of the Catholic church' in the Third Reich,[48] for the President of the German Conference of Bishops at that time it was on the contrary one of the decisive reasons for his unshakeable loyalty to Hitler.

In May 1945 the old cardinal certainly no longer represented the voice of the German bishops, far less that of the people of the church. To that degree it is quite inappropriate to make accusations against him or excuses for him for any reason whatsoever. What is clear from him, in addition to his particularly striking exemplification of Catholic obedience to the authorities, is the confusion, error and tragedy which he shared with countless Germans of his period.

# Judaism and Christianity in the Ideology and Politics of National Socialism, 1919-1945*

## 1. Preliminary comments on matters of principle

The following account begins from two presupposiitons:
1. The race question was the decisive basis of Hitler's world-view;
2. The transformation of the race question into a political world-view was essentially Hitler's work.

These theses reject the argument already put forward in Hitler's lifetime from both the conservative (Hermann Rauschning) and the Marxist (Franz Neumann) sides that Hitler's antisemitism was merely a means to an end and that the National Socialist world-view was above all a matter of propaganda. According to this thesis Hitler and his closest followers were power-seeking cynics who were themselves above antisemitism but exploited the traditional enmity towards the Jews to achieve their political ends. The Marxist interpretation in particular, which sees National Socialism as a species of European Fascism and is compelled to interpret it as an inevitable late form of monopolistic capitalism, can only attribute a functional and instrumental significance to the antisemitism of the régime.

Contrary to this, all the sources show that Hitler himself and his most important supporters – Goebbels, Bormann and Himmler – were convinced of the central significance of the race question and accordingly made it the foundation and criterion of all important political decisions. (Only Göring is an exception here. That could

*Originally published in *Papers presented to the International Symposium on Judaism and Christianity under the Impact of National Socialism (1919-1945)*, ed. Itzchak Mais, Jerusalem 1982, 183-200.

explain the gradual decline in his influence on Hitler and the Reich leadership.)

So if we want to speak of a functional relationship between the race question and rule in the period of National Socialism, we have to turn things the other way round: in its basic direction and in a wealth of individual decisions National Socialist politics was the implementation of the National Socialist world-view.

'The abundance of sources at our disposal contain nothing to indicate that Hitler saw "the final solution of the Jewish question" as an instrument in the service of other aims. Rather, they lead inexorably to the conclusion that the Final Solution did not serve a further purpose for Hitler but was in keeping with his values, specifically his conviction that the Jews were the deadly enemies of Germany, and that Germany would only be safe when Jewry had been obliterated from the surface of the earth.'[1]

## 2. The basic features of Hitler's world-view

The foundation of Hitler's world-view was a radical racial and ethical dualism: as it were a modern racialist form of Manichaeism. He was convinced that the hidden principle of world history was the fight between a good and an evil race, between Aryans and Jews, and that the outcome of this fight would also decide the outcome of world history. We already find this conception in the first of Hitler's political documents known to us, his letter to Adolf Gemlich of 16 September 1919. The same perspective in this or a similar form dominates almost all Hitler's speeches and articles over the next few years; these have now been made accessible for the first time in Eberhard Jäckel's edition.

The letter begins with a significant distinction between antisemitism as a mere 'emotional phenomenon' and true political antisemitism, which rests on 'clear knowledge', 'the knowledge of facts'. Among the facts Hitler, who was thirty at the time, includes the racial character of the Jewish question – Jewry is 'unconditionally a race and not a religious community' – and the irremovably different worth of the races. Hitler was being true to his basic conviction, which we find here already in its fully developed form, when he wrote: 'And thus the fact arises that a non-German, alien race lives among us, which is unwilling and indeed unable to sacrifice its racial characteristics, its own feelings, thoughts and strivings, and which nevertheless possess all the political rights that we do. If Jewish feeling already moves in the purely material sphere, Jewish thoughts and strivings do so even more. The dance around the golden calf becomes the inexorable struggle over all those possessions which our innermost feelings tell us are not meant to be the highest good on this earth, the only one that is worth striving for.' Hitler's conviction was that the activity of the Jews was destroying all the higher spiritual and moral values of the peoples and was ultimately preparing for their downfall. This led him to the following conclusion: 'Antisemitism for purely emotional reasons will find its ultimate expression in the form of pogroms (!). However, rational antisemitism must lead to a systematic legal fight against the Jews and the removal of their privileges... Its last, unshakeable aim must be the removal of the Jews.'

At the same time the functional relationship between world view and politics – politics as a means of implementing the aims of a world view – becomes clear when Hitler ends this section by saying: 'Only a government of national power, never a government of national impotence, is capable of both these things' – the planned legal fight against the Jews and finally their complete removal.[2]

In the meantime there has been a whole series of investigations into the origin of these convictions. They generally point to the historical line which is characterized by the names of Gobineau and Chamberlain. Possibly, however, the whole contribution of racist scientific reseach as been too little noted here. A work like that on the Rehoboth Bastards by the well known anthropologist Eugen Fischer, which appeared in 1913, was well suited for giving racist theory the semblance of objectivity.[3]

Hitler himself doubtless derived his ideas from the *völkisch* movement which at that time, under the impact of the loss of the War, was showing considerable signs of life in Munich, though more in the form of sectarian agitation and activity. Of course there was already an antisemitic trend in Germany in the nineteenth century. But it took a political catastrophe which was felt to be secular yet incomprehensible, like the loss of the First World War, to prepare the ground on which *völkisch* antisemitism could really spread.

There is no idea, no image, no argument of any significance in Hitler's early remarks which does not occur often in the *völkisch* writings of the time. So it does not make much sense to look for individual spiritual forebears for Hitler. These forebears are those to which the *völkisch* movement as a whole appealed. Nevertheless it would be wrong to see Hitler simply as a *völkisch* ideologist. Certainly he came from this movement, but he very quickly grew out of it, in two ways. With the extraordinary energy of his will and his special sense of political effect, he formed the various elements of the race question into a coherent political world-view with an unprecedented impact. And at the same time he understood that the presupposition for the victory of this world view lay in political organization. He developed both these things during the time when he was imprisoned in Landsberg. The most important source of this is *Mein Kampf*.

The two central chapters of this book are the last two chapters of the first volume: Chapter 11, 'Nation (Volk) and Race', and Chapter 12, 'The First Period of Development of the National Socialist German Workers' Party'. In Chapter 11 Hitler presents race theory as a natural law and applies its doctrines to the battle against Jewry. Here he makes clear how this question bears on the whole of his policy: 'Whether we consider questions of general justice or cankers of economic life, symptoms of cultural decline or processes of political degeneration, questions of faulty schooling or the bad influence exerted on grown-ups by the press, etc., everywhere and always it is fundamentally the disregard of the racial needs of our one's own people or failure to see a foreign racial menace.'[4]

However, Hitler did not stop at this insight into the connections which he thought he saw. Others, too, had that. The decisive thing, rather, was the way in which he associated these insights with a form of organization. It was only through this association that the National Socialist world-view came into being; and it was Hitler's own work. Therefore we read in italics in Chapter 12: 'Every philosophy of life, even if it is a thousand times correct and of highest benefit to humanity, will remain without significance for the practical shaping of a people's life, as long as its principles have not become the banner of a fighting movement which for its part in turn will be a party as long as its activity has not found completion in the victory of its ideas and its party dogmas have not become the new state principles of a people's community.'[5]

At this point the question arises: 'What role was conceived of for Christianity in this world view?'

### 3. Hitler's conception of antisemitism and Christianity

There can be hardly any doubt that in the first half of the 1920s, when Hitler was developing this conception, he saw Christianity as an ally. And on a superficial examination the broad anti-Jewish tradition which the Christian churches had handed down from the Middle Ages could encourage him in this.

The much discussed Article 24 of the Party programme of 1920, which while not Hitler's work was presented by him, makes this clear. What it postulates, albeit in a somewhat qualified form, is basically a kind of Aryan Christianity. In the requirement in the first paragraph of Article 24 of 'the freedom of all religious confessions in the state', on condition that 'they do not endanger its existence or offend against the sense of morality and moral feeling of the Germanic race', the condition is aimed solely at the Jewish religion, which is excluded from the requirement of freedom. And in the second paragraph of the article, the acknowledgment of a so-called 'positive Christianity' in connection with the fight against 'the Jewish-materialistic spirit within us and outside' shows that the young party counted on the support of Christianity for the implementation of its racist, antisemitic programme – not, however, Christianity *per se* but a particular form of Christianity which corresponded to 'the virtue and moral feeling of the Germanic race' and fought against 'the Jewish-materialistic spirit'.[6]

Hitler made clear what this involved in a programmatic speech in April 1922. He began the relevant section with a question which was decisive for this whole conception: whether as a Christian one could be antisemitic. Remarkably, he did not answer this question in the same way as the usual antisemitism of the time, by saying that although one was a Christian one could also be antisemitic – for whatever moral or economic reasons; he said that as a Christian one *had to be* antisemitic. For Hitler, here as always antisemitism was nothing to be apologized for: on the contrary, it was a political and moral imperative which he derived directly from the figure and fate of Jesus. 'I tell you,' he declared, 'that my Christian feelings point me to the man who once in solitude, surrounded by only a few supporters, recognized these Jews and summoned people to fight against them...' 'But today, after two thousand years,' Hitler continued, 'I can recognize his tremendous battle for this world against the Jewish poison, and be most deeply and powerfully moved by the fact that he had to shed his blood for it on the cross.'[7]

Hitler here exploited for his conception the old theme of the 'murderers of Christ', which was doubtless familiar to much of the predominantly Catholic audience for this speech.

To what degree Hitler's closest followers interpreted the whole of church history in these terms in his name is clear from a book by his friend and mentor Dietrich Eckart which appeared in 1924: *Bolshevism from Moses to Lenin. A Conversation between Adolf Hitler and Me.* Although the actual conversation is hardly authentic, it does clarify the horizons of Hitler's thought during these years. In this work the picture of an Aryan Christianity is developed, the basic features of which had been familiar and current since Paul de Lagarde and Houston Stewart Chamberlain. Hitler and his conversation-partner Eckart gather up all the antisemitic traditions in Christian history to demonstrate that the anti-Jewish front has long been the true Christian front and only modern Christianity has forgotten this, to its detriment.[8]

All these convictions are summed up again in the famous sentences from *Mein Kampf*, often also quoted in the Third Reich as a key saying, in which Hitler claims God as the creator even of his conception: 'If, with the help of his Marxist creed, the Jew is victorious over the other peoples of the world, his crown will be the funeral wreath of humanity and this planet will, as it did millions of years ago, move through the ether devoid of men. Eternal nature inexorably avenges the infringement of her commands. Hence today I believe that I am acting in accordance with the will of the Almighty Creator: by defending myself against the Jew, I am fighting for the work of the Lord.'[9]

However, with *Mein Kampf* at the same time a decisive political shift takes place for Hitler. The Party Leader makes a basic decision of extraordinary significance for church politics. Although he is still convinced of his conception, in the new beginning after his release from prison he categorically forbids the Party to enter into controversies with the Christian churches over matters of principle. This is the logical conclusion of the insight he gained during his time in Landsberg into the quite decisive significance of an organization with closed ranks. Nothing, he rightly feared, would damage this solidarity more than disputes over church confessions. Any advocacy of the view that Jesus was the greatest antisemite or of antisemitism generally as the embodiment of Christianity would inevitably lead to vigorous controversy inside and outside the Party, which could neither be controlled nor decided on by the Party Leader with his political authority. Therefore over the next few years Hitler parted company with Ludendorff and his wife Mathilde von Kemnitz, who sought to set the Party on a religious-antisemitic line, and with his Thuringian Gauleiter Arthur Dinter. He continued to respect Dinter as an antisemitic writer (*The Sin against the Blood*), but he firmly rejected Dinter's attempt at a religious 'reformation' with the help of the Party.

This basic church-political decision, namely to keep the Party out of all church and religious controversies as far as possible, in no way changed Hitler's conviction that the Christian churches were called to fight against the Jews side by side with National Socialism. He merely refrained from demanding this directly and publicly measuring his relationship to the churches by it.

However, we may proceed on the assumption that beyond all church-political tactics which were necessitated by the politics of the day, Hitler was resolved to make the fundamental solution of the church question in the Third Reich dependent on whether the churches were willing to take his side on the issue of antisemitism.

In Hitler's view the only chance that the churches still had was to ally themselves with the modern world-view of racial antisemitism. In his first conversation as Reich Chancellor with a Catholic bishop – this was Bishop Berning of Osnabrück, in April 1933 – he made his expectations clear in this respect. After telling the bishop that in his – Hitler's – view Christianity had 'in recent centuries failed to exert its strength and its will to overcome the powers which are hostile to the state and Christianity', he went on to speak of the Jewish question and in so doing supported his Jewish policy with a reference to the Catholic church, which for 1500 years had seen the Jews as the culprits. Only 'in the time of liberalism' were people 'no longer aware of' this danger.[11] So evidently at this time Hitler still expected that the Catholic church would support his antisemitic legislation and administrative measures.

He was already talking much more critically a year later in a conversation with the Protestant bishops Wurm and Meiser: 'The church must get used to the doctrine of blood and race. Just as the Catholic church could not change the fact that the earth goes round the sun, so the church could not do away with the irrefutable facts which are given in blood and race. Unless they recognize that, developments will simply pass them by.'[12]

Hitler's remarks to Cardinal Faulhaber in their three-hour conversation in November 1936 pointed in the same direction. Here too Hitler called on the church to give up the battle against race legislation 'which rests on absolute scientific research'. And as for both Hitler and the cardinal Bolshevism and Judaism were largely identical concepts, Hitler's warning was also clear: 'Unless National Socialism gets the better of Bolshevism, then all will be up with Christianity and the church in Europe.'[13]

Until around 1937/38 Hitler may still have felt that there was a chance that the Christian churches in Germany would come round to sharing his insights and recognize racial antisemitism. As long as that was the case, his church policy was not yet directed towards annihilating Christianity and the churches but towards limiting their influence.

## 4. The reactions of the churches

These presumptuous demands put the Christian churches in Germany in a difficult situation. For centuries they had had an antisemitic tradition, but the basis of this was religious, not racial. As H.A.Oberman has again shown recently,[14] the traditional Christian hostility to the Jews was rooted in a situation of rivalry between two monotheistic religions, which from the beginning had found themselves in opposition to each other. In this context a central role was played by the concept of 'hardening': God himself, Christian doctrine held, had smitten the Jews with blindness so that they did not recognize the Messiah but pressed for his death, and this stubbornness and enmity would continue and be repeated in the Jewish people until the end of time. This view at the same time meant that any Jew who was converted from that perspective, i.e. allowed himself to be baptized, was freed from the spell of hardening and could without qualification be accepted into the Christian community. By contrast it was a mark and characteristic of the racist antisemitism put forward by Hitler that Jewry was not a religious community but a racial community, not a religious entity but a biological entity, which nothing – even baptism – could alter.

As far as I can see, complete clarity has yet to be arrived at as to the development of the relationship between religious and racial antisemitism in the nineteenth century. It is obvious that despite their different origins we must assume that there was a close connection. Possibly the linking factor is provided by the social and economic problems of the nineteenth century and in Germany, especially those of the Kaiser's Reich. At all events that is true for a man like Adolf Stöcker, who in 1881 combined the racial, religious and economic arguments in an extrarodinarily characteristic way in a lecture on 'The Significance of the Christian World-View for the Burning Questions of the Present': 'We want to, we must, remain Germans, Christians... Jewry is an alien drop in our blood!... Let us take the holy vow to see our Israelite fellow-citizens as citizens, the ruins of an old, glorious people, but one which rejected the Messiah and took up mammon...'[15]

Unfortunately, to my knowledge there are as yet no investigations into whether Christian antisemitism displayed any differences which went with a particular confession; whether it was equally widespread in the two great confessions or whether – as Hitler assumed and Friedrich Heer seems to suggest[16] – it was more broadly and deeply rooted in Catholicism.

In view of this tradition Hitler's excesses(!) could arouse a response in Christian Germany. In fact, with very few exceptions, there was hardly any active and direct opposition to the Jewish policy of the authorities anywhere in the churches during the period of the Third Reich.

On the other hand – and this is no less important – at no time did the two Christian churches as a whole deny their close and indissoluble connection with Israel. One example of this is the way in which they retained the Old Testament as a source of revelation. Hitler's hope that the churches would accept the conception of an Aryan Christianity, and thus identify themselves not only in practice but also in principle with the National Socialist ideology, was not fulfilled. This refusal led Hitler and his closest entourage in the leadership to see Christianity as being increasingly close to Judaism as time went on. Since Christianity was maintaining its Jewish roots, even if these were often broken, from the perspective of universal racial theory it was showing itself up to be a Jewish invention: this was the conclusion which began to force itself increasingly strongly upon Hitler after 1937.

The discussion of the possibility of an Aryan Christianity was carried on openly and explicitly only within Protestantism, as might have been expected from its greater openness. A conclusion had already been reached by the end of 1933.

The programme of a religion understood in racial terms entered the Protestant church officially for the first time in 1932 with the Guidelines of the German Christians. The relevant slogans were '*artgemäss* faith in Christ'; race, Volkstum and nation as God-given orders; and therefore rejection of 'the mixing of races', 'protection of the Volk from the incompetent and the inferior'; the rejection of the mission to the Jews because of the associated danger of 'blurring of race and bastardization'.[17] The origin and scope of these concepts are clear and need no interpretation. It is worth noting that the German Christians were able to make substantial inroads into the Protestant church with their Guidelines.

The discussion in theology and church which then began and was carried on in a very lively way did not always use such clear arguments as those which can be found in Dietrich Bonhoeffer's comments ('The Church and the Jewish Question', April 1933; The Bethel Confession, August 1933, para.6).[18] In fact it took the introduction of the Aryan paragraph by the Prussian General Synod on 5 September 1933 and thus the formal legalization in church law of a Christianity understood in racial terms to provoke really broad and extensive opposition. In the end, however, a decisive statement was made clearly and directly in point 5 of the declaration of commitment required by the Pastors' Emergency League: 'In such commitment I bear witness that the application of the Aryan paragraph within the sphere of the church of Christ is a violation of the state of confession.'[19]

The German Christian rally at the Sports Palace on 13 November, with the speech by Reinhold Krause, represented the last attempt to establish and give a home to Aryan Christianity in the church, overcoming all resistance as it were by a revolutionary procedure. For Krause's demand that the Old Testament should be disowned in principle and the New Testament purged of all Jewish and Pauline traces was precisely this conception.[20]

The reaction to the speech throughout the church made it clear that these demands were unacceptable even to the German Christians. In fact the much disputed Sports Palace scandal marked the beginning of the end of the German Christian movement – even if efforts continued up to 1945 to understand the relationship between Christianity and Judaism in racial terms.[21]

On the Catholic side the five sermons which Cardinal Faulhaber of Munich gave to enormous congregations of the faithful from the First Sunday in Advent until New Year's Eve 1933 had a similar significance to the broad church reaction to Krause's speech on the Protestant side. These sermons were published in 1934 under the title *Judaism, Christianity, Germanhood*. In view of the tense confessional situation in Germany it was quite extraordinary that a German cardinal should look over the hedge dividing the confessions and say: 'We extend a hand to our separated brethren in order to join them in defending the holy books of the Old Testament.' Faulhaber's sermons were not directed against the practical political antisemitism of the time but against its basic presuppositions, racial antisemitism, and its invasion of the church. Again, if we remember Hitler's expectation of particular support for his world view from the Catholic church, the Cardinal's sermon was a clear rebuff in this respect. Faulhaber declared that it was obvious that Christ rejected 'ties of blood' and called for 'ties of faith'. So the question was not: 'Was Christ born a Jew or an Aryan?', but rather: 'Are we incorporated into Christ through baptism and faith? "In Christ Jesus what matters is not whether one is a Jew or a non-Jew but only the new creation".'[22]

However little the Christian churches may have been involved in resistance to practical antisemitism in subsequent years, they never surrendered the Old Testament or the fact that the Christ was born of the Jewish race. And it was this point which for all their opportunism, blindness and weakness ultimately marked them off from the Third Reich.

However, the churches saw this very much less clearly than Hitler himself and his group of leaders: Bormann, Himmler and Goebbels.

## 5. Changes in Hitler's attitude to Christianity

Presumably it was during 1937 that Hitler came to the conclusion that he could not count on support for his world-view from the churches. This was not a sudden insight, but one which grew upon him gradually. His long and intensive conversation with Cardinal Faulhaber of Munich in November 1937 was the last attempt to bring the Catholic church into the fight against Bolshevism on his side – and here it must be remembered that Hitler used Bolshevism and Jewry as synonyms. If the reply of the German bishops at the end of 1936 had already been disappointing, Hitler must have regarded the encyclical *Mit brennender Sorge* in April 1937 almost as a snub. In fact it will have seemed to him to be the final rejection of his world-view by Catholicism.

At the same time, in February 1937, the Reich Church Minister's attempt to mediate between the Evangelical Chuch and the Third Reich also failed.

These two events, combined with his own growing certainty, will have led Hitler to cease cherishing any expectations that the churches would see the light as he wanted them to. A passing comment in a speech made to propaganda leaders in October 1937 takes on special significance in this context: 'Hitler declared that after hard inner struggles he had freed himself from the childish view of religion that was still around. "Now I feel as fresh as a colt in the meadow".'[23]

The refusal of the churches unconditionally to join the National Socialist side in the fight against world Jewry and Bolshevism was a serious disappointment for Hitler, who by this time was used to success. This was more of a passive refusal, simply a matter of holding on to the creed which had been handed down, but it was enough to put in question the totalitarian claim of the National Socialist world view. As Hitler was convinced that this world-view had been proved clearly and scientifically, he had to find an explanation for the churches' refusal. The one which he found was obvious, and matched his view that in the end all problems amounted to one and the same: the Jewish question. Those who did not support the National Socialist fight against Jewry must themselves have been contaminated by Judaism. That was true of Bolshevism, of capitalism and now also of Christianity.

For many reasons an open conflict with the churches in Germany was still unthinkable. But the church-political decisions of 1938 clearly indicate a harsher approach. To a growing degree Hitler now gave a free hand to Martin Bormann, who was his most loyal executive in this area. This led to Bormann's implementation in the newly-annexed territories of Austria and the Sudetenland of legislation which deprived the churches of their status under public law and made them subject to the law of associations – a prelude to the treatment of the church question in the so-called Warthegau, which ended up in complete oppression of and control over the churches.

Hitler's famous speech of 30 January 1939 showed that similar developments awaited the old Reich. After announcing 'the annihilation of the Jewish race in Europe' in a coming war, in the same context he turned to the churches with a warning that the National Socialist state was ready at any time to bring about 'a clear separation of church and state', in other words to subject the churches to the law of associations and to deprive them of all state support.[24]

Above all the war situation compelled Hitler to leave this threat unfulfilled for the moment. But he was basically resolved after annihilating the Jews and winning the war also to annihilate Christianity, so to speak as the last bastion of the Jewish spirit. His monologues in the Führer's headquarters in 1941/42 are unique evidence of this, with an unsurpassable clarity.

A Christianity which rejected the National Socialist world-view could only be a Jewish invention.

So on 11/12 July 1941 Hitler declared succinctly: 'Christianity is the hardest blow which ever hit humanity. Bolshevism is the bastard son of Christianity; both are a monstrous issue of the Jews.'[25] Only Jesus continued unchanged to be the Aryan who fought against Judaism, as Hitler already saw him in 1922. 'Christianity was all-destroying Bolshevism. But the Galilean who was later called Christ wanted something else. He was a leader of the people who opposed Jewry.' The Jew Paul was then the one who 'refined, falsified and exploited the teaching of the Galilean for his own ends'.[26] So both Christianity and Judaism become instruments for destroying the world: 'By turning the Aryan protest movement against Judaism in Palestine into the Christian religion transcending the state, the Jew ruined the Roman empire.'

The hope that Christianity could renew itself by some move in an Aryan direction had meanwhile been given up long since. As Hitler commented in December 1941: 'Minister Kerrl wanted to produce a synthesis between National Socialism and Christianity in the noblest sense. I do not believe that that is possible; the reason lies in Christianity itself... Pure Christianity, so-called earliest Christianity, ends up in the demonstration of Christian theory: it leads to the annihilation of mankind; it is naked Bolshevism in a metaphysical guise.'[27]

This logically led to the statement that the solution of the church question was his last great problem. 'The war will come to an end and I shall see my last task as clearing up the church problem. Only then will the German nation be completely safe... In my youth I had the view: dynamite! Today I see that one cannot break it over one's knee. It has to be cut off like a gangrenous limb.'[28]

For Hitler, Judaism was the root of all disaster and remained so. Therefore it was the Jew who first encountered his hatred and his destructive will. But the more time went on, the more Christianity followed Judaism as being a Jewish invention through and through.

Thus the Jewish question and the Christian question were much more closely connected in the Third Reich than the Christian churches ever realized. Only the downfall of Hitler prevented Christians from being brutally awakened to this fact.

# Notes

## Introduction

1. K.Scholder, Report, in *The Church in a Changing Society. Conflict, Reconciliation or Adjustment?*, Uppsala 1978, 334.
2. As an example of a completely ambivalent evaluation in connection with this cf. W.D.Hauschild, *Evangelische Kommentare* 19, 1986, 468f.; id., 'Zur Erforschung der Barmer Theologischen Erklärung von 1934', *Theologische Rundschau* 51, 1986, 130-65, esp. 134, 140, 151, 159; or E.Iserloh, *Theologische Revue* 82, 1986, 297f.
3. K.Scholder, 'Altes und Neues zur Vorgeschichte des Reichskonkordats. Erwiderung auf Konrad Repgen' (1978), reprinted with an introduction by K.O.von Aretin in *Die Kirchen zwischen Republik und Gewaltsherrschaft*, Berlin 1988, 171-203.
4. K. Scholder, *The Churches and the Third Reich*, Volume 1. *Preliminary History and the Time of Illusions 1918-1934*, London and Philadelphia 1987, x.
5. 'Über den Umgang mit unserer jüngsten Geschichte', reprinted in *Die Kirchen zwischen Republik und Gewaltsherrschaft* (n.3 above), 44-57.
6. The two quotations come from K.Scholder, 'Die theologische Grundlage des Kirchenkampfes. Zur Entstehung und Bedeutung der Barmer Erklärung', *Evangelische Theologie* 44, 1984, 523f. In this connection see also Scholder's argument with Helmut Gollwitzer over the theological standpoint of the journal *Evangelische Theologie* in *EvTh* 44, 1984, 193-205.
7. See n.5.
8. K.Scholder, 'Fate and Guilt in History', below 34.
9. Ibid.
10. K.Scholder and D.Kleinmann, *Protestantische Profile. Lebensbilder aus fünf Jahrhunderten*, Königstein im Taunus 1983, 11.

## 1. History and Hope

1. H.Luppe, *Mein Leben*, Quellen zur Geschichte und Kultur der Stadt Nürnberg, Vol.10, Nuremberg 1977, 279.
2. *Nürnberg 1933. Eine Sammlung der wichtigsten Reden auf dem Parteitag der NSDAP vom 30.August bis 3.September 1933*, Berlin 1933, 8.
3. H.Beer, *Widerstand gegen den Nationalsozialismus in Nürnberg 1933-1945*, Nürnberg Werkstücke zur Stadt- und Landesgeschichte 20, Nuremberg 1976, 33ff.

Notes 183

4. Ibid., table on p.39. For the behaviour of the electorate in the predominantlyProtestant areas see K.Scholder, *The Churches and the Third Reich* I, London
and Philadelphia 1987, 128ff.

5. J.W.Baird (ed.), 'Das politische Testament Julius Streichers', *Vierteljahrshefte für Zeitgeschichte* 26, 1978, 670.

6. For details of the development of völkisch antisemitism cf. Scholder,
*Churches*, I, 74ff.

7. A.Müller, *Geschichte der Juden in Nürnberg 1146-1945*, Nuremberg 1968,
184.

8. R.H.Phelps, ' "Before Hitler Came": Thule Society and German Orden',
*The Journal of Modern History* 53, 1963, 249.

9. H.Preiss, *Die Anfänge der völkischen Bewegung in Franken*, Erlangen
philosophical dissertation 1937, 69.

10. G.Pfeiffer (ed.), *Nürnberg. Geschichte einer europäischen Stadt*, Munich
1971, 456; J.W.Baird, 'Das politische Testament' (see n.5 above), 680ff.

11. A.Müller, *Geschichte der Juden* (n.7 above), 195ff.

12. Ibid., 201.

13. L.Riefenstahl, *Hinter den Kulissen des Reichsparteitag-Films*, Munich
1935, 11.

14. R.Karwehl, 'Politisches Messiastum. Zur Auseinandersetzung zwischen
Kirche und Nationalsozialismus', *Zwischen den Zeiten*, 1931, 542f.

15. H.T.Burden, *Die Programmierte Nation. Die Nürnberger Reichspartei-
tage*, Gütersloh 1967, 98f.; G.Pfeiffer, *Nürnberg* (n.10 above), 456.

16. A.Speer, *Inside the Third Reich*, London 1970, 96ff.

17. A.Speer, *Spandau. The Secret Diaries*, London and New York 1976, 428;
H.T.Burden, *Die programmierte Nation*, 223.

18. Speer, *Inside the Third Reich*, 99.

19. *Nürnberg 1933* (see n.2 above), 13.

20. M.Domarus, *Hitler. Reden und Proklamationen*, I.2, Munich 1962, 715.

21. A.Speer, *Spandau. The Secret Diaries*, 262.

22. B.Blau, *Das Ausnahmerecht für die Juden in den europäischen Ländern
1933-1945*, I, New York 1952, 29ff.; B.Lösener, 'Als Rassenreferent im Reichs-
ministerium des Innern', *Vierteljahrshefte für Zeitgeschichte* 9, 1961, esp. 272-
87; U.A.Adam, *Judenpolitik im Dritten Reich*, Düsseldorf 1972, 125-53.

23. This is the conclusion of H.Beer, *Widerstand gegen den Nationalsozialismus in Nürnberg 1933-1945* (n.3).

24. H.Baier, *Kirchenkampf in Nürnberg 1933-1945*, Nuremberg 1945, 20ff.

25. Ibid., 32.; A.Müller, *Geschichte der Juden* (n.7), 245.

26. K.Scholder, *Churches* I, 279.

27. H.T.Burden, *Programmierte Nation* (n.15 above), 238.

28. H.Rumpf, *Das war der Bomberkrieg*, Oldenburg 1961, 35.

29. M.Middlebrook, *Nuremberg Raid*, London ²1986, 87.

30. G.Pfeiffer, *Nürnberg* (n.5), 464; F.Nadler, *'Ich sah, wie Nürnberg
unterging...!'*, Nuremberg 1955.

31. Cf. also A.Verrier, *Bomberoffensive gegen Deutschland 1939-1945*,
Frankfurt 1970, 200.

32. G.E.Gründler and A.von Manikowsky, *Das Gericht der Sieger*, Oldenburg 1967, 70f.

33. Ibid., 42.

34. Ibid., 48f.

184     *A Requiem for Hitler*

## 2. Fate and Guilt in History

1. This lecture takes up a theme which Klaus Scholder also touched on at the annual reception of the Evangelische Akademie, Tutzing, on 17 January 1980; for the text see 'Über den Umgang mit unserer jüngsten Geschichte', in *Die Kirche zwischen Republik und Gewaltherrschaft*, Berlin 1988, 44-57.

2. P.Graf Kielmannsegg, *Deutschland und der Erste Weltkrieg*, Stuttgart ²1980, 697-730, is a good introduction to the most important literature. Since this is a lecture, with very few exceptions I have only provided references for the direct quotations.

3. For the discussion and the theses of Fritz Fischer see the summary now in F.Fischer, *Bündnis der Eliten. Zur Kontinuität der Machtstrukturen in Deutschland 1871-1945*, Düsseldorf 1979.

4. This is the predominant view of more recent German research, e.g. P.Graf Kielmannsegg (n.2), 7-22; A.Hillgruber, *Deutschlands Rolle in der Vorgeschichte der beiden Weltkriege*, Göttingen ²1979, esp. 54-8; T.Schieder, *Staatensystem als Vormacht der Welt 1848-1918*, Propyläen Geschichte Europas 5, Frankfurt, Berlin and Vienna 1977, 328f.; K.D.Erdmann, 'Die Zeit der Weltkriege', in Gebhardt and Grundmann, *Handbuch der deutschen Geschichte* 4.1, Stuttgart ⁹1973, 52-7.

5. Quoted from K.D.Erdmann (n.4), 54.

6. Aeschylus, *Agamemnon*, 1034-1330; Virgil, *Aeneid* II, 245f.

7. T.Schieder, *Staatensystem* (n.4), 330.

8. G.Berber, *Das Diktat von Versailles, Enstehung-Inhalt-Zerfall. Eine Darstellung in Dokumenten*, Essen 1939, article 231, p.1224; note of the German Peace Delegation, 1227; Allied covering note, 69ff.

9. From the lecture by Lord Lothian (i.e. Philip Kerr), 29 June 1937, ibid., 1224f.

10. M.Weber, 'Zum Thema der "Kriegsschuld"', *Frankfurter Zeitung*, 17 January 1919, in *Gesammelte Politische Schriften*, Tübingen ²1958, 478.

11. A.François-Ponçet, *Als Botschafter in Berlin 1931-1938*, Mainz 1947, 12. For English policy in the period between the wars cf. M.R.Gordon, *Conflict and Consensus in Labour's Foreign Policy 1914-1965*, Stanford 1969, 45-82.

12. K.Barth, letter to Professor Hromadka in Prague, 19 September 1938, in *Eine Schweizer Stimme 1938-1945*, Zurich 1945, 58f.; 'Fürchtet euch nicht! Ein Brief' (1950), in K. Kupisch (ed.), *Der Götze wackelt*, Berlin ²1964, 152.

13. K.D.Erdmann (n.3), 303-7.

14. Winston S.Churchill, *The Second World War* I, London 1948 reissued Harmondsworth 1985, 58f.; cf. also H.Brüning, *Memoiren 1918-1934*, Stuttgart 1970, 556-64.

15. Thus according to W.Niesel's account in W.-D.Zimmermann (ed.), *I knew Dietrich Bonhoeffer*, London 1966, 147. E.Bethge, *Dietrich Bonhoeffer, Theologian, Christian, Contemporary*, London and New York 1970, 586ff., differs.

16. D.Bonhoeffer, *Ethics*, London ⁵1985, 56.

17. Quoted from D.Irving, *The War Path. Hitler's Germany 1933-1939*, London 1978, 175.

18. F.P.Reck-Malleczewen, *Tagebuch eines Verzweifelten*, Lorch and Stuttgart 1947, 27f.

19. P.Hoffmann, *Widerstand, Staatsstreich, Attentat. Der Kampf der Oppo-*

*sition gegen Hitler*, Frankfurt, Berlin and Vienna 1974, 304ff., 333f., 340f., 477, etc.

20. H.Wilhelmy, *Aus meinem Leben*, Ebernburg 1977 (duplicated typescript).
21. H.Asmussen to Visser't Hooft, 13 December 1942; K.Ludwig, 'Karl Barths Dienst der Versöhnung. Zur Geschichte des Stuttgarter Schuldbekenntnisses', in *Zur Geschichte des Kirchenkampfes, Gesammelte Aufsätze II*, Göttingen 1971, 311ff.
22. Cited from B.Scheurig, *Henning von Tresckow, Eine Biographie*, Oldenburg ³1973, 191.
23. Text in G.Heidtmann (ed.), *Hat die Kirche geschwiegen? Das öffentliche Wort der evangelischen Kirche aus den Jahren 1954-1964*, Berlin ³1964, 19f.
24. Otto von Bismarck, *Die gesammelten Werke*, 14.II, Berlin 1933, 672.

## 3. Modern German History and Protestant Theology

1. *Anfänge der dialektischen Theologie*, ed. Jürgen Moltmann, *Teil 1: Karl Barth, Heinrich Barth, Emil Brunner*, Munich 1962; *Teil 2: Rudolf Bultmann, Friedrich Gogarten, Eduard Thurneysen*, Munich 1963. There is a partial English translation edited with an introduction by James M.Robinson, *The Beginnings of Dialectical Theology*, Richmond, Va 1968. Where there is no reference to the English translation, the passage in question does not appear in it.
2. Moltmann's further comment here, that 'It was, rather, itself in effect a power of judgment on a dead past and the opening up of a new future', seems to me to need some historical justification.
3. K.D.Bracher, *Die Auflösung der Weimarer Republik. Eine Studie zum Problem des Machtverfalls in der Demokratie*, ³1960; K.D.Bracher, W.Sauer and G.Schulz, *Die nationalsozialistische Machtergreifung. Studien zur Errichtung des totalitären Herrschaftssystems in Deutschland 1933/34*, Köln Opladen ²1962. Each has a detailed bibliography.
4. Kurt Sontheimer, *Antidemokratisches Denken in der Weimarer Republik. Die politischen Ideen des deutschen Nationalismus zwischen 1918 und 1933*, Munich 1962.
5. 'A representative part of those who supported the "conservative revolution" or a new nationalism were born between 1895 and 1905' (W.Bussmann, 'Politische Ideologien zwischen Monarchie und Weimarer Republik', *Historische Zeitschrift* 190, 1960, 64, see also 61.
6. Thus for example in 1932 Hans Zehrer argued in *Die Tat*: 'Look for the forms and formations which liberalism has produced and which are its most distinctive products. Nowadays one can paint a cross on each of them; it is doomed to downfall... Today the Bund belongs to the future, the Party to the past' (quoted from Sontheimer, *Antidemokratisches Denken* [n.4], 209).
7. Bussmann's closing observation is also very fine; 'If one thinks that the concept of tragedy is indissolubly bound up with that of guilt, the representatives of the "conservative revolution" may be said to be "tragic", i.e. at the same time doomed to failure. There are confessions of this guilt, and in such cases they simply confirm the experience that moral respectability and political failure are not mutually exclusive' ('Politische Ideologien' [n.5], 77).
8. See the section on anti-democratic thought against the cultural background of the time in Sontheimer, *Antidemokratisches Denken*, 42ff., and the references in Bussmann, 'Politische Ideologien', 67 and 71. I shall not be going more

closely here into the connection between this irrationalist movement and German history in the nineteenth century.

9. Christian Graf Krockow, *Die Entscheidung. Eine Untersuchung über Ernst Jünger, Carl Schmitt, Martin Heidegger*, Göttinger Abhandlungen zur Soziologie, 3, Stuttgart 1958.

10. Ernst Troeltsch, 'Die Ideen von 1914' (1916), in *Deutscher Geist und Westeuropa*, 1925, 437.

11. Ernst Troeltsch's *Spektator-Briefe. Aufsätze über die deutsche Revolution und die Weltpolitik 1918/1922*, Tübingen 1924, with an introduction by Friedrich Meinecke, is an example here, as is his article 'Naturrecht und Humanität in der Weltpolitik', in *Deutscher Geist und Westeuropa*, 3ff. For the whole question see also Bussmann, 'Politische Ideologien', 58ff.

12. Friedrich Georg Jünger in his article 'Krieg und Krieger' (1930), quoted in Bussmann, 'Politische Ideologien', 65.

13. Perhaps I may be allowed here, because of the criticism of Gogarten that follows (which I think that there is no way of avoiding), at the same time to say a word of personal admiration and gratitude. I gladly acknowledge that I owe much to Gogarten and my Göttingen semester – and certainly not least the freedom of theological criticism.

14. *Anfänge* 2, 95.

15. *Anfänge* 2, 94.; ET, 277.

16. *Anfänge* 2, 96f.; ET, 278f.

17. *Anfänge* 2, 98; ET, 279.

18. *Anfänge* 2, 98; ET, 279.

19. In the introduction to the *Politische Ethik*, Jena 1932, 1. Cf. the quotation from Ernst Jünger, above 79.

20. Here I would refer to the small 1918 booklet *Religion weither*, in which there is a contrast between 'experience' as the way of grasping reality and 'intellect', for which there is 'no reality' (32, etc.). The connections with life philosophy here are obvious.

21. *Politische Ethik*, passim. Cf. also the introduction to *Glaube und Wirklichkeit*, 1928, especially 4ff. Sontheimer associates the Jünger brothers, Hans Zehrer and Hans Freyer with Gogarten as representatives of this concept of freedom, cf. *Antidemokratisches Denken* (n.4), 338ff.

22. *Der Zerfall des Humanismus und die Gottesfrage*, 1937, 13ff.; quoted from Moltmann, *Anfänge* I, xivf.

23. *Anfänge* I, xv.

24. *Anfänge* I, 36; ET in Karl Barth, *The Word of God and the Word of Man*, New York 1928 reissued 1956, 327).

25. *Anfänge* 2, 100; ET, 281.

26. *Anfänge* 2, 101; ET, 282. Gogarten himself seems later to have noted the danger of this position when in the introduction to *Gericht oder Skepsis* (1937) he writes: 'This radical thought brought us dangerously close to the universal crisis which utterly shattered human life through the War and the post-War period, and to the mood of hopelessness and being at the end which came over many people at that time. There is no doubt that this general crisis was not without influence on the radicalism of our thought' (Moltmann, *Anfänge* 2, 337).

27. *Anfänge* I, 28; ET, 312.

28. *Anfänge* I, 32; ET, 319.

29. Cf. e.g. Ernst Troeltsch, *Spektator-Briefe* (n.11), 298, etc.

30. That Karl Barth was in principle open to the other possibility is perhaps shown by the fact that as early as September 1926 he was made a member of the 'Friends of the *Christliche Welt*' (Johannes Rathje, *Die Welt des freien Protestantismus*, Stuttgart 1952, 376).

31. *Karl Barth zum Kirchenkampf*, Theologische Existenz heute, NF 49, 1956, 91.

32. *Anfänge* 2, 332.

33. The same argument also appears in 'Abschied von "Zwischen den Zeiten"', in Moltmann, *Anfänge* 2 (see n.1 above), 313f.

34. 'Sozialismus und Christentum' (1923), ibid., 245.

35. See the critical comment by Paul Schempp in his 'Randglossen zum Barthianismus': 'Barth has a school because his theology is more in keeping with the current cultural situation than other theologies, because the *sacrificium* is a satisfaction to those who have sacrificed little here, because the paradox seems profound, because the criticism of the morbid is already an achievement for weaklings, because as a result of it theology has again become interesting, problematical, justified in its existence, a sanctuary for doubters and believers and the whole host of religious intermediaries' (ibid., 305).

36. For this see above all 'Naturrecht und Humanität in der Weltpolitik' (n.11 above), 3ff.

37. Ibid., 7f.

38. In 'Abschied von "Zwischen den Zeiten"', in Moltmann, *Anfänge* 2 (see n.1 above), 320f.

39. *Anfänge* 2, 320.

40. Gottfried Mehnert, *Evangelische Kirche und Politik 1917-1919. Die politischen Strömungen im deutschen Protestantismus von der Julikrise 1917 bis zum Herbst 1919*, Beiträge zur Geschichte des Parlamentarismus und der politischen Parteien 16, Düsseldorf 1959. Cf. my detailed review in *Zeitschrift für Kirchengeschichte* 73, 1962, 408ff.

41. E.Peterson, *Theologische Traktate* 1951, 301.

42. From *Meine Lebensgeschichte*, 1929, 404. Quoted from Mehnert, *Evangelische Kirche und Politik* (n.28), 233.

43. References in *Die Christliche Welt* 14, 1900, 977f.

44. Gerhard Kaiser, *Pietismus und Patriotismus im literarischen Deutschland. Ein Beitrag zum Problem der Säkularisation*, Veröffentlichungen des Instituts für Europäische Geschichte Mainz, Abteilung für abendländische Religionsgeschichte 24.VIII, Wiesbaden 1961. For this theme see also the earlier work by Koppel S.Pinson, *Pietism as a Factor in the Rise of German Nationalism*, New York 1934.

45. See the references in my article 'Romantik: kirchengeschichtlich', in *RGG*[3] V, cols.1178f.

46. Ernst Weymar, *Das Selbstverständnis der Deutschen. Ein Bericht über den Geist des Geschichtsunterrichts der höheren Schulen im 19. Jahrhundert*, Stuttgart 1962.

47. Weymar points out that Friedrich Neubauer, the editor of the fifteenth edition of Kohlrausch's *Kurzer Darstellung der deutschen Geschichte* (1822, [15]1894), continued its tradition in his own text books 'which were widely used in German Protestant schools until around 1930' (23 n.22).

48. Under this heading Weymar discusses above all the cultural-political

aspect of this question, i.e. the efforts of the state to make the teaching of religion and history serve its own higher aims.

49. *Karl Barth zum Kirchenkampf* (n.31 above), 93.

50. Ibid.

51. This was the heading under which in 1945 Friedrich Meinecke first raised the demand for new reflection (*Die deutsche Katastrophe*, Wiesbaden ²1949, 156f.). It has since been taken up many times.

52. In this connection Gerhard Schulz has raised the important question whether the 'revision of German "pictures of history" is conceivable and possible without a revision of history generally. 'Immediately after the collapse of 1945 the demand for a revision of the conceptuality of history was the only possible reaction, and it was basically an almost impulsive, and correct, intuition... In the long run historiography will not be able to avoid subjecting the manner of its research to critical examination also...' ('Der Stil der Historie und der Stand der Erfahrungen', in *Zur Geschichte und Problematik der Demokratie*, Festgabe Hans Herzfeld, Berlin, 1958, 160.

53. Hans Kohn, *The Mind of Germany. The Education of a Nation*, New York 1959.

54. Georg Lukacs, *Die Zerstörung der Vernunft*, Werke, Vol.9, Düsseldorf 1962. Cf. in this connection also the review of the 1954 edition which Kurt Sontheimer published under the title 'Deutsche Geschichte und Nationalsozialismus', *Zeitschrift für Religions- und Geistesgeschichte* IX, 1957, 287ff.

55. Here, as with Kohn, I must limit myself to drawing the basic outlines. A detailed discussion, which would doubtless be worth the work, would call for a separate extensive article.

56. Cf. also above all the chapter on neo-Hegelianism, in which Lukacs passionately defends Hegel against the 'irrationalist misunderstanding' of the neo-Hegelians.

57. Similarly Sontheimer in his review (see n.54), 291.

58. See nn.10, 36.

59. Carlo Antoni, *Der Kampf wider die Vernunft. Zur Entstehungsgeschichte des deutschen Freiheitsgedankens*, 1951, 5. The Italian edition of this brilliant investigation appeared as early as 1942 under the titel *La lotta contra la ragione*. The same author's *Vom Historismus zur Soziologie* (Dilthey, Troeltsch, Meinecke, Max Weber, Huizinga, Wölfflin), 1950, is a continuation.

## 4. Eugenio Pacelli and Karl Barth

1. *Katholische Kirche im Dritten Reich. Eine Aufsatzsammlung zum Verhältnis von Papstum, Episkopat und deutschen Katholiken zum Nationalsozialismus 1933-45*, ed. D.Albrecht; P.Leiber, *Pius XII*, Mainz 1976, 120.

2. Scholder has made a mistake here. These are not episcopal sees (Rothenburg is in Württemberg, Mainz in Hessen-Kassel), but church provinces, the seats of archbishops.

3. In his *allocutio* of 21 November 1921, Benedict XV stated that a concordat or church treaty would lapse if as a result of revolutions, peace treaties and so on, such great changes had taken place that the state that was partner to the treaty could no longer be recognized as the same body in law.

4. More than forty concordats and church treaties were concluded by Pius XI (1921-1939) and Pius XII (1939-1958). So this was not a German problem; the

Catholic church sought by means of treaties, especially with democratic states, to establish its rights and those of believers over against the state.

5. Otto Braun, *Von Weimar zu Hitler*, Hamburg 1949, 157.

6. The account is in H.Brüning, *Memoiren 1918-1934*, Stuttgart 1970, 338f. The account of this conversation and Brüning's information about the prehistory of the Reich concordat were the occasion for the Catholic side to dismiss Brüning's recollections with remarkable unanimity as untrustworthy. Although the style of publication of Brüning's memoirs was very unfortunate and hardly matched their historical claims, it is inappropriate for interested Catholic parties to represent the whole of the memoirs as untrustworthy. The historical-critical edition of these memoirs which is rightly called for by R.Mersag continues to be badly needed by contemporary research.

7. Cf. K.Scholder, 'Altes und Neues zur Vorgeschichte des Reichskonkordats. Erwiderung zu Konrad Repgen', *Vierteljahrshefte für Zeitgeschichte* 26, 1978, 535-70, reprinted with an introductory discussion by K.O.von Aretin in *Die Kirchen zwischen Republik und Gewaltherrschaft*, 171-203.

8. Article 32 of the Reich concordat was the so-called depoliticization article, which prohibited clergy and members of orders from joining political parties or being active in them; Article 23 guaranteed the existence of confessional schools. For the concordat see also K.Scholder, *The Churches and the Third Reich*, Vol.2, chapters 4 and 6, and the articles mentioned in the previous note.

9. *Die deutschen Konkordate und Kirchenverträge der Gegenwart* (an edition of the texts with the official justifications, supplementary regulations, comparative surveys, bibliographical references and a subject index), ed. Werner Weber, Göttingen 1962: 38-66 (Bavarian concordat); 152-67 (Bavarian church treaty); 67-91 (Prussian concordat); 168-83 (Prussian church treaty); 100-11 (Baden concordat); 189-94 (Baden church treaty).

10. Karl Barth, 'The Christian's Place in Society', in *The Word of God and the Word of Man*, New York 1928 reissued 1956, 273.

11. Ibid., 277.

12. Karl Barth, 'Biblical Questions, Insights, and Vistas', in *The Word of God and the Word of Man* (n.10 above), 67.

13. In: Karl Barth, *'Der Götze wackelt.' Zeitkritische Aufsätze und Briefe von 1930 bis 1960*, ed. Karl Kupisch, Berlin 1961, 27ff.

14. Thus in the lecture 'Roman Catholicism as a Question to the Protestant Church' (1928), in id., *Theology and Church*, London 1962, 307-33.

15. Ibid., 312.

16. Ibid., 322.

17. Ibid., 321.

18. Ibid., 314 n.1.

19. Ibid., 314.

20. *Quousque Tandem...?'* in *'Der Götze wackelt'* (n.13 above), 27.

21. Ibid., 28.

22. Ibid., 30.

23. Ibid., 31

24. See ibid., 33ff.

25. Ibid., 54.

26. Ibid., 62.

190      *A Requiem for Hitler*

*5. The Crisis of the 1930s as Questions to Christianity and the Churches*

1. This was originally a lecture given by the author on 10 January 1984 under the title 'Historical Reflections on the Theological Declaration of Barmen and its Influence up to the Present Day' to the Rhineland Landessynode in Bad Neuenahr. It was revised and provided with notes for the Tübingen lecture series on 'The Crisis of the 1930s and its Consequences'.

2. Surprisingly, the recent golden jubilee of the Barmen Declaration which I have since surveyed to some extent, did not make any new contribution to this historical question.

3. Here I am basically following my account in *The Churches and the Third Reich*, Vol.1, London and Philadelphia 1987.

4. Instead of giving extensive documentation which would go far beyond the framework of this lecture, I would refer here to my *The Churches and the Third Reich*, Vol. 2, *The Year of Disillusionment 1934. Barmen and Rome*, London and Philadelphia 1988, especially 7ff.

5. Karl Barth to Wilhelm Niesel, 21 May 1934, Karl Barth archive, Basel. I am grateful to the director of this Archive, Dr Hinrich Stoevesandt, for much help. Up to 1984 historical study of the prehistory of the Barmen declaration was in a quite desolate state. The last comprehensive works on it had been written by Gerhard Niemöller in 1952 and 1959: Gerhard Niemöller, *Die erste Bekenntnissynode der Deutschen Evangelischen Kirche zu Barmen*, Vol.1, *Geschichte, Kritik und Bedeutung der Synode und ihrer Theologischen Erklärung*; Vol.2, *Text–Dokumente–Berichte*, Göttingen 1954, 1959. Its inadequacy hardly needs to be pointed out. In the meantime the stimulus of the jubilee has in fact changed things. Here I would refer above all to the rich collection of material in Wolf-Dieter Hauschild, Georg Kretschmar and Carsten Nicolaisen (eds.), *Die lutherischen Kirchen und die Bekenntnissynode von Barmen, Referate des Internationalen Symposiums auf der Reisenburg 1983*, Göttingen 1984. In particular, the contribution by Carsten Nicolaisen, 'Der lutherische Beitrag zur Entstehung der Barmer Theologischen Erklärung', ibid., 13-38, describes for the first time the dramatic prehistory of the Theological Declaration in the lead-up to the synod. See now also C.Nicolaisen, *Der Weg nach Barmen. Die Entstehungsgeschichte der Theologischen Erklärung von 1934*, Neukirchen-Vluyn 1985.

6. The original was translated as *Theological Existence Today*, and published in London in 1933 (cited below as *TET*). Meanwhile a new edition in German has appeared, with an excellent commentary by Hinrich Stoevesandt: Karl Barth, *Theologische Existenz heute*, Munich 1984 (cited below as *TEh*). For the significance of this work in summer 1933 see also Scholder, *The Churches and the Third Reich* 1, 435-40.

7. *TET*, 11 (though the translation does not in fact bring it out; *TEh*, 27.

8. *TET*, 11, 14; *TEh*, 27 ,29.

9. *TET*, 14f.; *TEh*, 30.

10. *TET*, 17; *TEh*, 31.

11. *TET*, 69; *TEh*, 73.

12. *TET*,78; *TEh*, 81f.

13. There is no recent account of this unfortunate reception. There is a collection of material, albeit somewhat one-sided, in Wilhelm Niemöller, *Hitler und die evangelischen Kirchenführer (Zum 25.Januar 1934)*, Bielefeld 1959;

## Notes

## Notes                                                                             191

id., 'Epilog zur Kanzlerempfang', in Wilhelm Niemöller, *Wort und Tat im Kirchenkampf. Beiträge zur neuesten Kirchengeschichte*, Munich 1969, 80-99.

14. The first Free Synods felt themselves to be such a sign: cf. e.g. Joachim Beckmann, *Rheinische Bekenntnissynoden im Kirchenkampf. Eine Dokumentation aus den Jahren 1933-1945*, Neukirchen 1975, esp. 59-90 (Free Evangelical Synod in Rhineland at Barmen-Gemarke on 18 and 19 February 1934); 103-23 (Rhineland Westphalia Community Day 'Under the Word' on 18 March 1934 at Westfalenhalle, Dortmund; 124-50 (conference of the Westphalian Confessing Synod and the Free Evangelical Synod in the Rhineland on Sunday 29 April 1934, in Dortmund).

15. Quoted from Carsten Nicolaisen, 'Zur Entstehungsgeschichte der Barmer Theologischen Erklärung', in A.Burgsmüller and R.Weth (eds.), *Die Barmer Theologische Erklärung. Einführung und Dokumentation*, with an introduction by Eduard Lohse, Neukirchen 1983, 24.

16. There is a translation of the complete German text in John H.Leith, *Creeds of the Churches*, Atlanta ³1982, 518-22. Cf. also Beckmann, *Rheinische Bekenntnissynoden im Kirchenkampf* (n.14 above), 34-46.

17. Thus the first thesis of the January declaration, Beckmann, 34; cf. also Asmussen's commentary on the first thesis of the May Theological Declaration in A.Burgsmüller and R.Weth, *Barmer Theologische Erklärung* (n.15), 48.

18. For thesis I.2 see Leith, 520; Beckmann, 36.

19. Thesis I.3: Leith, 520; Beckmann, 36f.

20. Thesis V.4: Leith, 521; Beckmann, 45.

21. Thesis III.2: Leith, 532; Beckmann, 41.

22. For these plans and ideas of which previously only fragments were known, and for the following remarks, see K.Scholder, *The Churches and the Third Reich*, Vol.2, 6ff., 14ff.

23. Kurt Meier, *Der evangelische Kirchenkampf. Gesamtdarstellung in drei Bänden*, 1: *Der Kampf um die Reichskirche*, Göttingen 1976, 154-65. For the Chancellor's reception on 25 January 1934 see n.13 above.

24. There are extracts from the protocol of this session in *Dokumentation zum Kirchenkampf in Hessen und Nassau*, Vol.2, Darmstadt 1979, 231-4.

25. Zur Lage, Erwägung von Haehnelt und Wolter, Strassburg, EZA Berlin, KKA no.14/13.

26. Beckmann, *Rheinische Bekenntnissynoden* (n.14), 66f.

27. Ibid., 89.

28. For this development, which began in Frankfurt on 19 March and led directly to the Synod of Barmen, see also Nicolaisen, 'Der lutherische Beitrag zur Entstehung der Barmer Theologischen Erklärung' (n.5 above), 17-21.

29. Text, etc., in Kurt D.Schmidt, *Die Bekenntnisse und grundsätzlichen Aüsserungen zur Kirchenfrage*, Vol.2, *Das Jahr 1934*, Göttingen 1935, 62f.

30. Cf. Niemöller, *Die erste Bekenntnissynode* 1 (n.5 above), 67.

31. For the arguments in the period before the synod see now Nicolaisen, 'Der lutherische Beitrag zur Entstehung der Barmer Theologischen Erklärung' (n.5 above), 27ff.; M.Wittenberg, 'Hermann Sasse und "Barmen"', in Hauschild, Kretschmar and Nicolaisen, 'Die lutherischen Kirchen und die Bekenntnissynode' (above n.5), 84-106.

32. Minutes of the third session of the Nuremberg Committee on 7 May 1934, LKA Bielefeld, 5,1, no.704 fasc.2.

33. Text in Burgsmüller/Weth (eds.), *Die Barmer Theologische Erklärung* (n.15 above), 30, 33.

34. This is how the report of the Württemberg synod member Otto Seiz summed up the points in dispute: Otto Seiz, Bericht über die erste Bekenntnissynode der DEK, LKA Stuttgart D 1, 49, p.41.

35. Text in Burgsmüller and Weth, *Die Barmer Theologische Erklärung*, 34.

36. See above, 78f.

37. Burgsmüller and Weth, *Die Barmer Theologische Erklärung*, 48.

38 Text of the second thesis, ibid., 35; Leith, 520; Asmussen's report, ibid., 50.

39. Text of the second thesis, ibid., 38; Leith, 520.

40. Dietrich Bonhoeffer, 'Die Kirche vor der Judenfrage', a lecture given in April 1933, in *Gesammelte Schriften* 2, Munich 1959, 46; English text, 'The Church and the Jewish Question', in E.H.Robertson (ed.), *No Rusty Swords*, London 1970, 219.

41. As n.39.

42. Burgsmüller and Weth, *Die Barmer theologische Erklärung*, 55.


## 7. *Political Resistance or Self-assertion as a Problem of Church Governments*

1. For the negotiations over the Reich concordat in Rome see L.Volk, *Das Reichskonkordat vom 20 Juli 1933. Von den Ansätzen in der Weimarer Republik bis zur Ratifizierung am 10.September 1933*, Veröffentlichungen der Kommission für Zeitgeschichte (cited henceforward as VKZ), Reihe B, Vol.5, Mainz 1972, esp. 90ff.; K.Scholder, *The Churches and the Third Reich*, Volume 1, London and Philadelphia 1987, 385ff.

2. For Pacelli's efforts see D.Albrecht, 'Der heiliger Stuhl und das Dritte Reich', in K.Gotto and K.Repgen (eds.), *Kirche, Katholiken und Nationalsozialismus*, Topos Taschenbücher 96, Mainz 1980, 39f.

3. For Cardinal Bertram's so-called 'petitionary policy' see Ludwig Volk, 'Der deutsche Episkopat', in *Das Reichkonkordat* (n.1 above), 54ff.

4. For this see also Heinz Hürten, 'Selbstbehauptung und Widerstand der katholischen Kirche', in J.Schmädeke and P.Steinbach (eds.), *Der Widerstand gegen den Nationalsozialismus. Die deutsche Gesellschaft und der Widerstand gegen Hitler*, Munich and Zurich 1985, 240-53.

5. Karl Otmar von Aretin, 'Der deutsche Widerstand gegen Hitler', in Ulrich Cartarius, *Opposition gegen Hitler* (= *Deutscher Widerstand 1933-1945*), Berlin 1984, 9.

6. Martin Höllen, *Heinrich Wienken. Der 'unpolitische' Kirchenpolitiker. Eine Biographie aus drei Epochen des deutschen Katholizismus* (= VKZ, Reihe B, Vol.33), Mainz 1981, 73ff.

7. Archives of the Diocese of Osnabrück 04-62-33. For the events see also W.Adolph, *Erich Klausener*, Berlin 1955.

8. S.Kirchmann (i.e. W.Gurian), *St Ambrosius und die deutschen Bischöfe*, Lucerne 1934, 20.

9. Ibid., 6. Cf. also H.Hürten, *Waldemar Gurian. Ein Zeuge der Krise unserer Welt in der ersten Hälfte des 20 Jahrhunderts*, VKZ, Reihe B, Vol.11, Mainz 1972, 92ff.

10. The text is in the report by the Ordinariat of Berlin (source as in n.7).

11. Preysing to Bertram, 18 October 1936: L.Volk (ed.), *Akten deutscher*

*Bischöfe über die Lage der Kirche 1933-1945*, 4, *1936-1939*, VKZ, Reihe A, Vol.30, Mainz 1981, 365.

12. Memorandum by W.Adolph in Walter Adolph, *Geheime Aufzeichnungen aus dem nationalsozialistischen Kirchenkampf 1935-1943*, VKZ, Reihe B, Vol.33, Mainz 1979, 170f.

13. Bertram to Preysing, 21 October 1937: L.Volk (ed.), *Akten deutscher Bischöfe* (n.11 above), no.413.

14. For the history of this pastoral letter see L.Volk, 'Die Fuldaer Bischofskonferenz von der Enzyklika "Mit brennender Sorge" bis zum Ende der NS-Herrschaft', in D.Albrecht (ed.), *Katholische Kirche im Dritten Reich. Eine Aufsatzsammlung zum Verhältnis von Papsttum, Episkopat und deutschen Katholiken zum Nationalsozialismus 1933-1945*, Topos Taschenbücher 45, Mainz 1976, esp. 81ff.

15. Text of the draft of 15 November 1941 in L.Volk (ed.), *Akten Kardinal Michael von Faulhabers 1917-1945*, 2, *1935-1945*, VKZ Reihe A, Vol.26, Mainz 1978, no.845a.

16. Ibid., 838.

17. Thus according to Berning's report to the members of the Kevelaer conference of 12 March 1982, ibid., 877. See also the report from the Committee for Matters relating to Orders, 14 June 1942, ibid., 936.

18. Bertram to Faulhaber, 3 July 1941, ibid., 759f. For Bertram's attitude see also 'A Requiem for Hitler', below, 157-67.

19. The following events have often been described. There is a short survey of developments in the article 'The Church Struggle', above, 94-129.

20. There is a text of the memorandum of early 1936 e.g. in J.Beckmann (ed.), *Kirchliches Jahrbuch für die Evangelische Kirche in Deutschland 1933-1944*, Gütersloh ²1976, 132-7.

21. On this see W.Niemöller, *Die Bekennende Kirche sagt Hitler die Wahrheit. Die Geschichte der Denkschrift der vorläufigen Leitung von Mai 1936*, Bielefeld 1954, 30f.; E.C.Helmreich, 'Die Veröffentlichung der "Denkschrift der vorläufigen Leitung der Deutschen Evangelischen Kirche an den Führer und Reichskanzler. 28 Mai 1936', in *Zeitschrift für Kirchengeschichte* 87, 1976, 40-53.

22. W.Niemöller, *Die Bekennende Kirche* (n.21 above), 32.

23. Ibid., 36.

24. Ibid., 37.

25. Text of the liturgy in J.Beckmann (ed.), *Kirchliches Jahrbuch* (n.20 above), 256-8.

26. P.Hoffmann, *Widerstand – Staatsstreich – Attentat. Der Kampf der Opposition gegen Hitler*, Frankfurt-Berlin-Vienna ²1976, 74ff.

27. Thus according to a letter from the 'Provisional Government' to the Landeskirche governments and Land councils of brethren which were under it, dated 18 October 1938, J.Beckmann (ed.), *Kirchliches Jahrbuch*, 258f.

28. H.Hermelink, *Kirche im Kampf. Dokumente des Widerstands und des Aufbaus der Evangelischen Kirche in Deutschland von 1933-1945*, Tübingen and Stuttgart 1950, 455.

29. Ibid., 457.

30. Wurm to Frick, 19 July 1940. G.Schäfer, *Landesbischof D.Wurm und der nationalsozialistische Staat 1940-1945*, Stuttgart 1968, 119-24.

31. On the Protestant side there is the well-known example of Dietrich Bonhoeffer, to whom the Confessing Church refused a place on its list of

intercessions (E.Bethge, *Dietrich Bonhoeffer, Theologian, Christian, Contemporary*, London and New York 1970, 834). On the Catholic side, in 1946 eleven out of the sixteen priests from the archdiocese of Freiburg who had survived concentration camps made vigorous attacks on the Freiburg church authorities; they accused them, among other things, of having the attitude that 'a priest was more popular with the church authorities, the less he came into contact with the Gestapo' (H.Ott, 'Möglichkeit und Formen kirchlichen Widerstands gegen das Dritte Reich von seiten der Kirchenbehörde und des Pfarrklerus, dargestellt am Beispiel der Erzdiözese Freiburg im Breisgau', *Historisches Jahrbuch der Görres-Gesellschaft* 92, 1972, 312-33; the quotation is on 328.

32. E.Klügel, *Die lutherische Landeskirche Hannovers und ihr Bischof 1933-1945. Dokumente*, Berlin and Hamburg 1965, 213.

33. Adenauer to Pastor Bernhard Custodis, 23 February 1946, in Adenauer, *Briefe 1945-1947*, Rhöndorf Edition, Berlin 1983, 172f.

## 8. Politics and Church Politics in the Third Reich

1. K, Scholder, 'Die evangelische Kirche in der Sicht der nationalsozialistichen Führung bis zum Kriegsausbruch', in VZG 16, 1968, 15-35.

2. *Akten zur deutschen auswärtigen Politik* (ADAP), Serie D, 1937-1945, Vol. III.1.

3. Although many details are still obscure, here I am following the account of events by H.-H.Abendroth, 'Hitlers Entscheidung', in W.Schieder and C.Dipper (eds.), *Der spanische Bürgerkrieg in der internationalen Politik (1936-1939)*, Munich 1976, 76-128, here above all 90ff.; id., 'Deutschlands Rolle im spanischen Bürgerkrieg', in M.Funke (ed.), *Hitler, Deutschland und die Mächte*, Düsseldorf 1976, 471-88, here esp. 474.

4. H.Thomas, *The Spanish Civil War*, [3]1977, 370.

5. Thus with an extensive justification, H.-H.Abendroth, 'Hitlers Entscheidung', in Scheider and Dipper, *Der spanische Bürgerkrieg* (n.3 above), 92ff. With qualifications, also H.Wohlfeil, 'Der spanische Bürgerkrieg', ibid., 18, and W.Schieder, 'Spanischer Bürgerkrieg und Vierteljahresplan', ibid., 168. For the whole complex cf. H.-H.Abendroth, *Hitler in der spanischen Arena. Die deutsch-spanischen Beziehungen im Spannungsfeld der europäischen Interessenpolitik 1936-1939*, Paderborn 1973, 15ff.

6. ADAP D III, no.4 (n.1).

7. Text of the speech, VZG 3, 1955, 204-10.

8. For details see Thomas, *Spanish Civil War* (n.4 above), 258-81.

9. H.Domarus, *Hitler. Reden und Proklamationen 1932-1945*, Vol.I/2, Munich 1965, 646f.

10. There is a careful and impressive account of these events in H.G.Hockerts, *Die Sittlichkeitsprozesse gegen katholische Ordensangehörige und Priester 1936. Eine Studie zur nationalsozialistischen Herrschaftstechnik und zum Kirchenkampf*, Mainz 1971.

11. Detailed figures in H.Thomas, *Spanish Civil War*, 470.

12. Cf. ibid., 286f., 511f.

13. Text: B.Stasiewski (ed.), *Akten deutscher Bischofe über die Lage der Kirche 1933 bis 1945*, Vol. III, 1935-1936, Mainz 1979, 478-83.

14. Ibid.

15. L.Volk, *Akten Kardinal Michael von Faulhabers 1917-1945*, Vol.II, *1935-1945*, Mainz 1978, 185.

16. Ibid., 193. Cf. also W.Adolph, *Geheime Aufzeichnungen aus dem nationalsozialistischen Kirchenkampf 1935-1943*, Mainz 1979, 120: 'Hitler regarded the offer to Faulhaber as the last occasion for making peace with the church.'

17. K.Deschner, *Mit Gott und den Faschisten. Der Vatikan im Bunde mit Mussolini, Franco, Hitler und Pavelic*, Stuttgart 1965, 1 and passim.

18. P.E.Schramm (ed.), *H.Picker, Hitlers Tischgespräche im Führer Hauptquartier 1941-1942*, Stuttgart ²1965, 179f. Now also in W.Jochmann (ed.), *Adolf Hitler, Monologe im Führerhauptquartier 1941-1944. Die Aufzeichungen H.Heims*, Hamburg 1980, 284.

19. P.E.Schramm (ed.), *Tischgespräche*, 34.

20. Text: L.Volk, *Faulhaber-Akten* II, no.592.

21. Ibid., 599.

22. H.-A.Raem, *Pius XI und der Nationalsozialismus. Die Enzyklika 'Mit brenneder Sorge' vom 14. März 1937*, Paderborn, etc. 1979, 27f.

23. K.Scholder, *The Churches and the Third Reich*, Vol.1, London and Philadelphia 1987, 303f., 307f..

24. A report by the doctor treating Hitler on 1 October 1936, in BA Koblenz NS 10/29: letter of 28 September on resuming work on 5 November 1936, ibid.

25. Text: J.Beckmann (ed.), *Kirchliches Jahrbuch 1933-1944*, ²1976, 146f.

26. Text of the draft ordinance of 29 January 1937 in BA Koblenz R 22/4008.

27. K.D.Schmidt, *Dokumente des Kirchenkampfes II. Die Zeit des Reichkirchenausschusses 1935-1937*, II, Göttingen 1965, 1355.

28. Hitler's daily activities from January 30, 1934 to June 30, 1943, Institut für Zeitgeschichte, Munich F 19/13.

29. Goebbels' diaries now provide confirmation of this hypothesis, which was developed some years ago. Cf. H.G.Hockerts, 'Die Goebbels-Tagebücher 1932-1941', in *Festschrift für Konrad Repgen*, Berlin 1983, 372f.

30. Cf. Scholder, op.cit., (n.1 above), 30.

31. Text: J.Beckmann (ed.), *Kirchliches Jahrbuch* (n.25 above), 160.

32. Ibid., 163f.

33. For the mood in the Vatican after the conclusion of the Reich concordat see K.Scholder, 'Altes und neues zur Vorgeschichte des Reichkonkordats. Erwiderung auf Konrad Repgen', in *Die Kirchen zwischen Republik und Gewaltherrschaft*, 171-203.

34. Cited from H.A.Raem, *Pius XI* (n.22 above), 32.

35. L.Volk, *Faulhaber-Akten* II (n.15 above), 284.

36. The text of *Divini Redemptoris*, etc., is in E.Marmy, *Mensch und Gemeinschaft in christlicher Schau*, Freiburg im Breisgau 1945, 131-209.

37. L.Volk, *Faulhaber-Akten* II (n.15 above), 281.

38. Text in D.Albrecht, *Der Notenwechsel zwischen dem Hl.Stuhl und der deutschen Reichsregierung* I, Mainz 1965, 409f.

39. For details see H.-A.Raem, *Pius XI* (n.22 above), 62ff. and 106f.

40. BA Koblenz, R43 II/153a.

41. M.Domarus, *Hitler* 1/2 (n.9 above), 748ff.

42. Ibid., 645.

## 9. A Requiem for Hitler

1. W.Adolph, *Hirtenamt und Hitler-Diktatur*, Berlin 1965.

2. L.Volk, 'Die Fuldaer Bischofskonferenz von Hitlers Machtergreifung bis zur Enzyklika "Mit brennender Sorge"', *Stimmen der Zeit* 183, 1969, 10-31; id., 'Die Fuldaer Bischofskonferenz von der Enzyklika "Mit brennende Sorge" bis zum Ende der NS-Herrschaft', ibid. 178, 1966, 241-67. Both articles are now in D.Albrecht (ed.), *Katholische Kirche im Dritten Reich. Eine Aufsatzsammlung zum Verhältnis von Papstttum, Episkopat und deutschen Katholiken zum Nationalsozialismus 1933-1945*, Mainz 1976, 35-102.

3. K.Gotto, 'Katholische Kirche und Nationalsozialismus', in *Staatslexikon der Görres-Gesellschaft*, sixth edition, supplementary volume 2, 1970, col.490.

4. L.Volk (ed.), *Akten Kardinal Michael von Faulhabers 1917-1945*, II, *1935-1945*, Mainz 1978.

5. W.Adolph, *Geheime Aufzeichnungen aus dem nationalsozialistischen Kirchenkampf 1935-1943*, Mainz 1979.

6. K.Gotto, H.G.Hockerts and Konrad Repgen, 'Nationalsozialistische Herausforderung und kirchliche Antwort. Eine Bilanz', in K.Gotto und K.Repgen, *Kirche, Katholiken und Nationalsozialismus*, Mainz 1980, 101-18.

7. Ibid., 110f.

8. K.Scholder, *The Churches and the Third Reich*, Volume 1, London and Philadelphia 1987, 393ff.

9. Adolph, *Geheime Aufzeichnungen* (n.5), 51.

10. Ibid., 53.

11. Ibid., 165.

12. Ibid., 170f.

13. Archivum Archiecejalne Wroclaw (=AAW) Registratur I A 25, Fürstbischof Adolf Kardinal Bertram.

14. Cf. e.g. Adolph, *Geheime Aufzeichnungen* (n.5), 51.

15. Ibid., 213. See also 52.

16. Ibid., 218.

17. U.von Hehl, *Katholische Kirche und Nationalsozialismus im Erzbistum Köln 1933-1945*, Mainz 1977, 168f.

18. Cf. Faulhaber's memorandum of 24 August 1937, in L.Volk, *Akten Cardinal Michael von Faulhabers*, II (n. 4 above), 387ff.; also Adolph, *Geheime Aufzeichnungen* (n.5 above), 143.

19. Ibid., 229.

20 Cf. e.g. ibid., 238 (Preysing) with 279 (Bertram).

21. Note by Weizsäcker on a report of Greiser's dated 8 April 1938, Archiv des Auswärtigen Amtes Bonn, Pal III (Hl.Stuhl) PoZ, Band 5. Against K.Gotto et al., 'Nationalsozialistische Herausforderung' (n. 6 above), 112.

22. B.Schneider (ed), *Die Briefe Pius' XII an die deutschen Bischöfe 1939-1944*, Mainz 1966, 318. Cf also 299.

23. Ibid. 340f. and 318.

24. D.Albrecht (ed.), *Der Notenwechsel zwischen dem Hl.Stuhl und der deutschen Reichsregierung*, Vol. III, *Der Notenwechsel und die Demarchen des Nuntius Orsenigo 1933-1945*, Mainz 1980, 305.

25. Cf. the memoranda by Bertram and Faulhaber for Pius XII in B.Schneider, *Die Briefe Pius' XII* (n.22 above), 300-14.

26. W.Adolph, *Hirtenamt und Hitler-Diktatur* (n.1 above), 161f.

27. L.Volk in Albrecht, *Katholische Kirche im Dritten Reich* (n.2), 75.

28. W.Adolph, *Hirtenamt und Hitler-Diktatur* (n.1 above), 164-8.
29. Pius XII to Preysing, 12 June 1940. B.Schneider, *Die Briefe Pius' XII*, 74f.
30. Ibid., and 88f.
31. W.Adolph, *Geheime Aufzeichnungen*, 274.
32. U.von Hehl, *Katholische Kirche und Nationalsocialismus* (n.17 above), 208.
33. L.Volk, *Akten Kardinal Michael von Faulhabers* II (n.4 above), 826f.
34. Ibid., 833f.
35. Ibid., 838.
36. Ibid., 850ff.
37. Ibid.
38. Ibid., 936.
39. For the confusion over the pastoral letter and its recall cf. ibid., 888ff.
40. Ibid., 759.
41. AAW I A 25 z 19.
42. *Adolf Hitler. Monologe im Führerhauptquartier 1941-1944*, ed. W.Jochmann, Hamburg 1980, 150f., etc.
43. *Hitler's Mein Kampf*, translated by Ralph Manheim with an introduction by D.C.Watt, London 1974, 5
44. K.Engelbert (ed.), *Geschichte des Breslauer Domkapitels im Rahmen der Diözesangeschichte vom Beginn des 19.Jahrhunderts bis zum Ende des Zweiten Weltkriegs*, Hildesheim 1964, 242.
45. M.Domarus, *Hitler, Reden von 1932-1945*, Vol. II 2, Munich 1965, 2250.
46. AAW I A 25, line 19.
47. L.Eisenhofer, *Handbuch der Liturgik* II, Freiburg 1933, 14.
48. K.Repgen, 'Über die Entstehung der Reichskonkordats-Offerte im Frühjahr 1933 und die Bedeutung des Reichskonkordats', *Vierteljahrshefte für Zeitgeschichte* 26, 1978, 533.

## 10. Judaism and Christianity in the Ideology and Politics of National Socialism 1919-1945

1. E.Goldhagen, 'Weltanschauung und Endlösung. Zum Antisemitismus der nationalsozialistischen Führungsschicht', *VZG* 24, 1976, 397.
2. E.Jäckel (ed.), *Hitler. Sämtliche Aufzeichnungen 1905-1924*, Stuttgart 1980, 88-90.
3. E.Fischer, *Die Rehobother Bastards und das Bastardierungsproblem beim Menschen. Anthropologische und ethnographische Studien am Rehobother Bastardvolk in Deutsch-Südwest-Afrika*, Jena 1913.
4. *Hitler's Mein Kampf* (see Chapter 9 n.43 above), 297.
5. Ibid., 345f. [Here Scholder has made a mistake: the passage to which he refers in fact appears in the first chapter of Volume 2].
6. W.Hofer, *Der Nationalsozialismus. Dokumente 1933-1945*, Frankfurt 1957, 28-31.
7. E.Jäckel (ed.), *Hitler* (n.2 above), 623.
8. D.Eckart, *Der Bolschewismus von Moses bis Lenin. Zwiegespräch zwischen Adolf Hitler und mir*, Munich 1924.
9. *Hitler's Mein Kampf*, 60.

198     *A Requiem for Hitler*

10. For Hitler's basic decision on church policy see K.Scholder, *The Churches and the Third Reich*, Vol.1, 92-8.

11. B.Stasiewski, *Akten deutscher Bischöfe über die Lage der Kirche 1933-1945*, II, *1935-1945*, 185, 187.

14. H.A.Oberman, *Wurzeln des Antisemitismus*, Berlin 1981.

15. A.Stöcker, *Christlich-Sozial. Reden und Aufsätze*, Berlin ²1890, 272.

16. F.Heer, *Der Glaube des Adolf Hitler. Anatomie einer politischen Religiosität*, Munich and Esslingen 1969.

17. J.Gauger, *Chronik der Kirchenwirren*, I Teil, Elberfeld 1934, 67.

18. Dietrich Bonhoeffer, *Gesammelte Schriften* II, Munich 1959, 44-53, 115-17; *No Rusty Swords* (see Chapter 5, n.40 above), 217-25, 227, 276.

19. K.Scholder, *The Churches and the Third Reich*, Vol.I, 482f.

20. Ibid., 552-4.

21. Cf. also e.g. *Christentum und Judentum. Studien zur Erforschung ihres gegenseitigen Verhältnisses. Sitzungsberichte der ersten Arbeitstagung des Instituts zur Erforschung des jüdischen Einflusses auf das deutsche kirchliche Leben*, ed. W.Grundmann, Leipzig 1940.

22. M.von Faulhaber, *Judentum, Christentum, Germanentum* (Advent sermons given in St Michael's Church, Munich, 1933), Munich (1934), 20, 23.

23. M.Domarus, *Hitler, Reden und Proklamationen 1932-1945*, I 2, Munich 1965, 745.

24. Ibid., II 1, 1058-60.

25. W.Jochmann (ed.), *Adolf Hitler. Monologe im Führerhauptquartier 1941-1944*, Hamburg 1980, 41.

26. Ibid., 96-98.

27. Ibid,. 152.

28. Ibid., 150.

# Index